Learning React
Functional Web Development
with React and Redux

Alex Banks and Eve Porcello

Beijing · Boston · Farnham · Sebastopol · Tokyo

Learning React

by Alex Banks and Eve Porcello

Published by O'Reilly Media, Inc., 1005 Gravenstein Highway North, Sebastopol, CA 95472.

O'Reilly books may be purchased for educational, business, or sales promotional use. Online editions are also available for most titles (*http://oreilly.com/safari*). For more information, contact our corporate/institutional sales department: 800-998-9938 or *corporate@oreilly.com*.

Editor: Allyson MacDonald
Production Editor: Melanie Yarbrough
Copyeditor: Colleen Toporek
Proofreader: Rachel Head

Indexer: WordCo Indexing Services
Interior Designer: David Futato
Cover Designer: Karen Montgomery
Illustrator: Rebecca Demarest

May 2017:   First Edition

Revision History for the First Edition
2017-04-26:   First Release
2018-02-09:   Second Release

See *http://oreilly.com/catalog/errata.csp?isbn=9781491954621* for release details.

978-1-491-95462-1

[LSI]

Table of Contents

literally just array shite

Preface

This book is for developers who want to learn the React library while learning the latest techniques currently emerging in the JavaScript language. This is an exciting time to be a JavaScript developer. The ecosystem is exploding with new tools, syntax, and best practices that promise to solve many of our development problems. Our aim with this book is to organize these techniques, so you can get to work with React right away. We'll get into Redux, React Router, and build tooling, so we promise not to introduce only the basics and then throw you to the wolves.

This book does not assume any knowledge of React at all. We'll introduce all of React's basics from scratch. Similarly, we won't assume that you've worked with ES6 or any of the latest JavaScript syntax. This will be introduced in Chapter 2 as foundation for the rest of the chapters.

You'll be better prepared for the contents of the book if you're comfortable with HTML, CSS, and JavaScript. It's almost always best to be comfortable with these big three before diving into a JavaScript library.

Along the way, check out the GitHub repository (*http://github.com/moonhighway/learning-react*). All of the examples are there and will allow you to practice with hands-on examples.

Conventions Used in This Book

The following typographical conventions are used in this book:

Italic
> Indicates new terms, URLs, email addresses, filenames, and file extensions.

`Constant width`
> Used for program listings, as well as within paragraphs to refer to program elements such as variable or function names, databases, data types, environment variables, statements, and keywords.

Constant width bold

> Shows commands or other text that should be typed literally by the user.

Constant width italic

> Shows text that should be replaced with user-supplied values or by values determined by context.

This element signifies a tip or suggestion.

This element signifies a general note.

This element indicates a warning or caution.

Using Code Examples

Supplemental material (code examples, exercises, etc.) is available for download at *https://github.com/moonhighway/learning-react*.

This book is here to help you get your job done. In general, if example code is offered with this book, you may use it in your programs and documentation. You do not need to contact us for permission unless you're reproducing a significant portion of the code. For example, writing a program that uses several chunks of code from this book does not require permission. Selling or distributing a CD-ROM of examples from O'Reilly books does require permission. Answering a question by citing this book and quoting example code does not require permission. Incorporating a significant amount of example code from this book into your product's documentation does require permission.

We appreciate, but do not require, attribution. An attribution usually includes the title, author, publisher, and ISBN. For example: "*Learning React* by Alex Banks and Eve Porcello (O'Reilly). Copyright 2017 Alex Banks, Eve Porcello, 978-1-491-95462-1."

If you feel your use of code examples falls outside fair use or the permission given above, feel free to contact us at *permissions@oreilly.com*.

O'Reilly Safari

 *Safari* (formerly Safari Books Online) is a membership-based training and reference platform for enterprise, government, educators, and individuals.

Members have access to thousands of books, training videos, Learning Paths, interactive tutorials, and curated playlists from over 250 publishers, including O'Reilly Media, Harvard Business Review, Prentice Hall Professional, Addison-Wesley Professional, Microsoft Press, Sams, Que, Peachpit Press, Adobe, Focal Press, Cisco Press, John Wiley & Sons, Syngress, Morgan Kaufmann, IBM Redbooks, Packt, Adobe Press, FT Press, Apress, Manning, New Riders, McGraw-Hill, Jones & Bartlett, and Course Technology, among others.

For more information, please visit *http://oreilly.com/safari*.

How to Contact Us

Please address comments and questions concerning this book to the publisher:

O'Reilly Media, Inc.
1005 Gravenstein Highway North
Sebastopol, CA 95472
800-998-9938 (in the United States or Canada)
707-829-0515 (international or local)
707-829-0104 (fax)

We have a web page for this book, where we list errata, examples, and any additional information. You can access this page at *http://bit.ly/learning-react-2e*.

To comment or ask technical questions about this book, send email to *bookquestions@oreilly.com*.

For more information about our books, courses, conferences, and news, see our website at *http://www.oreilly.com*.

Find us on Facebook: *http://facebook.com/oreilly*

Follow us on Twitter: *http://twitter.com/oreillymedia*

Watch us on YouTube: *http://www.youtube.com/oreillymedia*

Acknowledgments

Our journey with React wouldn't have started without some good old fashioned luck. We used YUI when we created the training materials for the full stack JavaScript program that we taught internally at Yahoo. Then in August 2014, development on YUI ended. We had to change all of our course files, but to what? What were we supposed to use on the front end now? The answer: React. We didn't fall in love with React immediately, it took us couple of hours to get hooked. It looked like React could potentially change everything. We got in early and got really lucky.

This book would not have been possible without the support of Ally MacDonald who helped us every step of the way and was monumentally patient with us through several library updates. We're grateful to Melanie Yarbrough, Colleen Toporek, and Rachel Head for their amazing attention to detail. Thanks to Sarah Ronau for proofreading this book well before it was ready for human eyes and to Bonnie Eisenman for her great advice and overall delightfulness. Thanks also to Stoyan Stefanov, who was nice enough to provide a technical review even though he's really busy building cool stuff at Facebook.

There's also no way this book could have existed without the Sharon Adams and Marilyn Messineo. They conspired to purchase Alex's first computer, a Tandy TRS 80 Color Computer. It also wouldn't have made it to book form without the love, support, and encouragement of Jim and Lorri Porcello, and Mike and Sharon Adams.

We'd also like to acknowledge Coffee Connexion in Tahoe City, California for giving us the coffee we needed to finish this book, and its owner, Robin, who gave us the timeless advice: "A book on programming? Sounds boring!"

CHAPTER 1

Welcome to React

React is a popular library used to create user interfaces. It was built at Facebook to address some of the challenges associated with large-scale, data-driven websites. When React was released in 2013, the project was initially viewed with some skepticism because the conventions of React are quite unique.

In an attempt to not intimidate new users, the core React team wrote an article called "Why React?" that recommended that you "Give It [React] Five Minutes." They wanted to encourage people to work with React first before thinking that their approach was too crazy.

Yes, React is a small library that doesn't come with everything you might need out of the box to build your application. Give it five minutes.

Yes, in React, you write code that looks like HTML right in your JavaScript. And yes, those tags require preprocessing to run in a browser. And you'll probably need a build tool like webpack for that. Give it five minutes.

If you read that article—as we did—you may have been dazzled by the promise of a new JavaScript library—a library that would solve all of our problems with the DOM; a library that would always be easy to work with and would never hurt us.

Then the questions start to arise: how do I convert this JSX? How do I load data? Where does the CSS go? What is declarative programming? Every path leads to more questions about how to incorporate this library in your actual day to day work. Every conversation introduces new terminology, new techniques, and more questions.

Obstacles and Roadblocks

By taking a few minutes to learn about React components, you've opened a door to a different way of thinking about and approaching web development. However, there are some learning obstacles that you'll have to overcome to begin writing production code with React.

React Is a Library

First, the React library is small and it is only used for one part of the job. It doesn't ship with all of the tools that you'd expect from a traditional JavaScript framework. A lot of the decisions about which tools from the ecosystem to use are left up to the developer. Also, new tools emerge all the time, and old ones are cast aside. There are so many different library names continually being added to the discussion that it may feel like it's impossible to keep up.

New ECMAScript Syntax

React has come of age in an important but chaotic time in the history of JavaScript. The ECMA used to release specifications infrequently. It would sometimes take up to 10 years to release a spec. This meant that developers wouldn't need to learn new syntax very often.

As of 2015, new language features and syntax additions will be released every year. This replaces a numbered release system (ECMAScript3, ECMAScript 5) with a yearly one (ECMAScript 2016, ECMAScript 2017). As the language evolves, the early adopters in the React community tend to use the new syntax. This often means that documentation assumes knowledge of the latest ECMAScript syntax. If you are not familiar with the latest spec, looking at React code can be daunting.

Popularity of Functional JavaScript

In addition to the changes emerging at a language level, there is a lot of momentum around functional JavaScript programming. JavaScript isn't necessarily a functional language, but functional techniques can be used in JavaScript code. React emphasizes functional programming over object-oriented programming. This shift in thinking can lead to benefits in areas like testability and performance. But when a lot of React materials assume an understanding of the paradigm, it can be hard to learn so much at once.

JavaScript Tooling Fatigue

It's a cliche at this point to talk about JavaScript Fatigue (*http://bit.ly/2pSiuE4*), but the source of this fake illness can be traced back to the building process. In the past, you just added JavaScript files to your page. Now the JavaScript file has to be built, usually with an automated continuous delivery process. There's emerging syntax that has to be transpiled to work in all browsers. There's JSX that has to be converted to JavaScript. There's SCSS that you might want to preprocess. These components need to be tested, and they have to pass. You might love React, but now you also need to be a webpack expert, handling code splitting, compression, testing, and on and on.

Why React Doesn't Have to Be Hard to Learn

The goal of this book is to avoid confusion in the learning process by putting things in sequence and building a strong learning foundation. We'll start with a syntax upgrade to get you acquainted with the latest JavaScript features, especially the ones that are frequently used with React. Then we'll give an introduction to functional JavaScript so you can apply these techniques immediately and understand the paradigm that gave birth to React.

From there, we will cover foundational React knowledge including your first components and how and why we need to transpile our code. With the basics in place, we will break ground on a new application that allows users to save and organize colors. We will build this application using React, improve the code with advanced React techniques, introduce Redux as the client data container, and finish off the app by incorporating Jest testing and routing with the React Router. In the final chapter, we will introduce universal and isomorphic code and enhance the color organizer by rendering it on the server.

We hope to get you up to speed with the React ecosystem faster by approaching it this way—not just to scratch the surface, but to equip you with the tools and skills necessary to build real world React applications.

React's Future

React is still new. It has reached a place where core functionality is fairly stable, but even that can change. Future versions of React will include Fiber, a reimplementation of React's core algorithm which is aimed at increasing rendering speed. It's a little early to hypothesize about how this will affect React developers, but it will definitely affect the speed at which apps are rendered and updated.

Many of these changes have to do with the devices that are being targeted. This book covers techniques for developing single-page web applications with React, but we shouldn't assume that web browsers are the only place that React apps can run. React Native, released in 2015, allows you to take the benefits of React applications into iOS and Android native apps. It's still early, but React VR, a framework for building interactive, virtual reality apps, has emerged as a way to design 360 degree experiences using React and JavaScript. A command of the React library will set you up to rapidly develop experiences for a range of screen sizes and types.

We hope to provide you with a strong enough foundation to be able to adapt to the changing ecosystem and build applications that can run on platforms beyond the web browser.

Keeping Up with the Changes

As changes are made to React and related tools, sometimes there are breaking changes. In fact, some of the future versions of these tools may break some of the example code in this book. You can still follow along with the code samples. We'll provide exact version information in the *package.json* file, so that you can install these packages at the correct version.

Beyond this book, you can stay on top of changes by following along with the official React blog (*https://facebook.github.io/react/blog/*). When new versions of React are released, the core team will write a detailed blog post and changelog about what is new.

There are also a variety of popular React conferences that you can attend for the latest React information. If you can't attend these in person, React conferences often release the talks on YouTube following the events. These include:

React Conf (http://conf.reactjs.com)
    Facebook-sponsored conference in the Bay Area

React Rally (http://www.reactrally.com)
    Community conference in Salt Lake City

ReactiveConf (https://reactiveconf.com)
    Community conference in Bratislava, Slovakia

React Amsterdam (http://react.amsterdam)
    Community conference in Amsterdam

Working with the Files

In this section, we will discuss how to work with the files for this book and how to install some useful React tools.

File Repository

The GitHub repository associated with this book (*https://github.com/moonhighway/learning-react*) provides all of the code files organized by chapter. The repository is a mix of code files and JSBin samples. If you've never used JSBin before, it's an online code editor similar to CodePen and JSFiddle.

One of the main benefits of JSBin is that you can click the link and immediately start tinkering with the file. When you create or start editing a JSBin, it will generate a unique URL for your code sample, as in Figure 1-1.

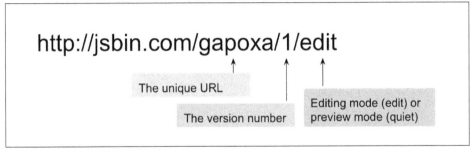

Figure 1-1. JSBin URL

The letters that follow *jsbin.com* represent the unique URL key. After the next slash is the version number. In the last part of the URL, there will be one of two words: *edit* for editing mode or *quiet* for preview mode.

React Developer Tools

There are several developer tools that can be installed as browser extensions or add-ons that you may find useful as well:

react-detector (http://bit.ly/2mwcoXR)
> react-detector is a Chrome extension that lets you know which websites are using React and which are not.

show-me-the-react
> This is another tool, available for Firefox (*http://bit.ly/2nvM0il*) and Chrome (*http://bit.ly/2nvKz3y*), that detects React as you browse the internet.

React Developer Tools (http://bit.ly/2nvFKar) (see Figure 1-2)
> This is a plugin that can extend the functionality of the browser's developer tools. It creates a new tab in the developer tools where you can view React elements.
>
> If you prefer Chrome, you can install it as an extension (*http://bit.ly/1O5DTlX*); you can also install it as an add-on for Firefox (*https://mzl.la/2mMVgi5*).

Figure 1-2. Viewing the React Developer Tools

Any time you see react-detector or show-me-the-react as active, you can open the developer tools and get an understanding of how React is being used on the site.

Installing Node.js

Node.js is JavaScript without the browser. It is a runtime environment used to build full-stack JavaScript applications. Node is open source and can be installed on Windows, macOS, Linux, and other platforms. We will be using Node in Chapter 12 when we build an Express server.

You do not need to use Node to use React. However, when working with React, you need to use the Node package manager, npm, to install dependencies. This is automatically installed with the Node installation.

If you're not sure if Node.js is installed on your machine, you can open a Terminal or Command Prompt window and type:

```
$ node -v
```

```
Output: v7.3.0
```

Ideally, you will have a Node version number of 4 or higher. If you type the command and see an error message that says "Command not found," Node.js is not installed. This can be done directly from the Node.js website (*http://nodejs.org*). Just go through the automated steps of the installer, and when you type in the node -v command again, you'll see the version number.

Dependency Management with Yarn

An optional alternative for npm is Yarn. It was released in 2016 by Facebook, in collaboration with Exponent, Google, and Tilde. The project helps Facebook and other companies manage their dependencies more reliably, and when using it to install packages, you'll likely notice that it's much faster. You can compare npm and Yarn's performance at the Yarn website (*https://yarnpkg.com/en/compare*).

If you're familiar with the npm workflow, getting up to speed with Yarn is fairly simple. First, install Yarn globally with npm.

```
npm install -g yarn
```

Then, you are ready to install packages. When installing dependencies from the package.json, in place of npm install, you can run yarn.

When installing specific packages, Instead of running npm install --save [package-name], run:

```
yarn add [package-name]
```

To remove a dependency, the command is familiar too:

```
yarn remove [package-name]
```

Yarn is used in production by Facebook and is included in projects like React, React Native, and create-react-app. If you ever find a project that contains a *yarn.lock* file, the project uses yarn. Similar to the npm install command, you can install all of the dependencies of the project by typing **yarn install** or simply **yarn**.

Now that you have your environment set up for React development, we are ready to begin overcoming learning obstacles. In Chapter 2, we will address ECMA, and get up to speed with the latest JavaScript syntax that is most commonly found in React code.

Emerging JavaScript

Since its release in 1995, JavaScript has gone through many changes. At first, it made adding interactive elements to web pages much simpler. Then it got more robust with DHTML and AJAX. Now, with Node.js, JavaScript has become a language that is used to build full-stack applications. The committee that is and has been in charge of shepherding the changes to JavaScript is the European Computer Manufacturers Association (ECMA).

Changes to the language are community-driven. They originate from proposals that community members write. Anyone can submit a proposal (*https://tc39.github.io/ process-document/*) to the ECMA committee. The responsibility of the ECMA committee is to manage and prioritize these proposals in order to decide what is included in each spec. Proposals are taken through clearly defined stages, from stage 0, which represents the newest proposals, up through stage 4, which represents the finished proposals.

The most recent major update to the specification was approved in June 2015[1] and is called by many names: ECMAScript 6, ES6, ES2015, and ES6Harmony. Based on current plans, new specs will be released on a yearly cycle. The 2016 release was relatively small, but it already looks like ES2017 will include quite a few useful features. We'll be using many of these new features in the book and will opt to use emerging JavaScript whenever possible.

Many of these features are already supported by the newest browsers. We will also be covering how to convert your code from emerging JavaScript syntax to ES5 syntax that will work today in almost all browsers. The kangax compatibility table (*http://*

---

1 Abel Avram, "ECMAScript 2015 Has Been Approved" (*http://bit.ly/2nvMJjJ*), InfoQ, June 17, 2015.

kangax.github.io/compat-table/esnext/) is a great place to stay informed about the latest JavaScript features and their varying degrees of support by browsers.

In this chapter, we will show you all of the emerging JavaScript that we'll be using throughout the book. If you haven't made the switch to the latest syntax yet, now would be a good time to get started. If you are already comfortable with ES.Next language features, skip to the next chapter.

Declaring Variables in ES6

Prior to ES6, the only way to declare a variable was with the var keyword. We now have a few different options that provide improved functionality.

const

A constant is a variable that cannot be changed. Like other languages had done before it, JavaScript introduced constants with ES6.

Before constants, all we had were variables, and variables could be overwritten:

```
var pizza = true
pizza = false
console.log(pizza) // false
```

We cannot reset the value of a constant variable, and it will generate a console error (Figure 2-1) if we try to overwrite the value:

```
const pizza = true
pizza = false
```

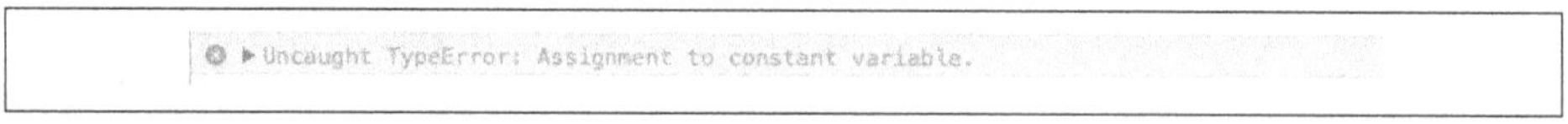

```
⊘ ▶ Uncaught TypeError: Assignment to constant variable.
```

Figure 2-1. An attempt at overwriting a constant

let

JavaScript now has *lexical variable scoping*. In JavaScript, we create code blocks with curly braces ({}). With functions, these curly braces block off the scope of variables. On the other hand, think about if/else statements. If you're coming from other languages, you might assume that these blocks would also block variable scope. This is not the case.

If a variable is created inside of an if/else block, that variable is not scoped to the block:

```
var topic = "JavaScript"

if (topic) {
  var topic = "React"
```

```
  console.log('block', topic)        // block React
}

console.log('global', topic)         // global React
```

The `topic` variable inside the `if` block resets the value of `topic`.

With the `let` keyword, we can scope a variable to any code block. Using `let` protects the value of the global variable:

```
var topic = "JavaScript"

if (topic) {
  let topic = "React"
  console.log('block', topic)        // React
}

console.log('global', topic)         // JavaScript
```

The value of `topic` is not reset outside of the block.

Another area where curly braces don't block off a variable's scope is in `for` loops:

```
var div,
    container = document.getElementById('container')

for (var i=0; i<5; i++) {
  div = document.createElement('div')
  div.onclick = function() {
      alert('This is box #' + i)
    }
  container.appendChild(div)
}
```

In this loop, we create five `div`s to appear within a container. Each `div` is assigned an `onclick` handler that creates an alert box to display the index. Declaring `i` in the `for` loop creates a global variable named `i`, and then iterates it until its value reaches 5. When you click on any of these boxes, the alert says that `i` is equal to 5 for all `div`s, because the current value for the global `i` is 5 (Figure 2-2).

Figure 2-2. i is equal to 5 for each box

Declaring the loop counter i with let instead of var does block off the scope of i. Now clicking on any box will display the value for i that was scoped to the loop iteration (Figure 2-3):

```
var div, container = document.getElementById('container')
for (let i=0; i<5; i++) {
  div = document.createElement('div')
  div.onclick = function() {
      alert('This is box #: ' + i)
   }
  container.appendChild(div)
}
```

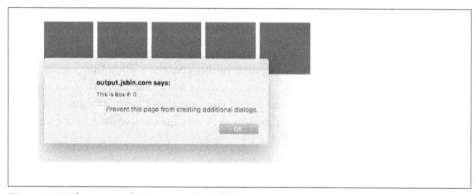

Figure 2-3. The scope of i is protected with let

Template Strings

Template strings provide us with an alternative to string concatenation. They also allow us to insert variables into a string.

Traditional string concatenation uses plus signs to compose a string using variable values and strings:

```
console.log(lastName + ", " + firstName + " " + middleName)
```

With a template, we can create one string and insert the variable values by surrounding them with ${ }:

```
console.log(`${lastName}, ${firstName} ${middleName}`)
```

Any JavaScript that returns a value can be added to a template string between the $ { } in a template string.

Template strings honor whitespace, making it easier to draft up email templates, code examples, or anything else that contains whitespace. Now you can have a string that spans multiple lines without breaking your code. Example 2-1 illustrates using tabs, line breaks, spaces, and variable names in an email template.

Example 2-1. Template strings honor whitespace

```
`

Hello ${firstName},

Thanks for ordering ${qty} tickets to ${event}.

Order Details
  ${firstName} ${middleName} ${lastName}
  ${qty} x $${price} = $${qty*price} to ${event}

You can pick your tickets up at will call 30 minutes before
the show.

Thanks,

${ticketAgent}

`
```

Previously, using an HTML string directly in our JavaScript code was not so easy to do because we'd need to run it together on one line. Now that the whitespace is recognized as text, you can insert formatted HTML that is easy to understand:

```
document.body.innerHTML = `
<section>
  <header>
      <h1>The HTML5 Blog</h1>
  </header>
  <article>
      <h2>${article.title}</h2>
      ${article.body}
  </article>
  <footer>
      <p>copyright ${new Date().getYear()} | The HTML5 Blog</p>
```

```
        </footer>
    </section>
```

Notice that we can include variables for the page title and article text as well.

Default Parameters

Languages including C++ and Python allow developers to declare default values for function arguments. Default parameters are included in the ES6 spec, so in the event that a value is not provided for the argument, the default value will be used.

For example, we can set up default strings:

```
function logActivity(name="Shane McConkey", activity="skiing") {
  console.log( `${name} loves ${activity}` )
}
```

If no arguments are provided to the `logActivity` function, it will run correctly using the default values. Default arguments can be any type, not just strings:

```
var defaultPerson = {
    name: {
        first: "Shane",
        last: "McConkey"
    },
    favActivity: "skiing"
}

function logActivity(p=defaultPerson) {
    console.log(`${p.name.first} loves ${p.favActivity}`)
}
```

Arrow Functions

Arrow functions are a useful new feature of ES6. With arrow functions, you can create functions without using the `function` keyword. You also often do not have to use the `return` keyword. Example 2-2 shows the traditional function syntax.

Example 2-2. As a traditional function

```
var lordify = function(firstname) {
  return `${firstname} of Canterbury`
}

console.log( lordify("Dale") )      // Dale of Canterbury
console.log( lordify("Daryle") )    // Daryle of Canterbury
```

With an arrow function, we can simplify the syntax tremendously, as shown in Example 2-3.

Example 2-3. As an arrow function

```
var lordify = firstname => `${firstname} of Canterbury`
```

GROSS

Semicolons Throughout This Book

Semicolons are ~~optional in JavaScript~~. Our philosophy is, why put in semicolons ~~that~~ aren't required? ~~This book~~ takes a minimal ~~approach~~ that excludes unnecessary syntax.

With the arrow, we now have an entire function declaration on one line. The `func tion` keyword is removed. We also remove `return` because the arrow points to what should be returned. Another benefit is that if the function only takes one argument, we can remove the parentheses around the arguments.

More than one argument should be surrounded by parentheses:

```
// Old
var lordify = function(firstName, land) {
  return `${firstName} of ${land}`
}

// New
var lordify = (firstName, land) => `${firstName} of ${land}`

console.log( lordify("Dale", "Maryland") )    // Dale of Maryland
console.log( lordify("Daryle", "Culpeper") )  // Daryle of Culpeper
```

We can keep this as a one-line function because there is only one statement that needs to be returned.

More than one line needs to be surrounded with brackets:

```
// Old
var lordify = function(firstName, land) {

  if (!firstName) {
    throw new Error('A firstName is required to lordify')
  }

  if (!land) {
    throw new Error('A lord must have a land')
  }

  return `${firstName} of ${land}`
}

// New
var lordify = (firstName, land) => {

  if (!firstName) {
```

```
    throw new Error('A firstName is required to lordify')
  }

  if (!land) {
    throw new Error('A lord must have a land')
  }

  return `${firstName} of ${land}`
}

console.log( lordify("Kelly", "Sonoma") )   // Kelly of Sonoma
console.log( lordify("Dave") )              // ! JAVASCRIPT ERROR
```

These `if/else` statements are surrounded with brackets but still benefit from the shorter syntax of the arrow function.

Regular functions do not block `this`. For example, `this` becomes something else in the `setTimeout` callback, not the `tahoe` object:

```
var tahoe = {
  resorts: ["Kirkwood","Squaw","Alpine","Heavenly","Northstar"],
  print: function(delay=1000) {

    setTimeout(function() {
      console.log(this.resorts.join(", "))
    }, delay)

  }
}

tahoe.print() // Cannot read property 'join' of undefined
```

This error is thrown because it's trying to use the `.join` method on what `this` is. In this case, it's the window object. Alternatively, we can use the arrow function syntax to protect the scope of `this`:

```
var tahoe = {
  resorts: ["Kirkwood","Squaw","Alpine","Heavenly","Northstar"],
  print: function(delay=1000) {

    setTimeout(() => {
      console.log(this.resorts.join(", "))
    }, delay)

  }
}

tahoe.print() // Kirkwood, Squaw, Alpine, Heavenly, Northstar
```

This works correctly and we can `.join` the resorts with a comma. Be careful, though, that you're always keeping scope in mind. Arrow functions do not block off the scope of `this`:

```
var tahoe = {
  resorts: ["Kirkwood","Squaw","Alpine","Heavenly","Northstar"],
  print: (delay=1000) => {

    setTimeout(() => {
      console.log(this.resorts.join(","))
    }, delay)

  }
}
```

```
tahoe.print() // Cannot read property resorts of undefined
```

Changing the print function to an arrow function means that this is actually the window.

To verify, let's change the console message to evaluate whether this is the window:

```
var tahoe = {
  resorts: ["Kirkwood","Squaw","Alpine","Heavenly","Northstar"],
  print: (delay=1000)=> {

    setTimeout(() => {
      console.log(this === window)
    }, delay)

  }
}
```

```
tahoe.print()
```

It evaluates as true. To fix this, we can use a regular function:

```
var tahoe = {
  resorts: ["Kirkwood","Squaw","Alpine","Heavenly","Northstar"],
  print: function(delay=1000) {

    setTimeout(() => {
      console.log(this === window)
    }, delay)

  }
}
```

```
tahoe.print() // false
```

Transpiling ES6

Not all web browsers support ES6, and even those that do don't support everything. The only way to be sure that your ES6 code will work is to convert it to ES5 code before running it in the browser. This process is called *transpiling*. One of the most popular tools for transpiling is Babel (*http://www.babeljs.io*).

In the past, the only way to use the latest JavaScript features was to wait weeks, months, or even years until browsers supported them. Now, transpiling has made it possible to use the latest features of JavaScript right away. The transpiling step makes JavaScript similar to other languages. Transpiling is not compiling: our code isn't compiled to binary. Instead, it's transpiled into syntax that can be interpreted by a wider range of browsers. Also, JavaScript now has source code, meaning that there will be some files that belong to your project that don't run in the browser.

Example 2-4 shows some ES6 code. We have an arrow function, already covered, mixed with some default arguments for x and y.

Example 2-4. ES6 code before Babel transpiling

```
const add = (x=5, y=10) => console.log(x+y);
```

After we run the transpiler on this code, here is what the output will look like:

```
"use strict";

var add = function add() {
    var x = arguments.length <= 0 || arguments[0] === undefined ?
        5 : arguments[0];
    var y = arguments.length <= 1 || arguments[1] === undefined ?
        10 : arguments[1];
    return console.log(x + y);
};
```

The transpiler added a "use strict" declaration to run in strict mode. The variables x and y are defaulted using the arguments array, a technique you may be familiar with. The resulting JavaScript is more widely supported.

You can transpile JavaScript directly in the browser using the inline Babel transpiler. You just include the *browser.js* file, and any scripts with type="text/babel" will be converted (even though Babel 6 is the current version of Babel, only the CDN for Babel 5 will work):

```
<script
    src="https://cdnjs.cloudflare.com/ajax/libs/babel-core/5.8.23/browser.js">
</script>
<script src="script.js" type="text/babel">
</script>
```

Transpiling in the Browser

This approach means that the browser does the transpiling at runtime. This is not a good idea for production because it will slow your application down a lot. In Chapter 5, we'll go over how to do this in production. For now, the CDN link will allow us to discover and use ES6 features.

You may be thinking to yourself: "Great! When ES6 is supported by all browsers, we won't have to use Babel anymore!" However, by the time this happens, we will want to use features of the next version of the spec. Unless a tectonic shift occurs, we'll likely be using Babel in the foreseeable future.

ES6 Objects and Arrays

ES6 gives us new ways for working with objects and arrays and for scoping the variables within these datasets. These features include destructuring, object literal enhancement, and the spread operator.

Destructuring Assignment

The destructuring assignment allows you to locally scope fields within an object and to declare which values will be used.

Consider this sandwich object. It has four keys, but we only want to use the values of two. We can scope bread and meat to be used locally:

```
var sandwich = {
    bread: "dutch crunch",
    meat: "tuna",
    cheese: "swiss",
    toppings: ["lettuce", "tomato", "mustard"]
}

var {bread, meat} = sandwich

console.log(bread, meat) // dutch crunch tuna
```

const X = {a, b, c};

const {a, b} = X;

The code pulls bread and meat out of the object and creates local variables for them. Also, the bread and meat variables can be changed:

```
var {bread, meat} = sandwich

bread = "garlic"
meat = "turkey"

console.log(bread) // garlic
console.log(meat) // turkey

console.log(sandwich.bread, sandwich.meat) // dutch crunch tuna
```

We can also destructure incoming function arguments. Consider this function that would log a person's name as a lord:

```
var lordify = regularPerson => {
  console.log(`${regularPerson.firstname} of Canterbury`)
}
```

```
var regularPerson = {
  firstname: "Bill",
  lastname: "Wilson"
}

lordify(regularPerson)        // Bill of Canterbury
```

Instead of using dot notation syntax to dig into objects, we can destructure the values that we need out of `regularPerson`:

```
var lordify = ({firstname}) => {
  console.log(`${firstname} of Canterbury`)
}

lordify(regularPerson)        // Bill of Canterbury
```

Destructuring is also more declarative, meaning that our code is more descriptive about what we are trying to accomplish. By destructuring `firstname`, we declare that we will only use the `firstname` variable. We'll cover more on declarative programming in the next chapter.

Values can also be destructured from arrays. Imagine that we wanted to assign the first value of an array to a variable name:

```
var [firstResort] = ["Kirkwood", "Squaw", "Alpine"]

console.log(firstResort) // Kirkwood
```

We can also pass over unnecessary values with *list matching* using commas. List matching occurs when commas take the place of elements that should be skipped. With the same array, we can access the last value by replacing the first two values with commas:

```
var [,,thirdResort] = ["Kirkwood", "Squaw", "Alpine"]

console.log(thirdResort) // Alpine
```

Later in this section, we'll take this example a step further by combining array destructuring and the spread operator.

Object Literal Enhancement

Object literal enhancement is the opposite of destructuring. It is the process of restructuring or putting back together. With object literal enhancement, we can grab variables from the global scope and turn them into an object:

```
var name = "Tallac"
var elevation = 9738

var funHike = {name,elevation}

console.log(funHike) // {name: "Tallac", elevation: 9738}
```

name and `elevation` are now keys of the `funHike` object.

We can also create object methods with object literal enhancement or restructuring:

```
var name = "Tallac"
var elevation = 9738
var print = function() {
  console.log(`Mt. ${this.name} is ${this.elevation} feet tall`)
}

var funHike = {name,elevation,print}

funHike.print()     // Mt. Tallac is 9738 feet tall
```

Notice we use `this` to access the object keys.

When defining object methods, it is no longer necessary to use the `function` keyword (Example 2-5).

Example 2-5. Old versus new: Object syntax

```
// OLD
var skier = {
    name: name,
    sound: sound,
    powderYell: function() {
        var yell = this.sound.toUpperCase()
        console.log(`${yell} ${yell} ${yell}!!!`)
    },
    speed: function(mph) {
        this.speed = mph
        console.log('speed:', mph)
    }
}

// NEW
const skier = {
    name,
    sound,
    powderYell() {
        let yell = this.sound.toUpperCase()
        console.log(`${yell} ${yell} ${yell}!!!`)
    },
    speed(mph) {
        this.speed = mph
        console.log('speed:', mph)
    }
}
```

Object literal enhancement allows us to pull global variables into objects and reduces typing by making the `function` keyword unnecessary.

The Spread Operator

The spread operator is three dots (...) that perform several different tasks. First, the spread operator allows us to combine the contents of arrays. For example, if we had two arrays, we could make a third array that combines the two arrays into one:

```
var peaks = ["Tallac", "Ralston", "Rose"]
var canyons = ["Ward", "Blackwood"]
var tahoe = [...peaks, ...canyons]

console.log(tahoe.join(', '))  // Tallac, Ralston, Rose, Ward, Blackwood
```

All of the items from peaks and canyons are pushed into a new array called tahoe.

Let's take a look at how the spread operator can help us deal with a problem. Using the peaks array from the previous sample, let's imagine that we wanted to grab the last item from the array rather than the first. We could use the Array.reverse method to reverse the array in combination with array destructuring:

```
var peaks = ["Tallac", "Ralston", "Rose"]
var [last] = peaks.reverse()

console.log(last) // Rose
console.log(peaks.join(', ')) // Rose, Ralston, Tallac
```

See what happened? The reverse function has actually altered or mutated the array. In a world with the spread operator, we don't have to mutate the original array; we can create a copy of the array and then reverse it:

```
var peaks = ["Tallac", "Ralston", "Rose"]
var [last] = [...peaks].reverse()

console.log(last) // Rose
console.log(peaks.join(', '))  // Tallac, Ralston, Rose
```

Since we used the spread operator to copy the array, the peaks array is still intact and can be used later in its original form.

The spread operator can also be used to get some, or the rest, of the items in the array:

```
var lakes = ["Donner", "Marlette", "Fallen Leaf", "Cascade"]

var [first, ...rest] = lakes

console.log(rest.join(", ")) // "Marlette, Fallen Leaf, Cascade"
```

We can also use the spread operator to collect function arguments as an array. Here, we build a function that takes in *n* number of arguments using the spread operator, and then uses those arguments to print some console messages:

```
function directions(...args) {
  var [start, ...remaining] = args
  var [finish, ...stops] = remaining.reverse()

  console.log(`drive through ${args.length} towns`)
  console.log(`start in ${start}`)
  console.log(`the destination is ${finish}`)
  console.log(`stopping ${stops.length} times in between`)
}

directions(
    "Truckee",
    "Tahoe City",
    "Sunnyside",
    "Homewood",
    "Tahoma"
)
```

The directions function takes in the arguments using the spread operator. The first argument is assigned to the start variable. The last argument is assigned to a finish variable using Array.reverse. We then use the length of the arguments array to display how many towns we're going through. The number of stops is the length of the arguments array minus the finish stop. This provides incredible flexibility because we could use the directions function to handle any number of stops.

The spread operator can also be used for objects.[2] Using the spread operator with objects is similar to using it with arrays. In this example, we'll use it the same way we combined two arrays into a third array, but instead of arrays, we'll use objects:

```
var morning = {
  breakfast: "oatmeal",
  lunch: "peanut butter and jelly"
}

var dinner = "mac and cheese"

var backpackingMeals = {
  ...morning,
  dinner
}

console.log(backpackingMeals) // {  breakfast: "oatmeal",
                              //    lunch: "peanut butter and jelly",
                              //    dinner: "mac and cheese"}
```

---

2 Rest/Spread Properties (*https://github.com/tc39/proposals*)

Promises

Promises give us a way to make sense out of asynchronous behavior. When making an asynchronous request, one of two things can happen: everything goes as we hope or there's an error. There may be several different types of successful or unsuccessful requests. For example, we could try several ways to obtain the data to reach success. We could also receive multiple types of errors. Promises give us a way to simplify back to a simple pass or fail.

Let's create an asynchronous promise for loading data from the *randomuser.me* API. This API has information like email address, name, phone number, location, and so on for fake members and is great to use as dummy data.

The `getFakeMembers` function returns a new promise. The promise makes a request to the API. If the promise is successful, the data will load. If the promise is unsuccessful, an error will occur:

```
const getFakeMembers = count => new Promise((resolves, rejects) => {
  const api = `https://api.randomuser.me/?nat=US&results=${count}`
  const request = new XMLHttpRequest()
  request.open('GET', api)
  request.onload = () =>
      (request.status === 200) ?
       resolves(JSON.parse(request.response).results) :
       reject(Error(request.statusText))
  request.onerror = (err) => rejects(err)
  request.send()
})
```

With that, the promise has been created, but it hasn't been used yet. We can use the promise by calling the `getFakeMembers` function and passing in the number of members that should be loaded. The `then` function can be chained on to do something once the promise has been fulfilled. This is called composition. We'll also use an additional callback that handles errors:

```
getFakeMembers(5).then(
  members => console.log(members),
  err => console.error(
      new Error("cannot load members from randomuser.me"))
)
```

Promises make dealing with asynchronous requests easier, which is good, because we have to deal with a lot of asynchronous data in JavaScript. You'll also see promises used heavily in Node.js, so a solid understanding of promises is essential for the modern JavaScript engineer.

Classes

Previously in JavaScript, there were no official classes. Types were defined by functions. We had to create a function and then define methods on the function object using the prototype:

```javascript
function Vacation(destination, length) {
  this.destination = destination
  this.length = length
}

Vacation.prototype.print = function() {
    console.log(this.destination + " | " + this.length + " days")
}

var maui = new Vacation("Maui", 7)

maui.print() // Maui | 7 days
```

If you were used to classical object orientation, this probably made you mad.

ES6 introduces class declaration, but JavaScript still works the same way. Functions are objects, and inheritance is handled through the prototype, but this syntax makes more sense if you come from classical object orientation:

```javascript
class Vacation {

  constructor(destination, length) {
    this.destination = destination
    this.length = length
  }

  print() {
    console.log(`${this.destination} will take ${this.length} days.`)
  }

}
```

Capitalization Conventions

The rule of thumb with capitalization is that all types should be capitalized. Due to that, we will capitalize all class names.

Once you've created the class, you can create a new instance of the class using the new keyword. Then you can call the custom method on the class:

```javascript
const trip = new Vacation("Santiago, Chile", 7)

trip.print() // Chile will take 7 days.
```

Now that a class object has been created, you can use it as many times as you'd like to create new vacation instances. Classes can also be extended. When a class is extended, the subclass inherits the properties and methods of the superclass. These properties and methods can be manipulated from here, but as a default, all will be inherited.

You can use Vacation as an abstract class to create different types of vacations. For instance, an Expedition can extend the Vacation class to include gear:

```
class Expedition extends Vacation {

  constructor(destination, length, gear) {
   super(destination, length)
   this.gear = gear
  }

  print() {
    super.print()
    console.log(`Bring your ${this.gear.join(" and your ")}`)
  }
}
```

That's simple inheritance: the subclass inherits the properties of the superclass. By calling the print method of Vacation, we can append some new content onto what is printed in the print method of Expedition. Creating a new instance works the exact same way—create a variable and use the new keyword:

```
const trip = new Expedition("Mt. Whitney", 3,
                  ["sunglasses", "prayer flags", "camera"])

trip.print()

// Mt. Whitney will take 3 days.
// Bring your sunglasses and your prayer flags and your camera
```

Classes and Prototypal Inheritance

Using a class still means that you are using JavaScript's prototypal inheritance. Log Vacation.prototype, and you'll notice the constructor and print methods on the prototype.

We will use classes a bit in this book, but we're focusing on the functional paradigm. Classes have other features, like getters, setters, and static methods, but this book favors functional techniques over object-oriented techniques. The reason we're introducing these is because we'll use them later when creating React components.

ES6 Modules

A JavaScript *module* is a piece of reusable code that can easily be incorporated into other JavaScript files. Until recently, the only way to work with modular JavaScript was to incorporate a library that could handle importing and exporting modules. Now, with ES6, JavaScript itself supports modules.[3] *but mult modules/exports per file*

JavaScript modules are stored in separate files, one file per module. There are two options when creating and exporting a module: you can export multiple JavaScript objects from a single module, or one JavaScript object per module.

In Example 2-6, *text-helpers.js*, two functions are exported.

Example 2-6. ./text-helpers.js

```
export const print(message) => log(message, new Date())

export const log(message, timestamp) =>
    console.log(`${timestamp.toString()}: ${message}`)
```

export can be used to export any JavaScript type that will be consumed in another module. In this example the print function and log function are being exported. Any other variables declared in *text-helpers.js* will be local to that module.

Sometimes you may want to export only one variable from a module. In these cases you can use export default (Example 2-7).

Example 2-7. ./mt-freel.js

```
const freel = new Expedition("Mt. Freel", 2, ["water", "snack"])

export default freel
```

export default can be used in place of export when you wish to export only one type. Again, both export and export default can be used on any JavaScript type: primitives, objects, arrays, and functions.[4]

Modules can be consumed in other JavaScript files using the import statement. Modules with multiple exports can take advantage of object destructuring. Modules that use export default are imported into a single variable:

```
import { print, log } from './text-helpers'
import freel from './mt-freel'
```

---

3 Mozilla Developer Network, JavaScript Code Modules (*https://mzl.la/2nvHwIR*)

4 Mozilla Developer Network, "Using JavaScript Code Modules" (*https://mzl.la/2nvBS9r*).

```
print('printing a message')
log('logging a message')

freel.print()
```

You can scope module variables locally under different variable names:

```
import { print as p, log as l } from './text-helpers'

p('printing a message')
l('logging a message')
```

You can also import everything into a single variable using *:

```
import * as fns from './text-helpers
```

ES6 modules are not yet fully supported by all browsers. Babel does support ES6 modules, so we will be using them throughout this book.

CommonJS

CommonJS is the module pattern that is supported by all versions of Node.js.[5] You can still use these modules with Babel and webpack. With CommonJS, JavaScript objects are exported using module.exports, as in Example 2-8.

Example 2-8. ./txt-helpers.js

```
const print(message) => log(message, new Date())

const log(message, timestamp) =>
    console.log(`${timestamp.toString()}: ${message}`)

module.exports = {print, log}
```

CommonJS does not support an import statement. Instead, modules are imported with the require function:

```
const { log, print } = require('./txt-helpers')
```

JavaScript is indeed moving quickly and adapting to the increasing demands that engineers are placing on the language. Browsers are quickly implementing the features of ES6 and beyond, so it's a good idea to use these features now without hesitation.[6] Many of the features that are included in the ES6 spec are present because they

---

5 Node.js Documentation, "Modules" (*https://nodejs.org/docs/latest/api/modules.html*).

6 For up-to-date compatibility information, see the ES6 compatibility table (*http://kangax.github.io/compat-table/es6/*).

support functional programming techniques. In functional JavaScript, we can think about our code as being a collection of functions that can be composed into applications. In the next chapter, we'll explore functional techniques in more detail and will discuss why you might want to use them.

CHAPTER 3

Functional Programming with JavaScript

When you start to explore the world of React programming, you'll notice that the topic of functional programming comes up a lot. Functional techniques are being used more and more in JavaScript projects.

You may have already written functional JavaScript code without thinking about it. If you've mapped or reduced an array, then you're already on your way to becoming a functional programmer. React, Flux, and Redux all fit within the functional JavaScript paradigm. Understanding the basic concepts of functional programming will elevate your knowledge of structuring React applications.

If you are wondering where this functional trend came from, the answer is the 1930s, with the invention of *lambda calculus*, or λ-calculus.[1] Functions have been a part of calculus since it emerged in the 17th century. Functions can be sent to functions as arguments or returned from functions as results. More complex functions, called *higher-order functions*, can manipulate functions and use them as either arguments or results or both. In the 1930s, Alonzo Church was at Princeton experimenting with these higher-order functions when he invented lambda calculus.

In the late 1950s, John McCarthy took the concepts derived from λ-calculus and applied them to a new programming language called Lisp. Lisp implemented the concept of higher-order functions and functions as *first-class members* or first-class citizens. A function is considered a first-class member when it can be declared as a variable and sent to functions as an argument. These functions can even be returned from functions.

---

1 Data S. Scott, "λ-Calculus: Then & Now" (*http://turing100.acm.org/lambda_calculus_timeline.pdf*).

In this chapter, we are going to go over some of the key concepts of functional programming, and we'll cover how to implement functional techniques with JavaScript.

What It Means to Be Functional

JavaScript supports functional programming because JavaScript functions are first-class citizens. This means that functions can do the same things that variables can do. ES6 adds language improvements that can beef up your functional programming techniques, including arrow functions, promises, and the spread operator (see Chapter 2).

In JavaScript, functions can represent data in your application. You may have noticed that you can declare functions with the var keyword the same way you can declare strings, numbers, or any other variables:

```
var log = function(message) {
  console.log(message)
};

log("In JavaScript functions are variables")

// In JavaScript, functions are variables
```

With ES6, we can write the same function using an arrow function. Functional programmers write a lot of small functions, and the arrow function syntax makes that much easier:

```
const log = message => console.log(message)
```

Since functions are variables, we can add them to objects:

```
const obj = {
    message: "They can be added to objects like variables",
    log(message) {
        console.log(message)
    }
}

obj.log(obj.message)

// They can be added to objects like variables
```

Both of these statements do the same thing: they store a function in a variable called log. Additionally, the const keyword was used to declare the second function, which will prevent it from being overwritten.

We can also add functions to arrays in JavaScript:

```
const messages = [
    "They can be inserted into arrays",
    message => console.log(message),
```

```
      "like variables",
      message => console.log(message)
]

messages[1](messages[0])    // They can be inserted into arrays
messages[3](messages[2])    // like variables
```

Functions can be sent to other functions as arguments, just like other variables:

```
const insideFn = logger =>
  logger("They can be sent to other functions as arguments");


insideFn(message => console.log(message))

// They can be sent to other functions as arguments
```

They can also be returned from other functions, just like variables:

```
var createScream = function(logger) {
    return function(message) {
        logger(message.toUpperCase() + "!!!")
    }
}

const scream = createScream(message => console.log(message))

scream('functions can be returned from other functions')
scream('createScream returns a function')
scream('scream invokes that returned function')

// FUNCTIONS CAN BE RETURNED FROM OTHER FUNCTIONS!!!
// CREATESCREAM RETURNS A FUNCTION!!!
// SCREAM INVOKES THAT RETURNED FUNCTION!!!
```

The last two examples were of higher-order functions, functions that either take or return other functions. Using ES6 syntax, we could describe the same `createScream` higher-order function with arrows:

```
const createScream = logger => message =>
    logger(message.toUpperCase() + "!!!")
```

From here on out, we need to pay attention to the number of arrows used during function declaration. More than one arrow means that we have a higher-order function.

We can say that JavaScript is a functional language because its functions are first-class citizens. This means that functions are data. They can be saved, retrieved, or flow through your applications just like variables.

Imperative Versus Declarative

Functional programming is a part of a larger programming paradigm: *declarative programming*. Declarative programming is a style of programming where applications are structured in a way that prioritizes describing what should happen over defining how it should happen.

In order to understand declarative programming, we'll contrast it with *imperative programming*, or a style of programming that is only concerned with how to achieve results with code. Let's consider a common task: making a string URL-friendly. Typically, this can be accomplished by replacing all of the spaces in a string with hyphens, since spaces are not URL-friendly. First, let's examine an imperative approach to this task:

```
var string = "This is the midday show with Cheryl Waters";
var urlFriendly = "";

for (var i=0; i<string.length; i++) {
  if (string[i] === " ") {
    urlFriendly += "-";
  } else {
    urlFriendly += string[i];
  }
}

console.log(urlFriendly);
```

In this example, we loop through every character in the string, replacing spaces as they occur. The structure of this program is only concerned with how such a task can be achieved. We use a `for` loop and an `if` statement, and set values with an equality operator. Just looking at the code alone does not tell us much. Imperative programs require lots of comments in order to understand what is going on.

Now let's look at a declarative approach to the same problem:

```
const string = "This is the mid day show with Cheryl Waters"
const urlFriendly = string.replace(/ /g, "-")

console.log(urlFriendly)
```

Here we are using `string.replace` along with a regular expression to replace all instances of spaces with hyphens. Using `string.replace` is a way of describing what is supposed to happen: spaces in the string should be replaced. The details of how spaces are dealt with are abstracted away inside the `replace` function. In a declarative program, the syntax itself describes what should happen and the details of how things happen are abstracted away.

Declarative programs are easy to reason about because the code itself describes what is happening. For example, read the syntax in the following sample—it details what happens after members are loaded from an API:

```
const loadAndMapMembers = compose(
    combineWith(sessionStorage, "members"),
    save(sessionStorage, "members"),
    scopeMembers(window),
    logMemberInfoToConsole,
    logFieldsToConsole("name.first"),
    countMembersBy("location.state"),
    prepStatesForMapping,
    save(sessionStorage, "map"),
    renderUSMap
);

getFakeMembers(100).then(loadAndMapMembers);
```

The declarative approach is more readable and, thus, easier to reason about. The details of how each of these functions is implemented are abstracted away. Those tiny functions are named well and combined in a way that describes how member data goes from being loaded to being saved and printed on a map, and this approach does not require many comments. Essentially, declarative programming produces applications that are easier to reason about, and when it is easier to reason about an application, that application is easier to scale.[2]

Now, let's consider the task of building a document object model, or DOM (*https://www.w3.org/DOM/*). An imperative approach would be concerned with how the DOM is constructed:

```
var target = document.getElementById('target');
var wrapper = document.createElement('div');
var headline = document.createElement('h1');

wrapper.id = "welcome";
headline.innerText = "Hello World";

wrapper.appendChild(headline);
target.appendChild(wrapper);
```

This code is concerned with creating elements, setting elements, and adding them to the document. It would be very hard to make changes, add features, or scale 10,000 lines of code where the DOM is constructed imperatively.

Now let's take a look at how we can construct a DOM declaratively using a React component:

---

2 Additional details about the declarative programming paradigm can be found at the Declarative Programming wiki (*http://c2.com/cgi/wiki?DeclarativeProgramming*).

```
const { render } = ReactDOM

const Welcome = () => (
    <div id="welcome">
        <h1>Hello World</h1>
    </div>
)

render(
    <Welcome />,
    document.getElementById('target')
)
```

React is declarative. Here, the Welcome component describes the DOM that should be rendered. The render function uses the instructions declared in the component to build the DOM, abstracting away the details of how the DOM is to be rendered. We can clearly see that we want to render our Welcome component into the element with the ID of 'target'.

Functional Concepts

Now that you have been introduced to functional programming, and what it means to be "functional" or "declarative," we will move on to introducing the core concepts of functional programming: immutability, purity, data transformation, higher-order functions, and recursion.

Immutability

To mutate is to change, so to be *immutable* is to be unchangeable. In a functional program, data is immutable. It never changes.

If you need to share your birth certificate with the public, but want to redact or remove private information, you essentially have two choices: you can take a big Sharpie to your original birth certificate and cross out your private data, or you can find a copy machine. Finding a copy machine, making a copy of your birth certificate, and writing all over that copy with that big Sharpie would be preferable. This way you can have a redacted birth certificate to share and your original that is still intact.

This is how immutable data works in an application. Instead of changing the original data structures, we build changed copies of those data structures and use them instead.

To understand how immutability works, let's take a look at what it means to mutate data. Consider an object that represents the color lawn:

```
let color_lawn = {
    title: "lawn",
    color: "#00FF00",
```

```
    rating: 0
}
```

We could build a function that would rate colors, and use that function to change the rating of the `color` object:

```
function rateColor(color, rating) {
  color.rating = rating
  return color
}

console.log(rateColor(color_lawn, 5).rating)    // 5
console.log(color_lawn.rating)                  // 5
```

In JavaScript, function arguments are references to the actual data. Setting the color's rating like this is bad because it changes or mutates the original color object. (Imagine if you tasked a business with redacting and sharing your birth certificate and they returned your original birth certificate with black marker covering the important details. You'd hope that a business would have the common sense to make a copy of your birth certificate and return the original unharmed.) We can rewrite the `rate Color` function so that it does not harm the original goods (the `color` object):

```
var rateColor = function(color, rating) {
    return Object.assign({}, color, {rating:rating})
}

console.log(rateColor(color_lawn, 5).rating)    // 5
console.log(color_lawn.rating)                  // 4
```

Here, we used `Object.assign` to change the color rating. `Object.assign` is the copy machine; it takes a blank object, copies the color to that object, and overwrites the rating on the copy. Now we can have a newly rated color object without having to change the original.

We can write the same function using an ES6 arrow function along with the object spread operator. This `rateColor` function uses the spread operator to copy the color into a new object and then overwrite its rating:

```
const rateColor = (color, rating) =>
    ({
        ...color,
        rating
    })
```

This emerging JavaScript version of the `rateColor` function is exactly the same as the previous one. It treats color as an immutable object, does so with less syntax, and looks a little bit cleaner. Notice that we wrap the returned object in parentheses. With arrow functions, this is a required step since the arrow can't just point to an object's curly braces.

Let's consider an array of color names:

```
let list = [
    { title: "Rad Red"},
    { title: "Lawn"},
    { title: "Party Pink"}
]
```

We could create a function that will add colors to that array using `Array.push`:

```
var addColor = function(title, colors) {
  colors.push({ title: title })
  return colors;
}
```

```
console.log(addColor("Glam Green", list).length)        // 4
console.log(list.length)                                // 4
```

However, `Array.push` is not an immutable function. This `addColor` function changes the original array by adding another field to it. In order to keep the `colors` array immutable, we must use `Array.concat` instead:

```
const addColor = (title, array) => array.concat({title})
```

```
console.log(addColor("Glam Green", list).length)        // 4
console.log(list.length)                                // 3
```

`Array.concat` concatenates arrays. In this case, it takes a new object, with a new color title, and adds it to a copy of the original array.

You can also use the ES6 spread operator to concatenate arrays in the same way it can be used to copy objects. Here is the emerging JavaScript equivalent of the previous `addColor` function:

```
const addColor = (title, list) => [...list, {title}]
```

This function copies the original list to a new array and then adds a new object containing the color's title to that copy. It is immutable.

Pure Functions

A *pure function* is a function that returns a value that is computed based on its arguments. Pure functions take at least one argument and always return a value or another function. They do not cause side effects, set global variables, or change anything about application state. They treat their arguments as immutable data.

In order to understand pure functions, let's first take a look at an impure function:

```
var frederick = {
    name: "Frederick Douglass",
    canRead: false,
    canWrite: false
}
```

```
function selfEducate() {
    frederick.canRead = true
    frederick.canWrite = true
    return frederick
}

selfEducate()
console.log( frederick )

// {name: "Frederick Douglass", canRead: true, canWrite: true}
```

The selfEducate function is not a pure function. It does not take any arguments, and it does not return a value or a function. It also changes a variable outside of its scope: Frederick. Once the selfEducate function is invoked, something about the "world" has changed. It causes side effects:

```
const frederick = {
  name: "Frederick Douglass",
  canRead: false,
  canWrite: false
}

const selfEducate = (person) => {
  person.canRead = true
  person.canWrite = true
  return person
}

console.log( selfEducate(frederick) )
console.log( frederick )

// {name: "Frederick Douglass", canRead: true, canWrite: true}
// {name: "Frederick Douglass", canRead: true, canWrite: true}
```

Pure Functions Are Testable

Pure functions are naturally *testable*. They do not change anything about their environment or "world," and therefore do not require a complicated test setup or teardown. Everything a pure function needs to operate it accesses via arguments. When testing a pure function, you control the arguments, and thus you can estimate the outcome. You can find more on testing in Chapter 10.

This selfEducate function is also impure: it causes side effects. Invoking this function mutates the objects that are sent to it. If we could treat the arguments sent to this function as immutable data, then we would have a pure function.

Let's have this function take an argument:

```
const frederick = {
    name: "Frederick Douglass",
    canRead: false,
    canWrite: false
}

const selfEducate = person =>
    ({
        ...person,
        canRead: true,
        canWrite: true
    })

console.log( selfEducate(frederick) )
console.log( frederick )

// {name: "Frederick Douglass", canRead: true, canWrite: true}
// {name: "Frederick Douglass", canRead: false, canWrite: false}
```

Finally, this version of selfEducate is a pure function. It computes a value based on the argument that was sent to it: the person. It returns a new person object without mutating the argument sent to it and therefore has no side effects.

Now let's examine an impure function that mutates the DOM:

```
function Header(text) {
  let h1 = document.createElement('h1');
  h1.innerText = text;
  document.body.appendChild(h1);
}

Header("Header() caused side effects");
```

The Header function creates a heading—one element with specific text and adds it to the DOM. This function is impure. It does not return a function or a value, and it causes side effects: a changed DOM.

In React, the UI is expressed with pure functions. In the following sample, Header is a pure function that can be used to create heading—one elements just like in the previous example. However, this function on its own does not cause side effects because it does not mutate the DOM. This function will create a heading-one element, and it is up to some other part of the application to use that element to change the DOM:

```
const Header = (props) => <h1>{props.title}</h1>
```

Pure functions are another core concept of functional programming. They will make your life much easier because they will not affect your application's state. When writing functions, try to follow these three rules:

1. The function should take in at least one argument.

2. The function should return a value or another function.

---

3. The function should not change or mutate any of its arguments.

Data Transformations *Boring, Dull, Just Google it :-*

How does anything change in an application if the data is immutable? Functional programming is all about transforming data from one form to another. We will produce transformed copies using functions. These functions make our code less imperative and thus reduce complexity.

You do not need a special framework to understand how to produce one dataset that is based upon another. JavaScript already has the necessary tools for this task built into the language. There are two core functions that you must master in order to be proficient with functional JavaScript: `Array.map` and `Array.reduce`.

In this section, we will take a look at how these and some other core functions transform data from one type to another.

Consider this array of high schools:

```
const schools = [
  "Yorktown",
  "Washington & Lee",
  "Wakefield"
]
```

We can get a comma-delimited list of these and some other strings by using the `Array.join` function:

```
console.log( schools.join(", ") )

// "Yorktown, Washington & Lee, Wakefield"
```

`join` is a built-in JavaScript array method that we can use to extract a delimited string from our array. The original array is still intact; `join` simply provides a different take on it. The details of how this string is produced are abstracted away from the programmer.

If we wanted to create a function that creates a new array of the schools that begin with the letter "W", we could use the `Array.filter` method:

```
const wSchools = schools.filter(school => school[0] === "W")

console.log( wSchools )
// ["Washington & Lee", "Wakefield"]
```

`Array.filter` is a built-in JavaScript function that produces a new array from a source array. This function takes a *predicate* as its only argument. A predicate is a function that always returns a Boolean value: `true` or `false`. `Array.filter` invokes this predicate once for every item in the array. That item is passed to the predicate as an argument and the return value is used to decide if that item shall be added to the new array. In this case, `Array.filter` is checking every school to see if its name begins with a "W".

When it is time to remove an item from an array we should use `Array.filter` over `Array.pop` or `Array.splice` because `Array.filter` is immutable. In this next sample, the `cutSchool` function returns new arrays that filter out specific school names:

```
const cutSchool = (cut, list) =>
    list.filter(school => school !== cut)

console.log(cutSchool("Washington & Lee", schools).join(" * "))

// "Yorktown * Wakefield"

console.log(schools.join("\n"))

// Yorktown
// Washington & Lee
// Wakefield
```

In this case, the `cutSchool` function is used to return a new array that does not contain "Washington & Lee". Then the `join` function is used with this new array to create a star-delimited string out of the remaining two school names. `cutSchool` is a pure function. It takes a list of schools and the name of the school that should be removed and returns a new array without that specific school.

Another array function that is essential to functional programming is `Array.map`. Instead of a predicate, the `Array.map` method takes a function as its argument. This function will be invoked once for every item in the array, and whatever it returns will be added to the new array:

```
const highSchools = schools.map(school => `${school} High School`)

console.log(highSchools.join("\n"))

//  Yorktown High School
//  Washington & Lee High School
//  Wakefield High School

console.log(schools.join("\n"))

//  Yorktown
//  Washington & Lee
//  Wakefield
```

In this case, the `map` function was used to append "High School" to each school name. The `schools` array is still intact.

In the last example, we produced an array of strings from an array of strings. The map function can produce an array of objects, values, arrays, other functions—any JavaScript type. Here is an example of the map function returning an object for every school:

```
const highSchools = schools.map(school => ({ name: school }))

console.log( highSchools )

// [
//   { name: "Yorktown" },
//   { name: "Washington & Lee" },
//   { name: "Wakefield" }
// ]
```

An array containing objects was produced from an array that contains strings.

If you need to create a pure function that changes one object in an array of objects, map can be used for this, too. In the following example, we will change the school with the name of "Stratford" to "HB Woodlawn" without mutating the schools array:

```
let schools = [
    { name: "Yorktown"},
    { name: "Stratford" },
    { name: "Washington & Lee"},
    { name: "Wakefield"}
]

let updatedSchools = editName("Stratford", "HB Woodlawn", schools)

console.log( updatedSchools[1] )  // { name: "HB Woodlawn" }
console.log( schools[1] )         // { name: "Stratford" },
```

The schools array is an array of objects. The updatedSchools variable calls the edit Name function and we send it the school we want to update, the new school, and the schools array. This changes the new array but makes no edits to the original:

```
const editName = (oldName, name, arr) =>
    arr.map(item => {
        if (item.name === oldName) {
            return {
                ...item,
                name
            }
        } else {
            return item
        }
    })
```

Within editName, the map function is used to create a new array of objects based upon the original array. The editName function can be written entirely in one line. Here's an example of the same function using a shorthand if/else statement:

```
const editName = (oldName, name, arr) =>
    arr.map(item => (item.name === oldName) ?
        ({...item,name}) :
        item
    )
```

If you need to transform an array into an object, you can use Array.map in conjunction with Object.keys. Object.keys is a method that can be used to return an array of keys from an object.

Let's say we needed to transform schools object into an array of schools:

```
const schools = {
  "Yorktown": 10,
  "Washington & Lee": 2,
  "Wakefield": 5
}

const schoolArray = Object.keys(schools).map(key =>
        ({
            name: key,
            wins: schools[key]
        })
    )

console.log(schoolArray)

// [
//   {
//     name: "Yorktown",
//     wins: 10
//   },
//   {
//     name: "Washington & Lee",
//     wins: 2
//   },
//   {
//     name: "Wakefield",
//     wins: 5
//   }
// ]
```

In this example, Object.keys returns an array of school names, and we can use map on that array to produce a new array of the same length. The name of the new object will be set using the key, and wins is set equal to the value.

So far we've learned that we can transform arrays with `Array.map` and `Array.filter`. We've also learned that we can change arrays into objects by combining `Object.keys` with `Array.map`. The final tool that that we need in our functional arsenal is the ability to transform arrays into primitives and other objects.

The `reduce` and `reduceRight` functions can be used to transform an array into any value, including a number, string, boolean, object, or even a function.

Let's say we needed to find the maximum number in an array of numbers. We need to transform an array into a number; therefore, we can use `reduce`:

```
const ages = [21,18,42,40,64,63,34];

const maxAge = ages.reduce((max, age) => {
    console.log(`${age} > ${max} = ${age > max}`);
    if (age > max) {
        return age
    } else {
        return max
    }
}, 0)

console.log('maxAge', maxAge);

// 21 > 0 = true
// 18 > 21 = false
// 42 > 21 = true
// 40 > 42 = false
// 64 > 42 = true
// 63 > 64 = false
// 34 > 64 = false
// maxAge 64
```

The `ages` array has been reduced into a single value: the maximum age, 64. `reduce` takes two arguments: a callback function and an original value. In this case, the original value is 0, which sets the initial maximum value to 0. The callback is invoked once for every item in the array. The first time this callback is invoked, `age` is equal to 21, the first value in the array, and `max` is equal to 0, the initial value. The callback returns the greater of the two numbers, 21, and that becomes the `max` value during the next iteration. Each iteration compares each `age` against the `max` value and returns the greater of the two. Finally, the last number in the array is compared and returned from the previous callback.

If we remove the `console.log` statement from the preceding function and use a shorthand `if/else` statement, we can calculate the max value in any array of numbers with the following syntax:

```
const max = ages.reduce(
    (max, value) => (value > max) ? value : max,
```

```
      0
)
```

Array.reduceRight

Array.reduceRight works the same way as Array.reduce; the difference is that it starts reducing from the end of the array rather than the beginning.

Sometimes we need to transform an array into an object. The following example uses reduce to transform an array that contains colors into a hash:

```
const colors = [
    {
        id: '-xekare',
        title: "rad red",
        rating: 3
    },
    {
        id: '-jbwsof',
        title: "big blue",
        rating: 2
    },
    {
        id: '-prigbj',
        title: "grizzly grey",
        rating: 5
    },
    {
        id: '-ryhbhsl',
        title: "banana",
        rating: 1
    }
]

const hashColors = colors.reduce(
    (hash, {id, title, rating}) => {
        hash[id] = {title, rating}
        return hash
    },
    {}
)

console.log(hashColors);

// {
//    "-xekare": {
//      title:"rad red",
//      rating:3
//    },
//    "-jbwsof": {
```

```
//      title:"big blue",
//      rating:2
//    },
//    "-prigbj": {
//      title:"grizzly grey",
//      rating:5
//    },
//    "-ryhbhsl": {
//      title:"banana",
//      rating:1
//    }
// }
```

In this example, the second argument sent to the reduce function is an empty object. This is our initial value for the hash. During each iteration, the callback function adds a new key to the hash using bracket notation and sets the value for that key to the id field of the array. Array.reduce can be used in this way to reduce an array to a single value—in this case, an object.

We can even transform arrays into completely different arrays using reduce. Consider reducing an array with multiple instances of the same value to an array of distinct values. The reduce method can be used to accomplish this task:

```
const colors = ["red", "red", "green", "blue", "green"];

const distinctColors = colors.reduce(
    (distinct, color) =>
        (distinct.indexOf(color) !== -1) ?
            distinct :
            [...distinct, color],
    []
)

console.log(distinctColors)

// ["red", "green", "blue"]
```

In this example, the colors array is reduced to an array of distinct values. The second argument sent to the reduce function is an empty array. This will be the initial value for distinct. When the distinct array does not already contain a specific color, it will be added. Otherwise, it will be skipped, and the current distinct array will be returned.

map and reduce are the main weapons of any functional programmer, and JavaScript is no exception. If you want to be a proficient JavaScript engineer, then you must master these functions. The ability to create one dataset from another is a required skill and is useful for any type of programming paradigm.

Higher-Order Functions

The use of *higher-order functions* is also essential to functional programming. We've already mentioned higher-order functions, and we've even used a few in this chapter. Higher-order functions are functions that can manipulate other functions. They can take functions in as arguments, or return functions, or both.

The first category of higher-order functions are functions that expect other functions as arguments. `Array.map`, `Array.filter`, and `Array.reduce` all take functions as arguments. They are higher-order functions.[3]

Let's take a look at how we can implement a higher-order function. In the following example, we create an `invokeIf` callback function that will test a condition and invoke on callback function when it is true and another callback function when that condition is false:

```
const invokeIf = (condition, fnTrue, fnFalse) =>
    (condition) ? fnTrue() : fnFalse()

const showWelcome = () =>
    console.log("Welcome!!!")

const showUnauthorized = () =>
    console.log("Unauthorized!!!")

invokeIf(true, showWelcome, showUnauthorized)    // "Welcome"
invokeIf(false, showWelcome, showUnauthorized)   // "Unauthorized"
```

`invokeIf` expects two functions: one for true, and one for false. This is demonstrated by sending both `showWelcome` and `showUnauthorized` to `invokeIf`. When the condition is true, `showWelcome` is invoked. When it is false, `showUnauthorized` is invoked.

Higher-order functions that return other functions can help us handle the complexities associated with asynchronicity in JavaScript. They can help us create functions that can be used or reused at our convenience.

Currying is a functional technique that involves the use of higher-order functions.

The following is an example of currying. The `userLogs` function hangs on to some information (the username) and returns a function that can be used and reused when the rest of the information (the message) is made available. In this example, log messages will all be prepended with the associated username. Notice that we're using the `getFakeMembers` function that returns a promise from Chapter 2:

---

3 For more on higher-order functions, check out Chapter 5 of *Eloquent JavaScript* (*http://eloquentjavascript.net/05_higher_order.html*).

```
const userLogs = userName => message =>
    console.log(`${userName} -> ${message}`)

const log = userLogs("grandpa23")

log("attempted to load 20 fake members")
getFakeMembers(20).then(
    members => log(`successfully loaded ${members.length} members`),
    error => log("encountered an error loading members")
)

// grandpa23 -> attempted to load 20 fake members
// grandpa23 -> successfully loaded 20 members

// grandpa23 -> attempted to load 20 fake members
// grandpa23 -> encountered an error loading members
```

userLogs is the higher-order function. The log function is produced from userLogs, and every time the log function is used, "grandpa23" is prepended to the message.

Recursion

Recursion is a technique that involves creating functions that recall themselves. Often when faced with a challenge that involves a loop, a recursive function can be used instead. Consider the task of counting down from 10. We could create a for loop to solve this problem, or we could alternatively use a recursive function. In this example, countdown is the recursive function:

```
const countdown = (value, fn) => {
    fn(value)
    return (value > 0) ? countdown(value-1, fn) : value
}

countdown(10, value => console.log(value));

// 10
// 9
// 8
// 7
// 6
// 5
// 4
// 3
// 2
// 1
// 0
```

countdown expects a number and a function as arguments. In this example, it is invoked with a value of 10 and a callback function. When countdown is invoked, the callback is invoked, which logs the current value. Next, countdown checks the value to see if it is greater than 0. If it is, `countdown` recalls itself with a decremented value. Eventually, the value will be 0, and `countdown` will return that value all the way back up the call stack.

Browser Call Stack Limitations

Recursion should be used over loops wherever possible, but not all JavaScript engines are optimized for a large amount of recursion. Too much recursion can cause JavaScript errors. These errors can be avoided by implementing advanced techniques to clear the call stack and flatten out recursive calls. Future JavaScript engines plan to eliminate call stack limitations entirely.

Recursion is another functional technique that works well with asynchronous processes. Functions can recall themselves when they are ready.

The `countdown` function can be modified to count down with a delay. This modified version of the `countdown` function can be used to create a countdown clock:

```
const countdown = (value, fn, delay=1000) => {
    fn(value)
    return (value > 0) ?
        setTimeout(() => countdown(value-1, fn, delay), delay) :
        value
}

const log = value => console.log(value)
countdown(10, log);
```

In this example, we create a 10-second countdown by initially invoking `countdown` once with the number 10 in a function that logs the countdown. Instead of recalling itself right away, the `countdown` function waits one second before recalling itself, thus creating a clock.

Recursion is a good technique for searching data structures. You can use recursion to iterate through subfolders until a folder that contains only files is identified. You can also use recursion to iterate though the HTML DOM until you find an element that does not contain any children. In the next example, we will use recursion to iterate deeply into an object to retrieve a nested value:

```
var dan = {
    type: "person",
    data: {
      gender: "male",
      info: {
        id: 22,
        fullname: {
          first: "Dan",
          last: "Deacon"
```

```
        }
      }
     }
    }

  deepPick("type", dan);                      // "person"
  deepPick("data.info.fullname.first", dan);  // "Dan"
```

deepPick can be used to access Dan's type, stored immediately in the first object, or to dig down into nested objects to locate Dan's first name. Sending a string that uses dot notation, we can specify where to locate values that are nested deep within an object:

```
const deepPick = (fields, object={}) => {
   const [first, ...remaining] = fields.split(".")
   return (remaining.length) ?
       deepPick(remaining.join("."), object[first]) :
       object[first]
}
```

The deepPick function is either going to return a value or recall itself, until it eventually returns a value. First, this function splits the dot-notated fields string into an array and uses array destructuring to separate the first value from the remaining values. If there are remaining values, deepPick recalls itself with slightly different data, allowing it to dig one level deeper.

This function continues to call itself until the fields string no longer contains dots, meaning that there are no more remaining fields. In this sample, you can see how the values for first, remaining, and object[first] change as deepPick iterates through:

```
deepPick("data.info.fullname.first", dan);  // "Deacon"

// First Iteration
//    first = "data"
//    remaining.join(".") = "info.fullname.first"
//    object[first] = { gender: "male", {info} }

// Second Iteration
//    first = "info"
//    remaining.join(".") = "fullname.first"
//    object[first] = {id: 22, {fullname}}

// Third Iteration
//    first = "fullname"
//    remaining.join("." = "first"
//    object[first] = {first: "Dan", last: "Deacon" }

// Finally...
//    first = "first"
//    remaining.length = 0
//    object[first] = "Deacon"
```

Recursion is a powerful functional technique that is fun to implement. Use recursion over looping whenever possible.

Composition

Functional programs break up their logic into small pure functions that are focused on specific tasks. Eventually, you will need to put these smaller functions together. Specifically, you may need to combine them, call them in series or parallel, or compose them into larger functions until you eventually have an application.

When it comes to composition, there are a number of different implementations, patterns, and techniques. One that you may be familiar with is chaining. In JavaScript, functions can be chained together using dot notation to act on the return value of the previous function.

Strings have a replace method. The replace method returns a template string which also will have a replace method. Therefore, we can chain together replace methods with dot notation to transform a string.

```
const template = "hh:mm:ss tt"
const clockTime = template.replace("hh", "03")
      .replace("mm", "33")
      .replace("ss", "33")
      .replace("tt", "PM")

console.log(clockTime)

// "03:33:33 PM"
```

In this example, the template is a string. By chaining replace methods to the end of the template string, we can replace hours, minutes, seconds, and time of day in the string with new values. The template itself remain intact and can be reused to create more clock time displays.

Chaining is one composition technique, but there are others. The goal of composition is to "generate a higher order function by combining simpler functions."[4]

The both function is one function that pipes a value through two separate functions. The output of civilian hours becomes the input for appendAMPM, and we can change a date using both of these functions combined into one.

```
const both = date => appendAMPM(civilianHours(date))
```

However, this syntax is hard to comprehend and therefore tough to maintain or scale. What happens when we need to send a value through 20 different functions?

---

4 Functional.js Composition (*http://functionaljs.com/functions/compose/*)

A more elegant approach is to create a higher order function we can use to compose functions into larger functions.

```
const both = compose(
    civilianHours,
    appendAMPM
)

both(new Date())
```

This approach looks much better. It is easy to scale because we can add more functions at any point. This approach also makes it easy to change the order of the composed functions.

The compose function is a higher order function. It takes functions as arguments and returns a single value.

```
const compose = (...fns) =>
  (arg) =>
    fns.reduce(
      (composed, f) => f(composed),
      arg
    )
```

compose takes in functions as arguments and returns a single function. In this implementation, the spread operator is used to turn those function arguments into an array called fns. A function is then returned that expects one argument, arg. When this function is invoked, the fns array is piped starting with the argument we want to send through the function. The argument becomes the initial value for composed and then each iteration of the reduced callback returns. Notice that the callback takes two arguments: composed and a function f. Each function is invoked with compose which is the result of the previous function's output. Eventually, the last function will be invoked and the last result returned.

This is a simple example of a compose function designed to illustrate composition techniques. This function becomes more complex when it is time to handle more than one argument or deal with arguments that are not functions. Other implementations of compose[5] may use reduceRight which would compose the functions in reverse order. This is something to look out for if you use a compose function from a different library.

Putting It All Together

Now that we've been introduced to the core concepts of functional programming, let's put those concepts to work for us and build a small JavaScript application.

---

5 Another implementation of compose is found in Redux (*http://redux.js.org/docs/api/compose.html*)

Since JavaScript will let you slip away from the functional paradigm, and you do not have to follow the rules, you will need to stay focused. Following these three simple rules will help you stay on target.

1. Keep data immutable.
2. Keep functions pure—accept at least one argument, return data or another function.
3. Use recursion over looping (wherever possible).

Our challenge is to build a ticking clock. The clock needs to display hours, minutes, seconds and time of day in civilian time. Each field must always have double digits, meaning leading zeros need to be applied to single digit values like 1 or 2. The clock must also tick and change the display every second.

First, let's review an imperative solution for the clock.

```
// Log Clock Time every Second
setInterval(logClockTime, 1000);

function logClockTime() {

  // Get Time string as civilian time
  var time = getClockTime();

  // Clear the Console and log the time
  console.clear();
  console.log(time);
}

function getClockTime() {

  // Get the Current Time
  var date = new Date();
  var time = "";

  // Serialize clock time
  var time = {
    hours: date.getHours(),
    minutes: date.getMinutes(),
    seconds: date.getSeconds(),
    ampm: "AM"
  }

  // Convert to civilian time
  if (time.hours == 12) {
    time.ampm = "PM";
  } else if (time.hours > 12) {
    time.ampm = "PM";
    time.hours -= 12;
  }
```

```
// Prepend a 0 on the hours to make double digits
if (time.hours < 10) {
  time.hours = "0" + time.hours;
}

// prepend a 0 on the minutes to make double digits
if (time.minutes < 10) {
  time.minutes = "0" + time.minutes;
}

// prepend a 0 on the seconds to make double digits
if (time.seconds < 10) {
  time.seconds = "0" + time.seconds;
}

// Format the clock time as a string "hh:mm:ss tt"
return time.hours + ":"
      + time.minutes + ":"
      + time.seconds + " "
      + time.ampm;

}
```

This solution is pretty straight forward. It works, and the comments help us understand what is happening. However, these functions are large and complicated. Each function does a lot. They are hard to comprehend, they require comments and they are tough to maintain. Let's see how a functional approach can produce a more scalable application.

Our goal will be to break the application logic up into smaller parts, functions. Each function will be focused on a single task, and we will compose them into larger functions that we can use to create the clock.

First, let's create some functions that give us values and manage the console. We'll need a function that gives us one second, a function that gives us the current time, and a couple of functions that will log messages on a console and clear the console. In functional programs, we should use functions over values wherever possible. We will invoke the function to obtain the value when needed.

```
const oneSecond = () => 1000
const getCurrentTime = () => new Date()
const clear = () => console.clear()
const log = message => console.log(message)
```

Next we will need some functions for transforming data. These three functions will be used to mutate the Date object into an object that can be used for our clock:

serializeClockTime

Takes a date object and returns a object for clock time that contains hours minutes and seconds.

civilianHours

Takes the clock time object and returns an object where hours are converted to civilian time. For example: 1300 becomes 1 o'clock

appendAMPM

Takes the clock time object and appends time of day, AM or PM, to that object.

```
const serializeClockTime = date =>
    ({
        hours: date.getHours(),
        minutes: date.getMinutes(),
        seconds: date.getSeconds()
    })

const civilianHours = clockTime =>
    ({
        ...clockTime,
        hours: (clockTime.hours > 12) ?
            clockTime.hours - 12 :
            clockTime.hours
    })

const appendAMPM = clockTime =>
    ({
        ...clockTime,
        ampm: (clockTime.hours >= 12) ? "PM" : "AM"
    })
```

These three functions are used to transform data without changing the original. They treat their arguments as immutable objects.

Next we'll need a few higher order functions:

display

Takes a target function and returns a function that will send a time to the target. In this example the target will be console.log.

formatClock

Takes a template string and uses it to return clock time formatted based upon the criteria from the string. In this example, the template is "hh:mm:ss tt". From ther, formatClock will replaces the placeholders with hours, minutes, seconds, and time of day.

prependZero

Takes an object's key as an argument and prepends a zero to the value stored under that objects key. It takes in a key to a specific field and prepends values with a zero if the value is less than 10.

```
const display = target => time => target(time)

const formatClock = format =>
    time =>
        format.replace("hh", time.hours)
            .replace("mm", time.minutes)
            .replace("ss", time.seconds)
            .replace("tt", time.ampm)

const prependZero = key => clockTime =>
    ({
        ...clockTime,
        [key]: (clockTime[key] < 10) ?
            "0" + clockTime[key] :
            clockTime[key]
    })
```

These higher order functions will be invoked to create the functions that will be reused to format the clock time for every tick. Both format clock and `prependZero` will be invoked once, initially setting up the required template or key. The inner functions that they return will be invoked once every second to format the time for display.

Now that we have all of the functions required to build a ticking clock, we will need to compose them. We will use the compose function that we defined in the last section to handle composition:

convertToCivilianTime

A single function that will take clock time as an argument and transforms it into civilian time by using both civilian hours.

doubleDigits

A single function that will take civilian clock time and make sure the hours, minutes, and seconds display double digits by prepending zeros where needed.

startTicking

Starts the clock by setting an interval that will invoke a callback every second. The callback is composed using all of our functions. Every second the console is cleared, currentTime obtained, converted, civilianized, formatted, and displayed.

```
const convertToCivilianTime = clockTime =>
    compose(
        appendAMPM,
        civilianHours
    )(clockTime)
```

```
const doubleDigits = civilianTime =>
    compose(
        prependZero("hours"),
        prependZero("minutes"),
        prependZero("seconds")
    )(civilianTime)

const startTicking = () =>
    setInterval(
        compose(
            clear,
            getCurrentTime,
            serializeClockTime,
            convertToCivilianTime,
            doubleDigits,
            formatClock("hh:mm:ss tt"),
            display(log)
        ),
        oneSecond()
    )

startTicking()
```

This declarative version of the clock achieves the same results as the imperative version. However, there quite a few benefits to this approach. First, all of these functions are easily testable and reusable. They can be used in future clocks or other digital displays. Also, this program is easily scalable. There are no side effects. There are no global variables outside of functions themselves. There could still be bugs, but they will be easier to find.

In this chapter, we've introduced functional programming principles. Throughout the book when we discuss best practices in React and Flux, we will continue to demonstrate how these libraries are based in functional techniques. In the next chapter, we will dive into React officially with an improved understanding of the principles that guided its development.

CHAPTER 4

Pure React

In order to understand how React runs in the browser, we will be working purely with React in this chapter. We will not introduce JSX, or JavaScript as XML, until the next chapter. You may have worked with React in the past without ever looking at the pure React code that is generated when we transpile JSX into React. You can successfully use React without looking at pure React. However, if you take the time to understand what is going on behind the scenes, you will be more efficient, especially when it comes time to debug. That is our goal in this chapter: to look under the hood and understand how React works.

Page Setup

In order to work with React in the browser, we need to include two libraries: React and ReactDOM. React is the library for creating views. ReactDOM is the library used to actually render the UI in the browser.

ReactDOM

React and ReactDOM were split into two packages for version 0.14. The release notes state: "The beauty and the essence of React has nothing to do with browsers or the DOM... This [splitting into two packages] paves the way to writing components that can be shared between the web version of React and React Native."[1] Instead of assuming that React will render only in the browser, future releases will aim to support rendering for a variety of platforms.

---

1 Ben Alpert, "React v0.14" (*http://bit.ly/2nvPHEQ*), React blog, October 7, 2015.

We also need an HTML element that ReactDOM will use to render the UI. You can see how the scripts and HTML elements are added in Example 4-1. Both libraries are available as scripts from the Facebook CDN.

Example 4-1. HTML document setup with React

```
<!DOCTYPE html>
<html>
<head>
<meta charset="utf-8">
<title>Pure React Samples</title>
</head>
<body>

  <!-- Target container -->
  <div id="react-container"></div>

  <!-- React library & ReactDOM-->
  <script src="https://unpkg.com/react@15.4.2/dist/react.js"></script>
  <script src="https://unpkg.com/react-dom@15.4.2/dist/react-dom.js"></script>

  <script>

    // Pure React and JavaScript code

  </script>

</body>
</html>
```

These are the minimum requirements for working with React in the browser. You can place your JavaScript in a separate file, but it must be loaded somewhere in the page after React has been loaded.

The Virtual DOM

HTML is simply a set of instructions that a browser follows when constructing the document object model, or DOM. The elements that make up an HTML document become DOM elements when the browser loads HTML and renders the user interface.

Let's say that you have to construct an HTML hierarchy for a recipe. A possible solution for such a task might look something like this:

```
<section id="baked-salmon">
  <h1>Baked Salmon</h1>
  <ul class="ingredients">
      <li>1 lb Salmon</li>
      <li>1 cup Pine Nuts</li>
```

```
        <li>2 cups Butter Lettuce</li>
        <li>1 Yellow Squash</li>
        <li>1/2 cup Olive Oil</li>
        <li>3 cloves of Garlic</li>
    </ul>
    <section class="instructions">
        <h2>Cooking Instructions</h2>
        <p>Preheat the oven to 350 degrees.</p>
        <p>Spread the olive oil around a glass baking dish.</p>
        <p>Add the salmon, garlic, and pine nuts to the dish.</p>
        <p>Bake for 15 minutes.</p>
        <p>Add the yellow squash and put back in the oven for 30 mins.</p>
        <p>Remove from oven and let cool for 15 minutes.
        Add the lettuce and serve.</p>
    </section>
</section>
```

In HTML, elements relate to each other in a hierarchy that resembles a family tree. We could say that the root element has three children: a heading, an unordered list of ingredients, and a section for the instructions.

Traditionally, websites have consisted of independent HTML pages. When the user navigated these pages, the browser would request and load different HTML documents. The invention of AJAX brought us the single-page application, or SPA (*https:// en.wikipedia.org/wiki/Single-page_application*). Since browsers could request and load tiny bits of data using AJAX, entire web applications could now run out of a single page and rely on JavaScript to update the user interface.

In an SPA, the browser initially loads one HTML document. As users navigate through the site, they actually stay on the same page. JavaScript destroys and creates a new user interface as the user interacts with the application. It may feel as though you are jumping from page to page, but you are actually still on the same HTML page and JavaScript is doing the heavy lifting.

The DOM API (*https://mzl.la/2m1oQDJ*) is a collection of objects that JavaScript can use to interact with the browser to modify the DOM. If you have used `document.crea teElement` or `document.appendChild`, you have worked with the DOM API. Updating or changing rendered DOM elements in JavaScript is relatively easy.[2] However, the process of inserting new elements is painfully slow.[3] This means if web developers are meticulous about how they make changes to UI, they can improve the performance of their applications.

Managing DOM changes with JavaScript efficiently can become very complicated and time-consuming. From a coding perspective, it is easier to clear all the children

---

2 Lindsey Simon, "Minimizing Browser Reflow" (*http://bit.ly/2m1pa58*).

3 Steven Luscher, "Building User Interfaces with Facebook's React" (*http://bit.ly/2m1pEs3*), Super VanJS 2013.

of a particular element and reconstruct them than it would be to leave those child elements in place and attempt to efficiently update them.[4] The problem is that we may not have the time or the advanced knowledge of JavaScript to work efficiently with the DOM API every time we build a new application. The solution is React.

React is a library that is designed to update the browser DOM for us. We no longer have to be concerned with the complexities associated with building performant SPAs because React can do that for us. With React, we do not interact with the DOM API directly. Instead, we interact with a *virtual DOM*, or set of instructions that React will use to construct the UI and interact with the browser.[5]

The virtual DOM is made up of React elements, which conceptually seem similar to HTML elements, but are actually JavaScript objects. It is much faster to work directly with JavaScript objects than it is to work with the DOM API. We make changes to a JavaScript object, the virtual DOM, and React renders those changes for us using the DOM API as efficiently as possible.

React Elements

The browser DOM is made up of DOM elements. Similarly, the React DOM is made up of React elements. DOM elements and React elements may look the same, but they are actually quite different. A React element is a description of what the actual DOM element should look like. In other words, React elements are the instructions for how the browser DOM should be created.

We can create a React element to represent an h1 using `React.createElement`:

```
React.createElement("h1", null, "Baked Salmon")
```

The first argument defines the type of element that we wish to create. In this case, we want to create a heading-one element. The third argument represents the element's children, any nodes that are inserted between the opening and closing tag. The second argument represents the element's properties. This h1 currently does not have any properties.

During rendering, React will convert this element to an actual DOM element:

```
<h1>Baked Salmon</h1>
```

When an element has attributes, they can be described with properties. Here is a sample of an HTML h1 tag that has id and data-type attributes:

```
React.createElement("h1",
    {id: "recipe-0", 'data-type': "title"},
```

---

4 Mark Wilton-Jones, "Efficient JavaScript" (*http://opr.as/2m1f5Fr*), Dev.Opera, November 2, 2006.

5 React Docs, "Refs and the DOM" (*http://bit.ly/2m1faJf*).

```
        "Baked Salmon"
    )

    <h1 data-reactroot id="recipe-0" data-type="title">Baked Salmon</h1>
```

The properties are similarly applied to the new DOM element: the properties are added to the tag as attributes, and the child text is added as text within the element. You'll also notice data-reactroot, which identifies that this is the root element of your React component (Figure 4-1).

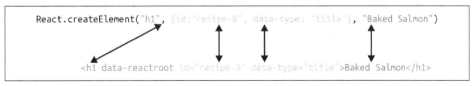

Figure 4-1. Relationship between createElement and the DOM element

data-reactroot

data-reactroot will always appear as an attribute of the root element of your React component. Prior to version 15, React IDs were added to each node that was a part of your component. This helped with rendering and keeping track of which elements needed to be updated. Now, there is only an attribute added to the root, and rendering is kept track of based on the hierarchy of elements.

So, a React element is just a JavaScript literal that tells React how to construct the DOM element. Example 4-2 shows the element that createElement call actually creates.

Example 4-2. Logging the title element

```
{
    $$typeof: Symbol(React.element),
    "type": "h1",
    "key": null,
    "ref": null,
    "props": {"children": "Baked Salmon"},
    "_owner": null,
    "_store": {}
}
```

This is a React element. There are fields that are used by React: _owner, _store, $$typeof. The key and ref fields are important to React elements, but we'll introduce those later, in Chapter 5. For now, let's take a closer look at the type and props fields in Example 4-2.

The `type` property of the React element tells React what type of HTML or SVG element to create. The `props` property represents the data and child elements required to construct a DOM element. The `children` property is for displaying other nested elements as text.

 A Note on Creating Elements

We are taking a peek at the object that `React.createElement` returns. There is never a case where you would create elements by hand-typing literals that look like this. You must always create React elements with the `React.createElement` function or factories, which are discussed at the end of this chapter.

ReactDOM

ReactDOM contains the tools necessary to render React elements in the browser. ReactDOM is where we will find the `render` method as well as the `renderToString` and `renderToStaticMarkup` methods that are used on the server. These will be discussed in greater detail in Chapter 12. All the tools necessary to generate HTML from the virtual DOM are found in this library.

We can render a React element, including its children, to the DOM with `ReactDOM.render`. The element that we wish to render is passed as the first argument and the second argument is the target node, where we should render the element:

```
var dish = React.createElement("h1", null, "Baked Salmon")

ReactDOM.render(dish, document.getElementById('react-container'))
```

Rendering the title element to the DOM would add a heading-one element to the `div` with the `id` of `react-container`, which we would already have defined in our HTML. In Example 4-3, we build this `div` inside the `body` tag.

Example 4-3. React added the h1 element to the target: react-container

```
<body>
    <div id="react-container">
        <h1>Baked Salmon</h1>
    </div>
</body>
```

All of the DOM rendering functionality in React has been moved to ReactDOM because we can use React to build native applications as well. The browser is just one target for React.

That's all you need to do. You create an element, and then you render it to the DOM. In the next section, we'll get an understanding of how to use `props.children`.

Children

ReactDOM allows you to render a single element to the DOM.[6] React tags this as `data-reactroot`. All other React elements are composed into a single element using nesting.

React renders child elements using `props.children`. In the previous section, we rendered a text element as a child of the h1 element, and thus `props.children` was set to `"Baked Salmon"`. We could render other React elements as children too, creating a tree of elements. This is why we use the term *component tree*. The tree has one root component from which many branches grow.

Let's consider the unordered list that contains ingredients in Example 4-4.

Example 4-4. Ingredients list

```
<ul>
    <li>1 lb Salmon</li>
    <li>1 cup Pine Nuts</li>
    <li>2 cups Butter Lettuce</li>
    <li>1 Yellow Squash</li>
    <li>1/2 cup Olive Oil</li>
    <li>3 cloves of Garlic</li>
</ul>
```

In this sample, the unordered list is the root element, and it has six children. We can represent this ul and its children with `React.createElement` (Example 4-5).

Example 4-5. Unordered list as React elements

```
React.createElement(
    "ul",
    null,
    React.createElement("li", null, "1 lb Salmon"),
    React.createElement("li", null, "1 cup Pine Nuts"),
    React.createElement("li", null, "2 cups Butter Lettuce"),
    React.createElement("li", null, "1 Yellow Squash"),
    React.createElement("li", null, "1/2 cup Olive Oil"),
    React.createElement("li", null, "3 cloves of Garlic")
)
```

---

6 Rendering Elements (*http://bit.ly/2nvR2vf*)

Every additional argument sent to the `createElement` function is another child element. React creates an array of these child elements and sets the value of `props.children` to that array.

If we were to inspect the resulting React element, we would see each list item represented by a React element and added to an array called `props.children`. Let's do that now (Example 4-6).

Example 4-6. Resulting React element

```
{
  "type": "ul",
  "props": {
    "children": [
      { "type": "li", "props": { "children": "1 lb Salmon" } … },
      { "type": "li", "props": { "children": "1 cup Pine Nuts"} … },
      { "type": "li", "props": { "children": "2 cups Butter Lettuce" } … },
      { "type": "li", "props": { "children": "1 Yellow Squash"} … },
      { "type": "li", "props": { "children": "1/2 cup Olive Oil"} … },
      { "type": "li", "props": { "children": "3 cloves of Garlic"} … }
    ]
    ...
  }
}
```

We can now see that each list item is a child. Earlier in this chapter, we introduced HTML for an entire recipe rooted in a `section` element. To create this using React, we'll use a series of `createElement` calls, as in Example 4-7.

Example 4-7. React Element tree

```
React.createElement("section", {id: "baked-salmon"},
    React.createElement("h1", null, "Baked Salmon"),
    React.createElement("ul", {"className": "ingredients"},
        React.createElement("li", null, "1 lb Salmon"),
        React.createElement("li", null, "1 cup Pine Nuts"),
        React.createElement("li", null, "2 cups Butter Lettuce"),
        React.createElement("li", null, "1 Yellow Squash"),
        React.createElement("li", null, "1/2 cup Olive Oil"),
        React.createElement("li", null, "3 cloves of Garlic")
    ),
    React.createElement("section", {"className": "instructions"},
        React.createElement("h2", null, "Cooking Instructions"),
        React.createElement("p", null, "Preheat the oven to 350 degrees."),
        React.createElement("p", null,
        "Spread the olive oil around a glass baking dish."),
        React.createElement("p", null, "Add the salmon, garlic, and pine..."),
        React.createElement("p", null, "Bake for 15 minutes."),
        React.createElement("p", null, "Add the yellow squash and put..."),
```

```
    React.createElement("p", null, "Remove from oven and let cool for 15 ....")
    )
)
```

className in React

Any element that has an HTML `class` attribute is using `className` for that property instead of `class`. Since `class` is a reserved word in JavaScript, we have to use `className` to define the `class` attribute of an HTML element.

This sample is what pure React looks like. Pure React is ultimately what runs in the browser. The virtual DOM is a tree of React elements all stemming from a single root element. React elements are the instructions that React will use to build a UI in the browser.

Constructing Elements with Data

The major advantage of using React is its ability to separate data from UI elements. Since React is just JavaScript, we can add JavaScript logic to help us build the React component tree. For example, ingredients can be stored in an array, and we can map that array to the React elements.

Let's go back and think about the unordered list in Example 4-8 for a moment.

Example 4-8. Unordered list

```
React.createElement("ul", {"className": "ingredients"},
    React.createElement("li", null, "1 lb Salmon"),
    React.createElement("li", null, "1 cup Pine Nuts"),
    React.createElement("li", null, "2 cups Butter Lettuce"),
    React.createElement("li", null, "1 Yellow Squash"),
    React.createElement("li", null, "1/2 cup Olive Oil"),
    React.createElement("li", null, "3 cloves of Garlic")
);
```

The data used in this list of ingredients can be easily represented using a JavaScript array (Example 4-9).

Example 4-9. items array

```
var items = [
    "1 lb Salmon",
    "1 cup Pine Nuts",
    "2 cups Butter Lettuce",
    "1 Yellow Squash",
    "1/2 cup Olive Oil",
```

```
    "3 cloves of Garlic"
]
```

We could construct a virtual DOM around this data using the `Array.map` function, as in Example 4-10.

Example 4-10. Mapping an array to li elements

```
React.createElement(
    "ul",
    { className: "ingredients" },
    items.map(ingredient =>
        React.createElement("li", null, ingredient)
    )
)
```

This syntax creates a React element for each ingredient in the array. Each string is displayed in the list item's children as text. The value for each ingredient is displayed as the list item.

When running this code, you'll see a console error, as shown in Figure 4-2.

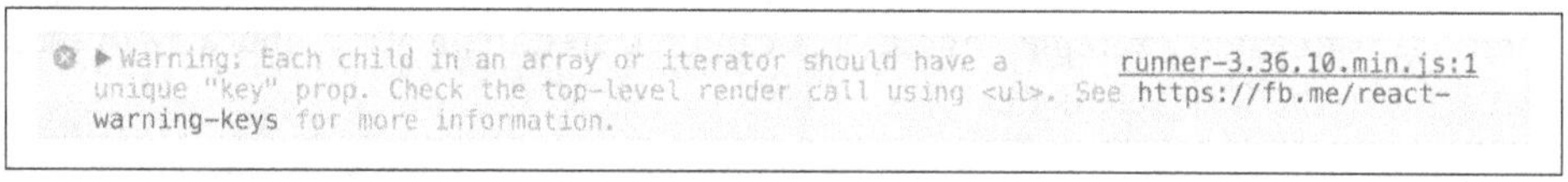

```
⊗ ▶ Warning: Each child in an array or iterator should have a          runner-3.36.10.min.js:1
     unique "key" prop. Check the top-level render call using <ul>. See https://fb.me/react-
     warning-keys for more information.
```

Figure 4-2. Console warning

When we build a list of child elements by iterating through an array, React likes each of those elements to have a key property. The key property is used by React to help it update the DOM efficiently. We will be discussing keys and why we need them in Chapter 5, but for now you can make this warning go away by adding a unique key property to each of the list item elements (Example 4-11). We can use the array index for each ingredient as that unique value.

Example 4-11. Adding a key property

```
React.createElement("ul", {className: "ingredients"},
    items.map((ingredient, i) =>
        React.createElement("li", { key: i }, ingredient)
)
```

React Components

Every user interface is made up of parts. The recipe example we'll use here has a few recipes, each made up of parts (Figure 4-3).

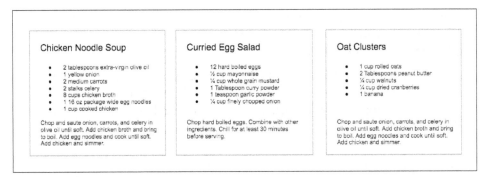

Figure 4-3. Recipes app

In React, we describe each of these parts as a *component*. Components allow us to reuse the same DOM structure for different recipes or different sets of data.

When considering a user interface that you want to build with React, look for opportunities to break down your elements into reusable pieces. For example, the recipes in Figure 4-4 each have a title, ingredients list, and instructions. All are part of a larger recipe or app component. We could create a component for each of the highlighted parts: ingredients, instructions, and so on.

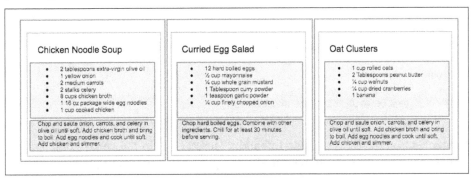

Figure 4-4. Each component is outlined: App, IngredientsList, Instructions

Think about how scalable this is. If we want to display one recipe, our component structure will support this. If we want to display 10,000 recipes, we'll just create new instances of that component.

Let's investigate the three different ways to create components: `createClass`, ES6 classes, and stateless functional components.

createClass

When React was first introduced in 2013, there was only one way to create a component: the `createClass` function.

New methods of creating components have emerged, but createClass is still used widely in React projects. The React team has indicated, however, that createClass may be deprecated in the future.

Let's consider the list of ingredients that are included in each recipe. As shown in Example 4-12, we can create a React component using React.createClass that returns a single unordered list element that contains a child list item for each ingredient in an array.

Example 4-12. Ingredients list as a React component

```
const IngredientsList = React.createClass({
  displayName: "IngredientsList",
  render() {
    return React.createElement("ul", {"className": "ingredients"},
        React.createElement("li", null, "1 lb Salmon"),
        React.createElement("li", null, "1 cup Pine Nuts"),
        React.createElement("li", null, "2 cups Butter Lettuce"),
        React.createElement("li", null, "1 Yellow Squash"),
        React.createElement("li", null, "1/2 cup Olive Oil"),
        React.createElement("li", null, "3 cloves of Garlic")
    )
  }
})

const list = React.createElement(IngredientsList, null, null)

ReactDOM.render(
  list,
  document.getElementById('react-container')
)
```

Components allow us to use data to build a reusable UI. In the render function, we can use the this keyword to refer to the component instance, and properties can be accessed on that instance with this.props.

Here, we have created an element using our component and named it Ingredients List:

```
<IngredientsList>
    <ul className="ingredients">
        <li>1 lb Salmon</li>
        <li>1 cup Pine Nuts</li>
        <li>2 cups Butter Lettuce</li>
        <li>1 Yellow Squash</li>
        <li>1/2 cup Olive Oil</li>
        <li>3 cloves of Garlic</li>
    </ul>
</IngredientsList>
```

Data can be passed to React components as properties. We can create a reusable list of ingredients by passing that data to the list as an array:

```
const IngredientsList = React.createClass({
  displayName: "IngredientsList",
  render() {
    return React.createElement("ul", {className: "ingredients"},
        this.props.items.map((ingredient, i) =>
            React.createElement("li", { key: i }, ingredient)
        )
    )
  }
})

const items = [
    "1 lb Salmon",
    "1 cup Pine Nuts",
    "2 cups Butter Lettuce",
    "1 Yellow Squash",
    "1/2 cup Olive Oil",
    "3 cloves of Garlic"
]

ReactDOM.render(
  React.createElement(IngredientsList, {items}, null),
  document.getElementById('react-container')
)
```

Now, let's look at ReactDOM. The data property items is an array with six ingredients. Because we made the li tags using a loop, we were able to add a unique key using the index of the loop:

```
<IngredientsList items=[...]>
    <ul className="ingredients">
        <li key="0">1 lb Salmon</li>
        <li key="1">1 cup Pine Nuts</li>
        <li key="2">2 cups Butter Lettuce</li>
        <li key="3">1 Yellow Squash</li>
        <li key="4">1/2 cup Olive Oil</li>
        <li key="5">3 cloves of Garlic</li>
    </ul>
</IngredientsList>
```

The components are objects. They can be used to encapsulate code just like classes. We can create a method that renders a single list item and use that to build out the list (Example 4-13).

Example 4-13. With a custom method

```
const IngredientsList = React.createClass({
  displayName: "IngredientsList",
```

```
  renderListItem(ingredient, i) {
    return React.createElement("li", { key: i }, ingredient)
  },
  render() {
    return React.createElement("ul", {className: "ingredients"},
        this.props.items.map(this.renderListItem)
    )
  }
})
```

This is also the idea of views in MVC languages. Everything that is associated with the UI for IngredientsList is encapsulated into one component; everything we need is right there.

Now we can create a React element using our component and pass it to the list of elements as a property. Notice that the element's type is now a string—it's the component class directly.

Component Classes as Types

When rendering HTML or SVG elements, we use strings. When creating elements with components, we use the component class directly. This is why IngredientsList is not surrounded in quotation marks; we are passing the class to createElement because it is a component. React will create an instance of our component with this class and manage it for us.

Using the IngredientsList component with this data would render the following unordered list to the DOM:

```
<ul data-react-root class="ingredients">
    <li>1 lb Salmon</li>
    <li>1 cup Pine Nuts</li>
    <li>2 cups Butter Lettuce</li>
    <li>1 Yellow Squash</li>
    <li>1/2 cup Olive Oil</li>
    <li>3 cloves of Garlic</li>
</ul>
```

ES6 Classes

As discussed in Chapter 2, one of the key features included in the ES6 spec are classes. React.Component is an abstract class that we can use to build new React components. We can create custom components through inheritance by extending this class with ES6 syntax. We can create IngredientsList using the same syntax (Example 4-14).

Example 4-14. IngredientsList as an ES6 class

```
class IngredientsList extends React.Component {

  renderListItem(ingredient, i) {
    return React.createElement("li", { key: i }, ingredient)
  }

  render() {
    return React.createElement("ul", {className: "ingredients"},
        this.props.items.map(this.renderListItem)
    )
  }

}
```

Stateless Functional Components

Stateless functional components are functions, not objects; therefore, they do not have a "this" scope. Because they are simple, pure functions, we'll use them as much as possible in our applications. There may come a point where the stateless functional component isn't robust enough and we must fall back to using `class` or `createClass`, but in general the more you can use these, the better.

Stateless functional components are functions that take in properties and return a DOM element. Stateless functional components are a good way to practice the rules of functional programming. You should strive to make each stateless functional component a pure function. They should take in props and return a DOM element without causing side effects. This encourages simplicity and makes the codebase extremely testable.

Stateless functional components will keep your application architecture simple, and the React team promises some performance gains by using them. If you need to encapsulate functionality or have a `this` scope, however, you can't use them.

In Example 4-15, we combine the functionality of `renderListItem` and `render` into a single function.

Example 4-15. Creating a stateless functional component

```
const IngredientsList = props =>
    React.createElement("ul", {className: "ingredients"},
        props.items.map((ingredient, i) =>
            React.createElement("li", { key: i }, ingredient)
        )
    )
```

We would render this component with `ReactDOM.render`, the exact same way we render components created with `createClass` or ES6 class syntax. This is just a function. The function collects data through the props arguments and returns an unordered list for each item that is sent to the props data.

One way we can improve this stateless functional component is through destructuring the properties argument (Example 4-16). Using ES6 destructuring syntax, we can scope the list property directly to this function, reducing the repetitive dot syntax. Now we'd use the `IngredientsList` the same way we render component classes.

Example 4-16. Destructuring the properties argument

```
const IngredientsList = ({items}) =>
    React.createElement("ul", {className: "ingredients"},
        items.map((ingredient, i) =>
            React.createElement("li", { key: i }, ingredient)
        )
    )
```

const with Stateless Functional Components

Each of these stateless functional components uses `const` instead of `var` when creating a component. This is a common practice but not a requirement. `const` declares this function as a constant and prevents us from redefining that variable later.

Aside from being slightly cleaner syntax, Facebook has hinted that in the future, stateless functional components might be faster than `createClass` or ES6 class syntax.

DOM Rendering

Since we are able to pass data to our components as props, we can separate our application's data from the logic that is used to create the UI. This gives us an isolated set of data that is much easier to work with and manipulate than the document object model. When we change any of the values in this isolated dataset, we change the state of our application.

Imagine storing all of the data in your application in a single JavaScript object. Every time you made a change to this object, you could send it to a component as props and rerender the UI. This means that `ReactDOM.render` is going to be doing a lot of heavy lifting.

In order for React to work in a reasonable amount of time, `ReactDOM.render` has to work smart, and it does. Instead of emptying and reconstructing the entire DOM,

`ReactDOM.render` leaves the current DOM in place and only applies the minimal amount of changes required to mutate the DOM.

Let's say we had an app that displayed the mood of our five team members using either a smiley face or a frowny face. We can represent the mood of all five individuals in a single JavaScript array:

```
["smile", "smile", "frown", "smile", "frown"];
```

This array of data may be used to construct a UI that looks something like this:

If something breaks and the team has to work all weekend, we can reflect the team's new mood simply by changing the data in this array, producing the result shown in the image that follows:

```
["frown", "frown", "frown", "frown", "frown"];
```

How many changes do we have to make to the first array to make it look like the second array of all frowns?

```
["smile", "smile", "frown", "smile", "frown"];
```

```
["frown", "frown", "frown", "frown", "frown"];
```

We would need to change the first, second, and fourth values from a smile to a frown.

Therefore, we can say that it would take three mutations to change the first array of data to match the second.

Now consider how we can update the DOM to reflect these changes. One inefficient solution to applying these changes to the UI is to erase the entire DOM and rebuild it, as in Example 4-17.

Example 4-17. Start with the current list

```
<ul>
    <li class="smile">smile</li>
    <li class="smile">smile</li>
    <li class="frown">frown</li>
    <li class="smile">smile</li>
```

```
  <li class="frown">frown</li>
</ul>
```

This involves the following steps:

1. Empty the current data:

   ```
   <ul>

   </ul>
   ```

2. Begin looping through data and build the first list item:

   ```
   <ul>
     <li class="frown">frown</li>
   </ul>
   ```

3. Build and add the second list item:

   ```
   <ul>
     <li class="frown">frown</li>
     <li class="frown">frown</li>
   </ul>
   ```

4. Build and append the third list item:

   ```
   <ul>
     <li class="frown">frown</li>
     <li class="frown">frown</li>
     <li class="frown">frown</li>
   </ul>
   ```

5. Build and append the fourth list item:

   ```
   <ul>
       <li class="frown">frown</li>
       <li class="frown">frown</li>
       <li class="frown">frown</li>
       <li class="frown">frown</li>
   </ul>
   ```

6. Build and append the fifth list item:

   ```
   <ul>
       <li class="frown">frown</li>
       <li class="frown">frown</li>
       <li class="frown">frown</li>
       <li class="frown">frown</li>
       <li class="frown">frown</li>
   </ul>
   ```

If we change the UI by erasing and rebuilding the DOM, we are creating and inserting five new DOM elements. Inserting an element into the DOM is one of the most costly DOM API operations—it's slow. In contrast, updating DOM elements that are already in place performs much more quickly than inserting new ones.

`ReactDOM.render` makes changes by leaving the current DOM in place and simply updating the DOM elements that need to be updated. In our example, there are only three mutations, so `ReactDOM.render` only needs to update three DOM elements (see Figure 4-5).

```
<ul>                                        <ul>
  <li class="smile">smile</li>                <li class="frown">frown</li>
  <li class="smile">smile</li>                <li class="frown">frown</li>
  <li class="frown">frown</li>                <li class="frown">frown</li>
  <li class="smile">smile</li>                <li class="frown">frown</li>
  <li class="frown">frown</li>                <li class="frown">frown</li>
</ul>                                       </ul>
```

Figure 4-5. Three DOM elements are updated

If new DOM elements need to be inserted, ReactDOM will insert them, but it tries to keep DOM insertions (the most costly operation) to a minimum.

This smart DOM rendering is necessary for React to work in a reasonable amount of time because our application state changes a lot. Every time we change that state, we are going to rely on `ReactDOM.render` to efficiently rerender the UI.

Factories

So far, the only way we have created elements has been with `React.createElement`. Another way to create a React element is to use factories. A `factory` is a special object that can be used to abstract away the details of instantiating objects. In React, we use factories to help us create React element instances.

React has built-in factories for all commonly supported HTML and SVG DOM elements, and you can use the `React.createFactory` function to build your own factories around specific components.

For example, consider our `h1` element from earlier in this chapter:

```
<h1>Baked Salmon</h1>
```

Instead of using `createElement`, we can create a React element with a built-in factory (Example 4-18).

Example 4-18. Using createFactory to create an h1

```
React.DOM.h1(null, "Baked Salmon")
```

In this case, the first argument is for the properties and the second argument is for the children. We can also use DOM factories to build an unordered list, as in Example 4-19.

Example 4-19. Building an unordered list with DOM factories

```
React.DOM.ul({"className": "ingredients"},
    React.DOM.li(null, "1 lb Salmon"),
    React.DOM.li(null, "1 cup Pine Nuts"),
    React.DOM.li(null, "2 cups Butter Lettuce"),
    React.DOM.li(null, "1 Yellow Squash"),
    React.DOM.li(null, "1/2 cup Olive Oil"),
    React.DOM.li(null, "3 cloves of Garlic")
)
```

In this case, the first argument is for the properties, where we define the `className`. Additional arguments are elements that will be added to the `children` array of the unordered list. We can also separate out the ingredient data and improve the preceding definition using factories (Example 4-20).

Example 4-20. Using map with factories

```
var items = [
    "1 lb Salmon",
    "1 cup Pine Nuts",
    "2 cups Butter Lettuce",
    "1 Yellow Squash",
    "1/2 cup Olive Oil",
    "3 cloves of Garlic"
]

var list = React.DOM.ul(
    { className: "ingredients" },
    items.map((ingredient, key) =>
        React.DOM.li({key}, ingredient)
    )
)

ReactDOM.render(
    list,
    document.getElementById('react-container')
)
```

Using Factories with Components

If you would like to simplify your code by calling components as functions, you need to explicitly create a factory (Example 4-21).

Example 4-21. Creating a factory with IngredientsList

```
const { render } = ReactDOM;

const IngredientsList = ({ list }) =>
    React.createElement('ul', null,
        list.map((ingredient, i) =>
            React.createElement('li', {key: i}, ingredient)
        )
    )

const Ingredients = React.createFactory(IngredientsList)

const list = [
    "1 lb Salmon",
    "1 cup Pine Nuts",
    "2 cups Butter Lettuce",
    "1 Yellow Squash",
    "1/2 cup Olive Oil",
    "3 cloves of Garlic"
]

render(
    Ingredients({list}),
    document.getElementById('react-container')
)
```

In this example, we can quickly render a React element with the `Ingredients` factory. `Ingredients` is a function that takes in properties and children as arguments just like the DOM factories.

If you are not working with JSX, you may find using factories preferable to numerous `React.createElement` calls. However, the easiest and most common way to define React elements is with JSX tags. If you use JSX with React, chances are you will never use a factory.

Throughout this chapter, we've used `createElement` and `createFactory` to build React components. In Chapter 5, we'll take a look at how to simplify component creation by using JSX.

React with JSX

In the last chapter, we looked at how the virtual DOM is a set of instructions that React follows when creating and updating a user interface. These instructions are made up of JavaScript objects called React elements. So far, we've learned two ways to create React elements: using `React.createElement` and using factories.

An alternative to typing out verbose `React.createElement` calls is JSX, a JavaScript extension that allows us to define React elements using syntax that looks similar to HTML. In this chapter, we are going to discuss how to use JSX to construct a virtual DOM with React elements.

React Elements as JSX

Facebook's React team released JSX when they released React to provide a concise syntax for creating complex DOM trees with attributes. They also hoped to make React more readable, like HTML and XML.

In JSX, an element's type is specified with a tag. The tag's attributes represent the properties. The element's children can be added between the opening and closing tags.

You can also add other JSX elements as children. If you have an unordered list, you can add child list item elements to it with JSX tags. It looks very similar to HTML (see Example 5-1).

Example 5-1. JSX for an unordered list

```
<ul>
    <li>1 lb Salmon</li>
    <li>1 cup Pine Nuts</li>
    <li>2 cups Butter Lettuce</li>
```

```
    <li>1 Yellow Squash</li>
    <li>1/2 cup Olive Oil</li>
    <li>3 cloves of Garlic</li>
</ul>
```

JSX works with components as well. Simply define the component using the class name. In Figure 5-1, we pass an array of ingredients to the IngredientsList as a property with JSX.

Figure 5-1. Creating the IngredientsList with JSX

When we pass the array of ingredients to this component, we need to surround it with curly braces. This is called a JavaScript *expression*, and we must use these when passing JavaScript values to components as properties. Component properties will take two types: either a string or a JavaScript expression. JavaScript expressions can include arrays, objects, and even functions. In order to include them, you must surround them in curly braces.

JSX Tips

JSX might look familiar, and most of the rules result in syntax that is similar to HTML. However, there are a few considerations that you should understand when working with JSX.

Nested components

JSX allows you to add components as children of other components. For example, inside the IngredientsList, we can render another component called Ingredient multiple times (Example 5-2).

Example 5-2. IngredientsList with three nested Ingredient components

```
<IngredientsList>
    <Ingredient />
    <Ingredient />
    <Ingredient />
</IngredientsList>
```

className

Since `class` is a reserved word in JavaScript, `className` is used to define the `class` attribute instead:

```
<h1 className="fancy">Baked Salmon</h1>
```

JavaScript expressions

JavaScript expressions are wrapped in curly braces and indicate where variables shall be evaluated and their resulting values returned. For example, if we want to display the value of the `title` property in an element, we can insert that value using a JavaScript expression. The variable will be evaluated and its value returned:

```
<h1>{this.props.title}</h1>
```

Values of types other than string should also appear as JavaScript expressions:

```
<input type="checkbox" defaultChecked={false} />
```

Evaluation

The JavaScript that is added in between the curly braces will get evaluated. This means that operations such as concatenation or addition will occur. This also means that functions found in JavaScript expressions will be invoked:

```
<h1>{"Hello" + this.props.title}</h1>

<h1>{this.props.title.toLowerCase().replace}</h1>

function appendTitle({this.props.title}) {
    console.log(`${this.props.title} is great!`)
}
```

Mapping arrays to JSX

JSX is JavaScript, so you can incorporate JSX directly inside of JavaScript functions. For example, you can map an array to JSX elements (Example 5-3).

Example 5-3. Array.map() with JSX

```
<ul>
    {this.props.ingredients.map((ingredient, i) =>
        <li key={i}>{ingredient}</li>
    )}
</ul>
```

JSX looks clean and readable, but it can't be interpreted with a browser. All JSX must be converted into `createElement` calls or factories. Luckily, there is an excellent tool for this task: Babel.

Babel

Most software languages allow you to compile your source code. JavaScript is an interpreted language: the browser interprets the code as text, so there is no need to compile JavaScript. However, not all browsers support the latest ES6 and ES7 syntax, and no browser supports JSX syntax. Since we want to use the latest features of JavaScript along with JSX, we are going to need a way to convert our fancy source code into something that the browser can interpret. This process is called transpiling, and it is what Babel (*https://babeljs.io/*) is designed to do.

The first version of the project was called 6to5, and it was released in September 2014. 6to5 was a tool that could be used to convert ES6 syntax to ES5 syntax, which is more widely supported by web browsers. As the project grew, it aimed to be a platform to support all of the latest changes in ECMAScript. It also grew to support transpiling JSX into pure React. The project was renamed to Babel in February 2015.

Babel is used in production at Facebook, Netflix, PayPal, Airbnb, and more. Previously, Facebook had created a JSX transformer that was their standard, but it was soon retired in favor of Babel.

There are many ways of working with Babel. The easiest way to get started is to include a link to the babel-core transpiler directly in your HTML, which will transpile any code in script blocks that have a type of "text/babel". Babel will transpile the source code on the client before running it. Although this may not be the best solution for production, it is a great way to get started with JSX (see Example 5-4).

Example 5-4. Including babel-core

```
<!DOCTYPE html>
<html>
  <head>
    <meta charset="utf-8">
    <title>React Examples</title>
  </head>
  <body>
    <div class="react-container"></div>

    <!-- React Library & React DOM -->
    <script src="https://unpkg.com/react@15.4.2/dist/react.js"></script>
    <script src="https://unpkg.com/react-dom@15.4.2/dist/react-dom.js"></script>
    <script
        src="https://cdnjs.cloudflare.com/ajax/libs/babel-core/5.8.29/browser.js">
    </script>

    <script type="text/babel">

        // JSX code here. Or link to separate JavaScript file that contains JSX.
```

```
  </script>

  </body>
</html>
```

Babel v5.8 Required

To transpile code in the browser, use Babel v. 5.8. Babel 6.0+ will
not work as an in-browser transformer.

Later in the chapter, we'll look at how we can use Babel with webpack to transpile our
JavaScript files statically. For now, using the in-browser transpiler will do.

Recipes as JSX

One of the reasons that we have grown to love React is that it allows us to write web
applications with beautiful code. It is extremely rewarding to create beautifully written modules that clearly communicate how the application functions. JSX provides us
with a nice, clean way to express React elements in our code that makes sense to us
and is immediately readable by the engineers that make up our community. The
drawback of JSX is that it is not readable by the browser. Before our code can be
interpreted by the browser, it needs to be converted from JSX into pure React.

The array in Example 5-5 contains two recipes, and they represent our application's
current state.

Example 5-5. Array of recipes

```
var data = [
  {
    "name": "Baked Salmon",
    "ingredients": [
      { "name": "Salmon", "amount": 1, "measurement": "l lb" },
      { "name": "Pine Nuts", "amount": 1, "measurement": "cup" },
      { "name": "Butter Lettuce", "amount": 2, "measurement": "cups" },
      { "name": "Yellow Squash", "amount": 1, "measurement": "med" },
      { "name": "Olive Oil", "amount": 0.5, "measurement": "cup" },
      { "name": "Garlic", "amount": 3, "measurement": "cloves" }
    ],
    "steps": [
      "Preheat the oven to 350 degrees.",
      "Spread the olive oil around a glass baking dish.",
      "Add the salmon, garlic, and pine nuts to the dish.",
      "Bake for 15 minutes.",
      "Add the yellow squash and put back in the oven for 30 mins.",
      "Remove from oven and let cool for 15 minutes. Add the lettuce and serve."
    ]
```

```
    },
    {
      "name": "Fish Tacos",
      "ingredients": [
        { "name": "Whitefish", "amount": 1, "measurement": "1 lb" },
        { "name": "Cheese", "amount": 1, "measurement": "cup" },
        { "name": "Iceberg Lettuce", "amount": 2, "measurement": "cups" },
        { "name": "Tomatoes", "amount": 2, "measurement": "large"},
        { "name": "Tortillas", "amount": 3, "measurement": "med" }
      ],
      "steps": [
        "Cook the fish on the grill until hot.",
        "Place the fish on the 3 tortillas.",
        "Top them with lettuce, tomatoes, and cheese."
      ]
    }
];
```

The data is expressed in an array of two JavaScript objects. Each object contains the name of the recipe, a list of the ingredients required, and a list of steps necessary to cook the recipe.

We can create a UI for these recipes with two components: a Menu component for listing the recipes and a Recipe component that describes the UI for each recipe. It's the Menu component that we will render to the DOM. We will pass our data to the Menu component as a property called recipes (Example 5-6).

Example 5-6. Recipe app code structure

```
// The data, an array of Recipe objects
var data = [ ... ];

// A stateless functional component for an individual Recipe
const Recipe = (props) => (
  ...
)

// A stateless functional component for the Menu of Recipes
const Menu = (props) => (
  ...
)

// A call to ReactDOM.render to render our Menu into the current DOM
ReactDOM.render(
    <Menu recipes={data} title="Delicious Recipes" />,
    document.getElementById("react-container")
)
```

The React elements within the Menu component are expressed as JSX (Example 5-7).
Everything is contained within an article element. A header element, an h1 element, and a div.recipes element are used to describe the DOM for our menu. The
value for the title property will be displayed as text within the h1.

Example 5-7. Menu component structure

```
const Menu = (props) =>
    <article>
        <header>
            <h1>{props.title}</h1>
        </header>
        <div className="recipes">
        </div>
    </article>
```

Inside of the div.recipes element, we add a component for each recipe
(Example 5-8).

Example 5-8. Mapping recipe data

```
<div className="recipes">
    {props.recipes.map((recipe, i) =>
        <Recipe key={i} name={recipe.name}
            ingredients={recipe.ingredients}
            steps={recipe.steps} />
    )}
</div>
```

In order to list the recipes within the div.recipes element, we use curly braces to
add a JavaScript expression that will return an array of children. We can use the map
function on the props.recipes array to return a component for each object within
the array. As mentioned previously, each recipe contains a name, some ingredients,
and cooking instructions (steps). We will need to pass this data to each Recipe as
props. Also remember that we should use the key property to uniquely identify each
element.

Using the JSX spread operator can improve our code. The JSX spread operator works
like the object spread operator discussed in Chapter 2. It will add each field of the

recipe object as a property of the Recipe component. The syntax in Example 5-9 accomplishes the same results.

Example 5-9. Enhancement: JSX spread operator

```
{props.recipes.map((recipe, i) =>
    <Recipe key={i} {...recipe} />
)}
```

Another place we can make an ES6 improvement to our Menu component is where we take in the props argument. We can use object destructuring to scope the variables to this function. This allows us to access the title and recipes variables directly, no longer having to prefix them with props (Example 5-10).

Example 5-10. Refactored Menu component

```
const Menu = ({ title, recipes }) => (
    <article>
        <header>
            <h1>{title}</h1>
        </header>
        <div className="recipes">
            {recipes.map((recipe, i) =>
                <Recipe key={i} {...recipe} />
            )}
        </div>
    </article>
)
```

Now let's code the component for each individual recipe (Example 5-11).

Example 5-11. Complete Recipe component

```
const Recipe = ({ name, ingredients, steps }) =>
    <section id={name.toLowerCase().replace(/ /g, "-")}>
        <h1>{name}</h1>
        <ul className="ingredients">
            {ingredients.map((ingredient, i) =>
                <li key={i}>{ingredient.name}</li>
            )}
        </ul>
        <section className="instructions">
            <h2>Cooking Instructions</h2>
            {steps.map((step, i) =>
                <p key={i}>{step}</p>
            )}
        </section>
    </section>
```

This component is also a stateless functional component. Each recipe has a string for the name, an array of objects for ingredients, and an array of strings for the steps. Using ES6 object destructuring, we can tell this component to locally scope those fields by name so we can access them directly without having to use props.name, or props.ingredients, props.steps.

The first JavaScript expression that we see is being used to set the id attribute for the root section element. It is converting the recipe's name to a lowercase string and globally replacing spaces with dashes. The result is that "Baked Salmon" will be converted to "baked-salmon" (and likewise, if we had a recipe with the name "Boston Baked Beans" it would be converted to "boston-baked-beans") before it is used as the id attribute in our UI. The value for name is also being displayed in an h1 as a text node.

Inside of the unordered list, a JavaScript expression is mapping each ingredient to an li element that displays the name of the ingredient. Within our instructions section, we see the same pattern being used to return a paragraph element where each step is displayed. These map functions are returning arrays of child elements.

The complete code for the application should look like Example 5-12.

Example 5-12. Finished code for recipe app

```
const data = [
  {
    "name": "Baked Salmon",
    "ingredients": [
      { "name": "Salmon", "amount": 1, "measurement": "l lb" },
      { "name": "Pine Nuts", "amount": 1, "measurement": "cup" },
      { "name": "Butter Lettuce", "amount": 2, "measurement": "cups" },
      { "name": "Yellow Squash", "amount": 1, "measurement": "med" },
      { "name": "Olive Oil", "amount": 0.5, "measurement": "cup" },
      { "name": "Garlic", "amount": 3, "measurement": "cloves" }
    ],
    "steps": [
      "Preheat the oven to 350 degrees.",
      "Spread the olive oil around a glass baking dish.",
      "Add the salmon, garlic, and pine nuts to the dish.",
      "Bake for 15 minutes.",
      "Add the yellow squash and put back in the oven for 30 mins.",
      "Remove from oven and let cool for 15 minutes. Add the lettuce and serve."
    ]
  },
  {
    "name": "Fish Tacos",
    "ingredients": [
      { "name": "Whitefish", "amount": 1, "measurement": "l lb" },
      { "name": "Cheese", "amount": 1, "measurement": "cup" },
```

```
      { "name": "Iceberg Lettuce", "amount": 2, "measurement": "cups" },
      { "name": "Tomatoes", "amount": 2, "measurement": "large"},
      { "name": "Tortillas", "amount": 3, "measurement": "med" }
    ],
    "steps": [
      "Cook the fish on the grill until hot.",
      "Place the fish on the 3 tortillas.",
      "Top them with lettuce, tomatoes, and cheese."
    ]
  }
]

const Recipe = ({ name, ingredients, steps }) =>
    <section id={name.toLowerCase().replace(/ /g, "-")}>
        <h1>{name}</h1>
        <ul className="ingredients">
            {ingredients.map((ingredient, i) =>
                <li key={i}>{ingredient.name}</li>
            )}
        </ul>
        <section className="instructions">
            <h2>Cooking Instructions</h2>
            {steps.map((step, i) =>
                <p key={i}>{step}</p>
            )}
        </section>
    </section>

const Menu = ({ title, recipes }) =>
    <article>
        <header>
            <h1>{title}</h1>
        </header>
        <div className="recipes">
            {recipes.map((recipe, i) =>
                <Recipe key={i} {...recipe} />
            )}
        </div>
    </article>


ReactDOM.render(
    <Menu recipes={data}
        title="Delicious Recipes" />,
    document.getElementById("react-container")
)
```

When we run this code in the browser, React will construct a UI using our instructions with the recipe data as shown in Figure 5-2.

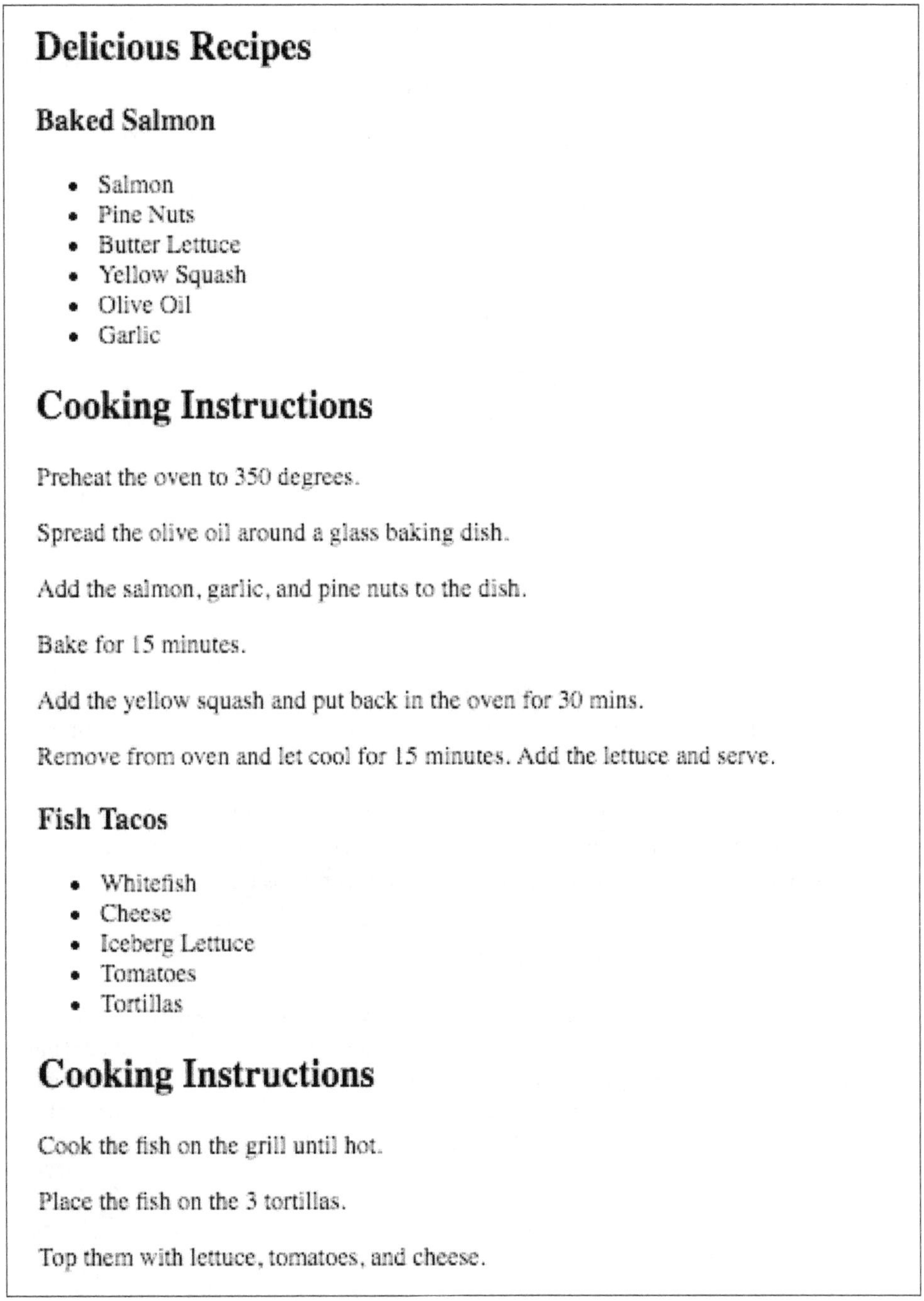

Delicious Recipes

Baked Salmon

- Salmon
- Pine Nuts
- Butter Lettuce
- Yellow Squash
- Olive Oil
- Garlic

Cooking Instructions

Preheat the oven to 350 degrees.

Spread the olive oil around a glass baking dish.

Add the salmon, garlic, and pine nuts to the dish.

Bake for 15 minutes.

Add the yellow squash and put back in the oven for 30 mins.

Remove from oven and let cool for 15 minutes. Add the lettuce and serve.

Fish Tacos

- Whitefish
- Cheese
- Iceberg Lettuce
- Tomatoes
- Tortillas

Cooking Instructions

Cook the fish on the grill until hot.

Place the fish on the 3 tortillas.

Top them with lettuce, tomatoes, and cheese.

Figure 5-2. Delicious Recipes output

If you are using Google Chrome and you have the React Developer Tools Extension installed, you can take a look at the present state of the virtual DOM. To do this, open the developer tools and select the React tab (Figure 5-3).

Figure 5-3. Resulting virtual DOM in React Developer Tools

Here we can see our Menu and its child elements. The data array contains two objects for recipes, and we have two Recipe elements. Each Recipe element has properties for the recipe name, ingredients, and steps.

The virtual DOM is constructed based on the application's state data being passed to the Menu component as a property. If we change the recipes array and rerender our Menu component, React will change this DOM as efficiently as possible.

Babel Presets

Babel 6 breaks possible transformations up into modules called *presets*. It requires engineers to explicitly define which transformations should be run by specifying which presets to use. The goal was to make everything more modular to allow developers to decide which syntax should be converted. The plugins fall into a few categories, and all are opt-in based on the needs of the application. The presets you're most likely to use are:

`babel-preset-es2015`
    Compiles ES2015, or ES6, to ES5.

`babel-preset-es2016`
    Compiles what is in ES2016 to ES2015

`babel-preset-es2017`
> Compiles what is in ES2017 to ES2016

`babel-preset-env`
> Compiles everything from ES2015, ES2016, ES2017. A catch-all for the previous three presets

`babel-preset-react`
> Compiles JSX to `React.createElement` calls.

When a new feature is proposed for inclusion in the ECMAScript spec, it goes through stages of acceptance from stage 0, Strawman (newly proposed and very experimental), to stage 4, Finished (accepted as part of the standard). Babel provides presets for each of these stages, so you can choose which stage you want to allow in your application:

- `babel-preset-stage-0`: Strawman
- `babel-preset-stage-1`: Proposal
- `babel-preset-stage-2`: Draft
- `babel-preset-stage-3`: Candidate

Intro to Webpack

Once we start working in production with React, there are a lot of questions to consider: How do we want to deal with JSX and ES6+ transformation? How can we manage our dependencies? How can we optimize our images and CSS?

Many different tools have emerged to answer these questions, including Browserify, Gulp, and Grunt. Due to its features and widespread adoption by large companies, *webpack* has also emerged as one of the leading tools for bundling CommonJS modules (see Chapter 2 for more on CommonJS).

Webpack is billed as a module bundler. A module bundler takes all of our different files (JavaScript, LESS, CSS, JSX, ES6, and so on) and turns them into a single file. The two main benefits of modular bundling are *modularity* and *network performance.*

Modularity will allow you to break down your source code into parts, or modules, that are easier to work with, especially in a team environment.

Network performance is gained by only needing to load one dependency in the browser, the bundle. Each `script` tag makes an HTTP request, and there is a latency penalty for each HTTP request. Bundling all of the dependencies into a single file allows you to load everything with one HTTP request, thereby avoiding additional latency.

Aside from transpiling, webpack also can handle:

Code splitting
Splits up your code into different chunks that can be loaded when you need them. Sometimes these are called *rollups* or *layers*; the aim is to break up code as needed for different pages or devices.

Minification
Removes whitespace, line breaks, lengthy variable names, and unnecessary code to reduce the file size.

Feature flagging
Sends code to one or more—but not all—environments when testing out features.

Hot Module Replacement (HMR)
Watches for changes in source code. Changes only the updated modules immediately.

Webpack Loaders

A *loader* is a function that handles the transformations that we want to put our code through during the build process. If our application uses ES6, JSX, CoffeeScript, and other languages that can't be read natively by the browser, we'll specify the necessary loaders in the *webpack.config.js* file to do the work of converting the code into syntax that can be read natively by the browser.

Webpack has a huge number of loaders that fall into a few categories. The most common use case for loaders is transpiling from one dialect to another. For example, ES6 and React code is transpiled by including the `babel-loader`. We specify the types of files that Babel should be run on, then webpack takes care of the rest.

Another popular category of loaders is for styling. The `css-loader` looks for files with the *.scss* extension and compiles them to CSS. The `css-loader` can be used to include CSS modules in your bundle. All CSS is bundled as JavaScript and automatically added when the bundled JavaScript file is included. There's no need to use `link` elements to include stylesheets.

Check out the full list of loaders (*https://webpack.js.org/concepts/loaders/*) if you'd like to see all of the different options.

Recipes App with a Webpack Build

The Recipes app that we built earlier in this chapter has some limitations that webpack will help us alleviate. Using a tool like webpack to statically build your client JavaScript makes it possible for teams to work together on large-scale web applications. We can also gain the following benefits by incorporating the webpack module bundler:

Modularity

Using the CommonJS module pattern in order to export modules that will later be imported or required by another part of the application makes our source code more approachable. It allows development teams to easily work together by allowing them to create and work with separate files that will be statically combined into a single file before sending to production.

Composing

With modules, we can build small, simple, reusable React components that we can compose efficiently into applications. Smaller components are easier to comprehend, test, and reuse. They are also easier to replace down the line when enhancing your applications.

Speed

Packaging all of the application's modules and dependencies into a single client bundle will reduce the load time of your application because there is latency associated with each HTTP request. Packaging everything together in a single file means that the client will only need to make a single request. Minifying the code in the bundle will improve load time as well.

Consistency

Since webpack will transpile JSX into React and ES6 or even ES7 into universal JavaScript, we can start using tomorrow's JavaScript syntax today. Babel supports a wide range of ESNext syntax, which means we do not have to worry about whether the browser supports our code. It allows developers to consistently use cutting-edge JavaScript syntax.

Breaking components into modules

Approaching the Recipes app with the ability to use webpack and Babel allows us to break our code down into modules that use ES6 syntax. Let's take a look at our stateless functional component for recipes (Example 5-13).

Example 5-13. Current Recipe component

```
const Recipe = ({ name, ingredients, steps }) =>
    <section id="baked-salmon">
        <h1>{name}</h1>
        <ul className="ingredients">
            {ingredients.map((ingredient, i) =>
                <li key={i}>{ingredient.name}</li>
            )}
        </ul>
```

```
    <section className="instructions">
        <h2>Cooking Instructions</h2>
        {steps.map((step, i) =>
            <p key={i}>{step}</p>
        )}
    </section>
</section>
```

This component is doing quite a bit. We are displaying the name of the recipe, con-structing an unordered list of ingredients, and displaying the instructions, with each step getting its own paragraph element.

A more functional approach to the `Recipe` component would be to break it up into smaller, more focused stateless functional components and compose them together. We can start by pulling the instructions out into their own stateless functional com-ponent and creating a module in a separate file that we can use for any set of instruc-tions (Example 5-14).

Example 5-14. Instructions component

```
const Instructions = ({ title, steps }) =>
    <section className="instructions">
        <h2>{title}</h2>
        {steps.map((s, i) =>
            <p key={i}>{s}</p>
        )}
    </section>

export default Instructions
```

Here we have created a new component called `Instructions`. We will pass the title of the instructions and the steps to this component. This way we can reuse this compo-nent for "Cooking Instructions," "Baking Instructions," "Prep Instructions", or a "Pre-cook Checklist"—anything that has steps.

Now think about the ingredients. In the `Recipe` component, we are only displaying the ingredient names, but each ingredient in the data for the recipe has an amount and measurement as well. We could create a stateless functional component to repre-sent a single ingredient (Example 5-15).

Example 5-15. Ingredient component

```
const Ingredient = ({ amount, measurement, name }) =>
    <li>
        <span className="amount">{amount}</span>
        <span className="measurement">{measurement}</span>
        <span className="name">{name}</span>
    </li>
```

```
export default Ingredient
```

Here we assume each ingredient has an amount, a measurement, and a name. We destructure those values from our props object and display them each in independent classed span elements.

Using the Ingredient component, we can construct an IngredientsList component that can be used any time we need to display a list of ingredients (Example 5-16).

Example 5-16. IngredientsList using Ingredient component

```
import Ingredient from './Ingredient'

const IngredientsList = ({ list }) =>
    <ul className="ingredients">
        {list.map((ingredient, i) =>
            <Ingredient key={i} {...ingredient} />
        )}
    </ul>

export default IngredientsList
```

In this file, we first import the Ingredient component because we are going to use it for each ingredient. The ingredients are passed to this component as an array in a property called list. Each ingredient in the list array will be mapped to the Ingredient component. The JSX spread operator is used to pass all of the data to the Ingredient component as props.

Using spread operator:

```
<Ingredient {...ingredient} />
```

is another way of expressing:

```
<Ingredient amount={ingredient.amount}
            measurement={ingredient.measurement}
            name={ingredient.name} />
```

So, given an ingredient with these fields:

```
let ingredient = {
    amount: 1,
    measurement: 'cup',
    name: 'sugar'
}
```

we get:

```
<Ingredient amount={1}
            measurement="cup"
            name="sugar"  />
```

Now that we have components for ingredients and instructions, we can compose recipes using these components (Example 5-17).

Example 5-17. Refactored Recipe component

```
import IngredientsList from './IngredientsList'
import Instructions from './Instructions'

const Recipe = ({ name, ingredients, steps}) =>
    <section id={name.toLowerCase().replace(/ /g, '-')}>
        <h1>{name}</h1>
        <IngredientsList list={ingredients} />
        <Instructions title="Cooking Instructions"
                      steps={steps} />
    </section>

export default Recipe
```

First we import the components that we are going to use, `IngredientsList` and `Instructions`. Now we can use them to create the `Recipe` component. Instead of a bunch of complicated code building out the entire recipe in one place, we have expressed our recipe more declaratively by composing smaller components. Not only is the code nice and simple, but it also reads well. This shows us that a recipe should display the name of the recipe, a list of ingredients, and some cooking instructions. We've abstracted away what it means to display ingredients and instructions into smaller, simple components.

In a modular approach with CommonJS, the `Menu` component would look pretty similar. The key difference is that it would live in its own file, import the modules that it needs to use, and export itself (Example 5-18).

Example 5-18. Completed Menu component

```
import Recipe from './Recipe'

const Menu = ({ recipes }) =>
    <article>
        <header>
            <h1>Delicious Recipes</h1>
        </header>
        <div className="recipes">
            { recipes.map((recipe, i) =>
                <Recipe key={i} {...recipe} />)
            }
        </div>
    </article>

export default Menu
```

We still need to use ReactDOM to render the Menu component. We will still have a *index.js* file, but it will look much different (Example 5-19).

Example 5-19. Completed index.js file

```
import React from 'react'
import { render } from 'react-dom'
import Menu from './components/Menu'
import data from './data/recipes'

window.React = React

render(
    <Menu recipes={data} />,
    document.getElementById("react-container")
)
```

The first four statements import the necessary modules for our app to work. Instead of loading react and react-dom via the script tag, we import them so webpack can add them to our bundle. We also need the Menu component, and a sample data array which has been moved to a separate module. It still contains two recipes: Baked Salmon and Fish Tacos.

All of our imported variables are local to the *index.js* file. Setting window.React to React exposes the React library globally in the browser. This way all calls to React.createElement are assured to work.

When we render the Menu component, we pass the array of recipe data to this component as a property. This single ReactDOM.render call will mount and render our Menu component.

Now that we have pulled our code apart into separate modules and files, let's create a static build process with webpack that will put everything back together into a single file.

Installing webpack dependencies

In order to create a static build process with webpack, we'll need to install a few things. Everything that we need can be installed with npm. First, we might as well install webpack globally so we can use the webpack command anywhere:

```
sudo npm install -g webpack
```

Webpack is also going to work with Babel to transpile our code from JSX and ES6 to JavaScript that runs in the browser. We are going to use a few loaders along with a few presets to accomplish this task:

```
npm install babel-core babel-loader babel-preset-env babel-preset-react
babel-preset-stage-0 --save-dev
```

Our application uses React and ReactDOM. We've been loading these dependencies with the script tag. Now we are going to let webpack add them to our bundle. We'll need to install the dependencies for React and ReactDOM locally:

```
npm install react react-dom --save
```

This adds the necessary scripts for react and react-dom to the *./node_modules* folder. Now we have everything needed to set up a static build process with webpack.

Webpack configuration

For this modular Recipes app to work, we are going to need to tell webpack how to bundle our source code into a single file. We can do this with configuration files, and the default webpack configuration file is always *webpack.config.js*.

The starting file for our Recipes app is *index.js*. It imports React, ReactDOM, and the *Menu.js* file. This is what we want to run in the browser first. Wherever webpack finds an import statement, it will find the associated module in the filesystem and include it in the bundle. *Index.js* imports *Menu.js*, *Menu.js* imports *Recipe.js*, *Recipe.js* imports *Instructions.js* and *IngredientsList.js*, and *IngredientsList.js* imports *Ingredient.js*. Webpack will follow this import tree and include all of these necessary modules in our bundle.

ES6 import Statements

We are using ES6 import statements, which are not presently supported by most browsers or by Node.js. The reason ES6 import statements work is because Babel will convert them into require('module/path'); statements in our final code. The require function is how CommonJS modules are typically loaded.

As webpack builds our bundle, we need to tell webpack to transpile JSX to pure React elements. We also need to convert any ES6 syntax to ES5 syntax. Our build process will initially have three steps (Figure 5-4).

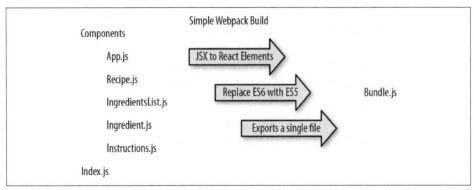

Figure 5-4. Recipe app build process

The *webpack.config.js* file is just another module that exports a JavaScript literal object that describes the actions that webpack should take. This file (Example 5-20) should be saved to the root folder of the project, right next to the *index.js* file.

Example 5-20. webpack.config.js

```
module.exports = {
    entry: "./src/index.js",
    output: {
        path: "dist/assets",
        filename: "bundle.js"
    },
    module: {
        rules: [
            {
                test: /\.js$/,
                exclude: /(node_modules)/,
                loader: ['babel-loader'],
                query: {
                    presets: ['env', 'stage-0', 'react']
                }
            }
        ]
    }
}
```

First, we tell webpack that our client entry file is *./src/index.js*. It will automatically build the dependency tree based upon import statements starting in that file. Next, we specify that we want to output a bundled JavaScript file to *./dist/assets/bundle.js*. This is where webpack will place the final packaged JavaScript.

The next set of instructions for webpack consists of a list of loaders to run on specified modules. The rules field is an array because there are many types of loaders that you can incorporate with webpack. In this example, we are only incorporating babel.

Each loader is a JavaScript object. The test field is a regular expression that matches the file path of each module that the loader should operate on. In this case, we are running the babel-loader on all imported JavaScript files except those found in the *node_modules* folder. When the babel-loader runs, it will use presets for ES2015 (ES6) and React to transpile any ES6 or JSX syntax into JavaScript that will run in most browsers.

Webpack is run statically. Typically bundles are created before the app is deployed to the server. Since you have installed webpack globally, you can run it from the command line:

```
$ webpack
  Time: 1727ms
  Asset     Size  Chunks          Chunk Names
  bundle.js  693 kB      0  [emitted]  main
    + 169 hidden modules
```

Webpack will either succeed and create a bundle, or fail and show you an error. Most errors have to do with broken import references. When debugging webpack errors, look closely at the filenames and file paths used in import statements.

Loading the bundle

We have a bundle, so now what? We exported the bundle to the *dist* folder. This folder contains the files that we want to run on the web server. The *dist* folder is where the *index.html* file (Example 5-21) should be placed. This file needs to include a target div element where the React Menu component will be mounted. It also requires a single script tag that will load our bundled JavaScript.

Example 5-21. index.html

```
<!DOCTYPE html>
<html>
<head>
<meta charset="utf-8">
<title>React Recipes App</title>
</head>
<body>
  <div id="react-container"></div>
  <script src="assets/bundle.js"></script>
</body>
</html>
```

This is the home page for your app. It will load everything it needs from one file, one HTTP request: *bundle.js*. You will need to deploy these files to your web server or build a web server application that will serve these files with something like Node.js or Ruby on Rails.

Source mapping

Bundling our code into a single file can cause some setbacks when it comes time to debug the application in the browser. We can eliminate this problem by providing a *source map*. A source map is a file that maps a bundle to the original source files. With webpack, all we have to do is add a couple of lines to our *webpack.config.js* file (Example 5-22).

Example 5-22. webpack.config.js with source mapping

```
module.exports = {
    entry: "./src/index.js",
    output: {
        path: "dist/assets",
        filename: "bundle.js",
        sourceMapFilename: 'bundle.map'
    },
    devtool: '#source-map',
    module: {
        rules: [
            {
                test: /\.js$/,
                exclude: /(node_modules)/,
                loader: ['babel-loader'],
                query: {
                    presets: ['env', 'stage-0', 'react']
                }
            }
        ]
    }
}
```

Setting the `devtool` property to `'#source-map'` tells webpack that you want to use source mapping. A `sourceMapFilename` is required. It is always a good idea to name your source map file after the target dependency. Webpack will associate the bundle with the source map during the export.

The next time you run webpack, you will see that two output files are generated and added to the *assets* folder: the original *bundle.js* and *bundle.map*.

The source map is going to let us debug using our original source files. In the Sources tab of your browser's developer tools, you should find a folder named *webpack://*. Inside of this folder, you will see all of the source files in your bundle (Figure 5-5).

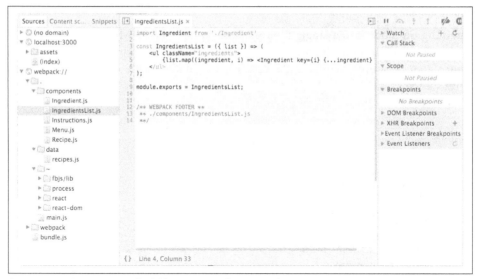

Figure 5-5. Sources panel of Chrome Developer Tools

You can debug from these files using the browser's step-through debugger. Clicking on any line number adds a breakpoint. Refreshing the browser will pause JavaScript processing when any breakpoints are reached in your source file. You can inspect scoped variables in the Scope panel or add variables to Watch in the watch panel.

Optimizing the bundle

The output bundle file is still simply a text file, so reducing the amount of text in this file will reduce the file size and cause it to load faster over HTTP. Some things that can be done to reduce the file size include removing all whitespace, reducing variable names to a single character, and removing any lines of code that the interpreter will never reach. Reducing the size of your JavaScript file with these tricks is referred to as *minifying* or *uglifying* your code.

Webpack has a built-in plugin that you can use to uglify the bundle. In order to use it, you will need to install webpack locally:

```
npm install webpack --save-dev
```

We can add extra steps to the build process using webpack plugins. In this example, we are going to add a step to our build process to uglify our output bundle, which will significantly reduce the file size (Example 5-23).

Example 5-23. webpack.config.js with Uglify plugin

```
var webpack = require("webpack");

module.exports = {
    entry: "./src/index.js",
    output: {
        path: "dist/assets",
        filename: "bundle.js",
        sourceMapFilename: 'bundle.map'
    },
    devtool: '#source-map',
    module: {
        rules: [
            {
                test: /\.js$/,
                exclude: /(node_modules)/,
                loader: ['babel-loader'],
                query: {
                    presets: ['env', 'stage-0', 'react']
                }
            }
        ]
    },
    plugins: [
        new webpack.optimize.UglifyJsPlugin({
            sourceMap: true,
            warnings: false,
            mangle: true
        })
    ]
}
```

To use the Uglify plugin, we need to require webpack, which is why we needed to install webpack locally.

`UglifyJsPlugin` is a function that gets instructions from its arguments. Once we uglify our code, it will become unrecognizable. We are going to need a source map, which is why `sourceMap` is set to `true`. Setting `warnings` to `false` will remove any console warnings from the exported bundle. Mangling our code means that we are going to reduce long variable names like `recipes` or `ingredients` to a single letter.

The next time you run webpack, you will see that the size of your bundled output file has been significantly reduced, and it's no longer recognizable. Including a source map will still allow you to debug from your original source even though your bundle has been minified.

Bundling CSS

Another nice feature of webpack is that it can bundle CSS into the same file as the bundled JavaScript. This allows your users to download a single file that contains all of the CSS and JavaScript necessary for your app.

CSS can be included into the bundle with `import` statements. These statements tell webpack to bundle up associated CSS files with a JavaScript module:

```
import Recipe from './Recipe'
import '../../stylesheets/Menu.css'

const Menu = ({ recipes }) =>
    <article>
        <header>
            <h1>Delicious Recipes</h1>
        </header>
        <div className="recipes">
            { recipes.map((recipe, i) =>
                <Recipe key={i} {...recipe} />)
            }
        </div>
    </article>

export default Menu
```

In order to implement CSS bundling in your webpack configuration, you will need to install some loaders:

```
npm install style-loader css-loader postcss-loader --save-dev
```

Finally, you have to incorporate this loader into your webpack configuration:

```
rules: [
  {
    test: /\.js$/,
    exclude: /(node_modules)/,
    loader: ['babel-loader'],
    query: {
      presets: ['env', 'stage-0', 'react']
    }
  },
  {
            test: /\.css$/,
            use: ['style-loader','css-loader', {
                loader: 'postcss-loader',
                options: {
                  plugins: () => [require('autoprefixer')]
                }}]
  }
]
```

> Bundling up CSS files with webpack will cause your site to load faster by reducing the number of requests that your browser needs to make for resources.

create-react-app

As the Facebook team mentions in their blog, "the React ecosystem has commonly become associated with an overwhelming explosion of tools."[1] In response to this, the React team launched `create-react-app` (*http://bit.ly/2mtQwNC*) a command-line tool that autogenerates a React project. `create-react-app` was inspired by the Ember CLI project (*https://ember-cli.com*), and it lets developers get started with React projects quickly without the manual configuration of webpack, Babel, ESLint, and associated tools.

To get started with `create-react-app`, install the package globally:

```
npm install -g create-react-app
```

Then, use the command and the name of the folder where you'd like the app to be created:

```
create-react-app my-react-project
```

This will create a React project in that directory with just three dependencies: React, ReactDOM, and `react-scripts`. `react-scripts` was also created by Facebook and is where the real magic happens. It installs Babel, ESLint, webpack, and more, so that you don't have to configure them manually. Within the generated project folder, you'll also find a *src* folder containing an *App.js* file. Here, you can edit the root component and import other component files.

From within the *my-react-project* folder, you can run `npm start`. If you prefer, you can also run `yarn start`. This will start your application on port 3000.

You can run tests with `npm test` or `yarn test`. This runs all of the test files in the project in an interactive mode.

You can also run the `npm run build` command. Using yarn, run `yarn build`.

This will create a production-ready bundle that has been transpiled and minified.

`create-react-app` is a great tool for beginners and experienced React developers alike. As the tool evolves, more functionality will likely be added, so you can keep an eye on the changes on GitHub.

---

1 Dan Abramov, "Create Apps with No Configuration" (*http://bit.ly/2ndUXzR*), React Blog, July 22, 2016.

CHAPTER 6

Props, State, and the Component Tree

In the last chapter, we talked about how to create components. We primarily focused on how to build a user interface by composing React components. This chapter is filled with techniques that you can use to better manage data and reduce time spent debugging applications.

Data handling within component trees is one of the key advantages of working with React. There are techniques that you can use when working with data in React components that will make your life much easier in the long run. Our applications will be easier to reason about and scale if we can manage data from a single location and construct the UI based on that data.

Property Validation

JavaScript is a loosely typed language, which means that the data type of a variable's value can change. For example, you can initially set a JavaScript variable as a string, then change its value to an array later, and JavaScript will not complain. Managing our variable types inefficiently can lead to a lot of time spent debugging applications.

React components provide a way to specify and validate property types. Using this feature will greatly reduce the amount of time spent debugging applications. Supplying incorrect property types triggers warnings that can help us find bugs that may have otherwise slipped through the cracks.

React has built-in automatic property validation (*http://bit.ly/2okjSzJ*) for the variable types, as shown in Table 6-1.

Table 6-1. React property validation

Type	Validator
Arrays	`React.PropTypes.array`
Boolean	`React.PropTypes.bool`
Functions	`React.PropTypes.func`
Numbers	`React.PropTypes.number`
Objects	`React.PropTypes.object`
Strings	`React.PropTypes.string`

In this section, we will create a `Summary` component for our recipes. The `Summary` component will display the title of the recipe along with counts for both ingredients and steps (see Figure 6-1).

Baked Salmon

5 Ingredients I 7 Steps

Figure 6-1. Summary component output for Baked Salmon

In order to display this data, we must supply the `Summary` component with three properties: a title, an array of ingredients, and an array of steps. We want to validate these properties to make sure the first is a string and the others are arrays, and supply defaults for when they are unavailable. How to implement property validation depends upon how components are created. Stateless functional components and ES6 classes have different ways of implementing property validation.

First, let's look at why we should use property validation and how to implement it in components created with `React.createClass`.

Validating Props with createClass

We need to understand why it is important to validate component property types. Consider the following implementation for the `Summary` component:

```
const Summary = createClass({
    displayName: "Summary",
    render() {
        const {ingredients, steps, title} = this.props
        return (
            <div className="summary">
                <h1>{title}</h1>
                <p>
                    <span>{ingredients.length} Ingredients</span> |
                    <span>{steps.length} Steps</span>
```

```
                    </p>
                </div>
            )
        }
    })
```

The `Summary` component destructures `ingredients`, `steps`, and `title` from the properties object and then constructs a UI to display that data. Since we expect both `ingredients` and `steps` to be arrays, we use `Array.length` to count the array's items.

What if we rendered this `Summary` component accidentally using strings?

```
render(
    <Summary title="Peanut Butter and Jelly"
            ingredients="peanut butter, jelly, bread"
            steps="spread peanut butter and jelly between bread" />,
    document.getElementById('react-container')
)
```

JavaScript will not complain, but finding the length will count the number of characters in each string (Figure 6-2).

Peanut Butter and Jelly

27 Ingredients | 44 Steps

Figure 6-2. Summary component output for Peanut Butter and Jelly

The output of this code is odd. No matter how fancy your peanut butter and jelly might be, it's doubtful that you are going to have 27 ingredients and 44 steps. Instead of seeing the correct number of steps and ingredients, we are seeing the length in characters of each string. A bug like this is easy to miss. If we validated the property types when we created the `Summary` component, React could catch this bug for us:

```
const Summary = createClass({
    displayName: "Summary",
    propTypes: {
        ingredients: PropTypes.array,
        steps: PropTypes.array,
        title: PropTypes.string
    },
    render() {
        const {ingredients, steps, title} = this.props
        return (
            <div className="summary">
                <h1>{title}</h1>
                <p>
                    <span>{ingredients.length} Ingredients | </span>
                    <span>{steps.length} Steps</span>
```

```
            </p>
          </div>
        )
      }
    })
```

Using React's built-in property type validation, we can make sure that both `ingredi`
`ents` and `steps` are arrays. Additionally, we can make sure that the `title` value is a
string. Now when we pass incorrect property types, we will see an error (Figure 6-3).

Figure 6-3. Property type validation warning

What would happen if we rendered the `Summary` component without sending it any
properties?

```
render(
  <Summary />,
  document.getElementById('react-container')
)
```

Rendering the `Summary` component without any properties causes a JavaScript error
that takes down the web app (Figure 6-4).

Figure 6-4. Error generated from missing array

This error occurs because the type of the `ingredients` property is undefined, and
undefined is not an object that has a length property like an array or a string. React
has a way to specify required properties. When those properties are not supplied,
React will trigger a warning in the console:

```
const Summary = createClass({
    displayName: "Summary",
    propTypes: {
        ingredients: PropTypes.array.isRequired,
        steps: PropTypes.array.isRequired,
        title: PropTypes.string
    },
    render() {
        ...
```

```
    }
})
```

Now when we render the Summary component without any properties, React directs our attention to the problem with a console warning just before the error occurs. This makes it easier to figure out what went wrong (Figure 6-5).

Figure 6-5. React warnings for missing properties

The Summary component expects an array for ingredients and an array for steps, but it only uses the length property of each array. This component is designed to display counts (numbers) for each of those values. It may make more sense to refactor our code to expect numbers instead, since the component doesn't actually need arrays:

```
import { createClass, PropTypes } from 'react'

export const Summary = createClass({
    displayName: "Summary",
    propTypes: {
        ingredients: PropTypes.number.isRequired,
        steps: PropTypes.number.isRequired,
        title: PropTypes.string
    },
    render() {
        const {ingredients, steps, title} = this.props
        return (
            <div className="summary">
                <h1>{title}</h1>
                <p>
                    <span>{ingredients} Ingredients</span> |
                    <span>{steps} Steps</span>
                </p>
            </div>
        )
    }
})
```

Using numbers for this component is a more flexible approach. Now the Summary component simply displays the UI; it sends the burden of actually counting ingredients or steps further up the component tree to a parent or ancestor.

Default Props

Another way to improve the quality of components is to assign default values for properties.[1] The validation behavior is similar to what you might expect: the default values you establish will be used if other values are not provided.

Let's say we want the Summary component to work even when the properties are not supplied:

```
import { render } from 'react-dom'

render(<Summary />, document.getElementById('react-container'))
```

With createClass, we can add a method called getDefaultProps that returns default values for properties that are not assigned:

```
const Summary = createClass({
    displayName: "Summary",
    propTypes: {
        ingredients: PropTypes.number,
        steps: PropTypes.number,
        title: PropTypes.string
    },
    getDefaultProps() {
        return {
            ingredients: 0,
            steps: 0,
            title: "[untitled recipe]"
        }
    },
    render() {
        const {ingredients, steps, title} = this.props
        return (
            <div className="summary">
                <h1>{title}</h1>
                <p>
                    <span>{ingredients} Ingredients | </span>
                    <span>{steps} Steps</span>
                </p>
            </div>
        )
    }
}
```

Now when we try to render this component without properties, we will see some default data instead, as in Figure 6-6.

---

1 React Docs, "Default Prop Values" (*http://bit.ly/2oYLr4r*)

> # [untitled recipe]
>
> 0 Ingredients | 0 Steps

Figure 6-6. Summary component output with default properties

Using default properties can extend the flexibility of your component and prevent errors from occurring when your users do not explicitly require every property.

Custom Property Validation

React's built-in validators are great for making sure that your variables are required and typed correctly. But there are instances that require more robust validation. For example, you may want to make sure that a number is within a specific range or that a value contains a specific string. React provides a way to build your own custom validation for such cases.

Custom validation in React is implemented with a function. This function should either return an error when a specific validation requirement is not met or `null` when the property is valid.

With basic property type validation, we can only validate a property based on one condition. The good news is that the custom validator will allow us to test the property in many different ways. In this custom function, we'll first check that the property's value is a string. Then we'll limit its length to 20 characters (Example 6-2).

Example 6-2. Custom prop validation

```
propTypes: {
    ingredients: PropTypes.number,
    steps: PropTypes.number,
    title: (props, propName) =>
        (typeof props[propName] !== 'string') ?
            new Error("A title must be a string") :
            (props[propName].length > 20) ?
                new Error(`title is over 20 characters`) :
                null
}
```

All property type validators are functions. To implement our custom validator, we will set the value of the `title` property, under the `propTypes` object, to a callback function. When rendering the component, React will inject the `props` object and the name of the current property into the function as arguments. We can use those arguments to check the specific value for a specific property.

In this case, we first check the title to make sure it is a string. If the title is not a string, the validator returns a new error with the message: "A title must be a string." If the title is a string, then we check its value to make sure it is not longer than 20 characters. If the title is under 20 characters, the validator function returns null. If the title is over 20 characters, then the validator function returns an error. React will capture the returned error and display it in the console as a warning.

Custom validators allow you to implement specific validation criteria. A custom validator can perform multiple validations and only return errors when specific criteria are not met. Custom validators are a great way to prevent errors when using and reusing your components.

ES6 Classes and Stateless Functional Components

In the previous sections, we discovered that property validation and default property values can be added to our component classes using `React.createClass`. This type checking also works for ES6 classes and stateless functional components, but the syntax is slightly different.

When working with ES6 classes, `propTypes` and `defaultProps` declarations are defined on the class instance, outside of the class body. Once a class is defined, we can set the `propTypes` and `defaultProps` object literals (Example 6-3).

Example 6-3. ES6 class

```
class Summary extends React.Component {
  render() {
   const {ingredients, steps, title} = this.props
     return (
         <div className="summary">
             <h1>{title}</h1>
             <p>
                 <span>{ingredients} Ingredients | </span>
                 <span>{steps} Steps</span>
             </p>
         </div>
     )
  }
}

Summary.propTypes = {
  ingredients: PropTypes.number,
  steps: PropTypes.number,
  title: (props, propName) =>
    (typeof props[propName] !== 'string') ?
        new Error("A title must be a string") :
        (props[propName].length > 20) ?
            new Error(`title is over 20 characters`) :
```

```
          null
}

Summary.defaultProps = {
    ingredients: 0,
    steps: 0,
    title: "[recipe]"
}
```

The `propTypes` and `defaultProps` object literals can also be added to stateless functional components (Example 6-4).

Example 6-4. Stateless functional component

```
const Summary = ({ ingredients, steps, title }) => {
  return <div>
    <h1>{title}</h1>
    <p>{ingredients} Ingredients | {steps} Steps</p>
  </div>
}

Summary.propTypes = {
  ingredients: React.PropTypes.number.isRequired,
  steps: React.PropTypes.number.isRequired
}

Summary.defaultProps = {
  ingredients: 1,
  steps: 1
}
```

With a stateless functional component, you also have the option of setting default properties directly in the function arguments. We can set default values for `ingredients`, `steps`, and `title` when we destructure the properties object in the function arguments as follows:

```
const Summary = ({ ingredients=0, steps=0, title='[recipe]' }) => {
  return <div>
    <h1>{title}</h1>
    <p>{ingredients} Ingredients | {steps} Steps</p>
  </div>
}
```

Class Static Properties

In the previous section, we looked at how `defaultProps` and `propTypes` are defined outside of the class. An alternative to this is emerging in one of the latest proposals to the ECMAScript spec: *Class Fields & Static Properties.*

Class static properties allow us to encapsulate `propTypes` and `defaultProps` inside of the class declaration. Property initializers also provide encapsulation and cleaner syntax:

```javascript
class Summary extends React.Component {

  static propTypes = {
    ingredients: PropTypes.number,
    steps: PropTypes.number,
    title: (props, propName) =>
      (typeof props[propName] !== 'string') ?
        new Error("A title must be a string") :
        (props[propName].length > 20) ?
          new Error(`title is over 20 characters`) :
          null
  }

  static defaultProps = {
    ingredients: 0,
    steps: 0,
    title: "[recipe]"
  }

  render() {
   const {ingredients, steps, title} = this.props
      return (
        <div className="summary">
          <h1>{title}</h1>
          <p>
            <span>{ingredients} Ingredients | </span>
            <span>{steps} Steps</span>
          </p>
        </div>
      )
  }
}
```

Property validation, custom property validation, and the ability to set default property values should be implemented in every component. This makes the component easier to reuse because any problems with component properties will show up as console warnings.

Refs

References, or *refs*, are a feature that allow React components to interact with child elements. The most common use case for refs is to interact with UI elements that collect input from the user. Consider an HTML form element. These elements are initially rendered, but the users can interact with them. When they do, the component should respond appropriately.

For the rest of this chapter, we are going to be working with an application that allows users to save and manage specific hexadecimal color values. This application, the color organizer, allows users to add colors to a list. Once a color is in the list, it can be rated or removed by the user.

We will need a form to collect information about new colors from the user. The user can supply the color's title and hex value in the corresponding fields. The AddColor Form component renders the HTML with a text input and a color input for collecting hex values from the color wheel (Example 6-5).

Example 6-5. AddColorForm

```
import { Component } from 'react'

class AddColorForm extends Component {
  render() {
    return (
      <form onSubmit={e=>e.preventDefault()}>
        <input type="text"
               placeholder="color title..." required/>
        <input type="color" required/>
        <button>ADD</button>
      </form>
    )
  }
}
```

The AddColorForm component renders an HTML form that contains three elements: a text input for the title, a color input for the color's hex value, and a button to submit the form. When the form is submitted, a handler function is invoked where the default form event is ignored. This prevents the form from trying to send a GET request once submitted.

Once we have the form rendered, we need to provide a way to interact with it. Specifically, when the form is first submitted, we need to collect the new color information and reset the form's fields so that the user can add more colors. Using refs, we can refer to the title and color elements and interact with them (Example 6-6).

Example 6-6. AddColorForm with submit method

```
import { Component } from 'react'

class AddColorForm extends Component {
  constructor(props) {
    super(props)
    this.submit = this.submit.bind(this)
  }
  submit(e) {
    const { _title, _color } = this.refs
    e.preventDefault();
    alert(`New Color: ${_title.value} ${_color.value}`)
    _title.value = '';
    _color.value = '#000000';
    _title.focus();
  }
  render() {
    return (
        <form onSubmit={this.submit}>
            <input ref="_title"
                   type="text"
                   placeholder="color title..." required/>
            <input ref="_color"
                   type="color" required/>
            <button>ADD</button>
        </form>
    )
  }
}
```

We needed to add a constructor to this ES6 component class because we moved sub mit to its own function. With ES6 component classes, we must bind the scope of the component to any methods that need to access that scope with this.

Next, in the render method, we've set the form's onSubmit handler by pointing it to the component's submit method. We've also added ref fields to the components that we want to reference. A ref is an identifier that React uses to reference DOM elements. Creating _title and _color ref attributes for each input means that we can access those elements with this.refs_title or this.refs_color.

When the user adds a new title, selects a new color, and submits the form, the component's submit method will be invoked to handle the event. After we prevent the form's default submit behavior, we send the user an alert that echoes back the data collected via refs. After the user dismisses the alert, refs are used again to reset the form values and focus on the title field.

> **Binding the 'this' Scope**
>
> When using `React.createClass` to create your components, there is no need to bind the `this` scope to your component methods. `React.createClass` automatically binds the `this` scope for you.

Inverse Data Flow

It's nice to have a form that echoes back input data in an alert, but there is really no way to make money with such a product. What we need to do is collect data from the user and send it somewhere else to be handled. This means that any data collected may eventually make its way back to the server, which we will cover in Chapter 12. First, we need to collect the data from the form component and pass it on.

A common solution for collecting data from a React component is *inverse data flow*.[2] It is similar to, and sometimes described as, *two-way data binding*. It involves sending a callback function to the component as a property that the component can use to pass data back as arguments. It's called inverse data flow because we send the component a function as a property, and the component sends data back as function arguments.

Let's say we want to use the color form, but when a user submits a new color we want to collect that information and log it to the console.

We can create a function called `logColor` that receives the title and color as arguments. The values of those arguments can be logged to the console. When we use the `AddColorForm`, we simply add a function property for `onNewColor` and set it to our `logColor` function. When the user adds a new color, `logColor` is invoked, and we've sent a function as a property:

```
const logColor = (title, color) =>
    console.log(`New Color: ${title} | ${value}`)

<AddColorForm onNewColor={logColor} />
```

To ensure that data is flowing properly, we will invoke `onNewColor` from `props` with the appropriate data:

```
submit() {
    const {_title, _color} = this.refs
    this.props.onNewColor(_title.value, _color.value)
    _title.value = ''
    _color.value = '#000000'
    _title.focus()
}
```

---

2 Pete Hunt, "Thinking in React" (*http://bit.ly/2nvMwgl*).

In our component, this means that we'll replace the `alert` call with a call to `this.props.onNewColor` and pass the new title and color values that we have obtained through refs.

The role of the `AddColorForm` component is to collect data and pass it on. It is not concerned with what happens to that data. We can now use this form to collect color data from users and pass it on to some other component or method to handle the collected data:

```
<AddColorForm onNewColor={(title, color) => {
    console.log(`TODO: add new ${title} and ${color} to the list`)
    console.log(`TODO: render UI with new Color`)
}} />
```

When we are ready, we can collect the information from this component and add the new color to our list of colors.

Optional Function Properties

In order to make two-way data binding optional, you must first check to see if the function property exists before trying to invoke it. In the last example, not supplying an `onNewColor` function property would lead to a JavaScript error because the component will try to invoke an undefined value.

This can be avoided by first checking for the existence of the function property:

```
if (this.props.onNewColor) {
    this.props.onNewColor(_title.value, _color.value)
}
```

A better solution is to define the function property in the component's `propTypes` and `defaultProps`:

```
AddColorForm.propTypes = {
    onNewColor: PropTypes.func
}

AddColorForm.defaultProps = {
    onNewColor: f=>f
}
```

Now when the property supplied is some type other than function, React will complain. If the `onNewColor` property is not supplied, it will default to this dummy function, `f=>f`. This is simply a placeholder function that returns the first argument sent to it. Although this placeholder function doesn't do anything, it can be invoked by JavaScript without causing errors.

Refs in Stateless Functional Components

Refs can also be used in stateless functional components. These components do not have this, so it's not possible to use this.refs. Instead of using string attributes, we will set the refs using a function. The function will pass us the input instance as an argument. We can capture that instance and save it to a local variable.

Let's refactor AddColorForm as a stateless functional component:

```
const AddColorForm = ({onNewColor=f=>f}) => {
    let _title, _color
    const submit = e => {
        e.preventDefault()
        onNewColor(_title.value, _color.value)
        _title.value = ''
        _color.value = '#000000'
        _title.focus()
    }
    return (
        <form onSubmit={submit}>
            <input ref={input => _title = input}
                   type="text"
                   placeholder="color title..." required/>
            <input ref={input => _color = input}
                   type="color" required/>
            <button>ADD</button>
        </form>
    )
}
```

In this stateless functional component, refs are set with a callback function instead of a string. The callback function passes the element's instance as an argument. This instance can be captured and saved into a local variable like _title or _color. Once we've saved the refs to local variables, they are easily accessed when the form is submitted.

React State Management

Thus far we've only used properties to handle data in React components. Properties are immutable. Once rendered, a component's properties do not change. In order for our UI to change, we would need some other mechanism that can rerender the component tree with new properties. React state is a built-in option for managing data that will change within a component. When application state changes, the UI is rerendered to reflect those changes.

Users interact with applications. They navigate, search, filter, select, add, update, and delete. When a user interacts with an application, the state of that application changes, and those changes are reflected back to the user in the UI. Screens and menus appear and disappear. Visible content changes. Indicators light up or are turned off. In React, the UI is a reflection of application state.

State can be expressed in React components with a single JavaScript object. When the state of a component changes, the component renders a new UI that reflects those changes. What can be more functional than that? Given some data, a React component will represent that data as the UI. Given a change to that data, React will update the UI as efficiently as possible to reflect that change.

Let's take a look at how we can incorporate state within our React components.

Introducing Component State

State represents data that we may wish to change within a component. To demonstrate this, we will take a look at a `StarRating` component (Figure 6-7).

Figure 6-7. The StarRating component

The `StarRating` component requires two critical pieces of data: the total number of stars to display, and the rating, or the number of stars to highlight.

We'll need a clickable `Star` component that has a `selected` property. A stateless functional component can be used for each star:

```
const Star = ({ selected=false, onClick=f=>f }) =>
    <div className={(selected) ? "star selected" : "star"}
        onClick={onClick}>
    </div>

Star.propTypes = {
    selected: PropTypes.bool,
    onClick: PropTypes.func
}
```

Every `Star` element will consist of a `div` that includes the class `'star'`. If the star is selected, it will additionally add the class `'selected'`. This component also has an optional `onClick` property. When a user clicks on any star `div`, the `onClick` property will be invoked. This will tell the parent component, the `StarRating`, that a `Star` has been clicked.

The `Star` is a stateless functional component. It says it right in the name: you cannot use state in a stateless functional component. Stateless functional components are meant to be the children of more complex, stateful components. It's a good idea to try to keep as many of your components as possible stateless.

The Star Is in the CSS

Our `StarRating` component uses CSS to construct and display a star. Specifically, using a *clip path*, we can clip the area of our `div` to look like a star. The clip path is collection of points that make up a polygon:

```
.star {
    cursor: pointer;
    height: 25px;
    width: 25px;
    margin: 2px;
    float: left;
    background-color: grey;
    clip-path: polygon(
        50% 0%,
        63% 38%,
        100% 38%,
        69% 59%,
        82% 100%,
        50% 75%,
        18% 100%,
        31% 59%,
        0% 38%,
        37% 38%
    );
}

.star.selected {
  background-color: red;
}
```

A regular star has a background color of grey, but a selected star will have a background color of red.

Now that we have a `Star`, we can use it to create a `StarRating`. `StarRating` will obtain the total number of stars to display from the component's properties. The rating, the value that the user can change, will be stored in the state.

First, let's look at how to incorporate state into a component defined with `create Class`:

```
const StarRating = createClass({
    displayName: 'StarRating',
    propTypes: {
        totalStars: PropTypes.number
    },
    getDefaultProps() {
```

```
            return {
                totalStars: 5
            }
        },
        getInitialState() {
            return {
                starsSelected: 0
            }
        },
        change(starsSelected) {
            this.setState({starsSelected})
        },
        render() {
            const {totalStars} = this.props
            const {starsSelected} = this.state
            return (
                <div className="star-rating">
                    {[...Array(totalStars)].map((n, i) =>
                        <Star key={i}
                            selected={i<starsSelected}
                            onClick={() => this.change(i+1)}
                        />
                    )}
                    <p>{starsSelected} of {totalStars} stars</p>
                </div>
            )
        }
    }
})
```

When using `createClass`, state can be initialized by adding `getInitialState` to the component configuration and returning a JavaScript object that initially sets the state variable, `starsSelected` to 0.

When the component renders, `totalStars` is obtained from the component's properties and used to render a specific number of `Star` elements. Specifically, the spread operator is used with the `Array` constructor to initialize a new array of a specific length that is mapped to `Star` elements.

The state variable `starsSelected` is destructured from `this.state` when the component renders. It is used to display the rating as text in a paragraph element. It is also used to calculate the number of selected stars to display. Each `Star` element obtains its `selected` property by comparing its index to the number of stars that are selected. If three stars are selected, the first three `Star` elements will set their `selected` property to `true` and any remaining stars will have a `selected` property of `false`.

Finally, when a user clicks a single star, the index of that specific `Star` element is incremented and sent to the `change` function. This value is incremented because it is assumed that the first star will have a rating of 1 even though it has an index of 0.

Initializing state in an ES6 component class is slightly different than using create Class. In these classes, state can be initialized in the constructor:

```
class StarRating extends Component {

    constructor(props) {
        super(props)
        this.state = {
            starsSelected: 0
        }
        this.change = this.change.bind(this)
    }

    change(starsSelected) {
        this.setState({starsSelected})
    }

    render() {
        const {totalStars} = this.props
        const {starsSelected} = this.state
        return (
            <div className="star-rating">
                {[...Array(totalStars)].map((n, i) =>
                    <Star key={i}
                            selected={i<starsSelected}
                            onClick={() => this.change(i+1)}
                    />
                )}
                <p>{starsSelected} of {totalStars} stars</p>
            </div>
        )
    }

}

StarRating.propTypes = {
    totalStars: PropTypes.number
}

StarRating.defaultProps = {
    totalStars: 5
}
```

When an ES6 component is mounted, its constructor is invoked with the properties injected as the first argument. Those properties are, in turn, sent to the superclass by invoking super. In this case, the superclass is React.Component. Invoking super initializes the component instance, and React.Component decorates that instance with functionality that includes state management. After invoking super , we can initialize our component's state variables.

Once the state is initialized, it operates as it does in `createClass` components. State can only be changed by calling `this.setState`, which updates specific parts of the state object. After every `setState` call, the `render` function is called, updating the state with the new UI.

Initializing State from Properties

We can initialize our state values using incoming properties. There are only a few necessary cases for this pattern. The most common case for this is when we create a reusable component that we would like to use across applications in different component trees.

When using `createClass`, a good way to initialize state variables based on incoming properties is to add a method called `componentWillMount`. This method is invoked once when the component mounts, and you can call `this.setState()` from this method. It also has access to `this.props`, so you can use values from `this.props` to help you initialize state:

```
const StarRating = createClass({
    displayName: 'StarRating',
    propTypes: {
        totalStars: PropTypes.number
    },
    getDefaultProps() {
        return {
            totalStars: 5
        }
    },
    getInitialState() {
        return {
            starsSelected: 0
        }
    },
    componentWillMount() {
        const { starsSelected } = this.props
        if (starsSelected) {
            this.setState({starsSelected})
        }
    },
    change(starsSelected) {
        this.setState({starsSelected})
    },
    render() {
        const {totalStars} = this.props
        const {starsSelected} = this.state
        return (
            <div className="star-rating">
                {[...Array(totalStars)].map((n, i) =>
                    <Star key={i}
```

```
                            selected={i<starsSelected}
                            onClick={() => this.change(i+1)}
                    />
                )}
            <p>{starsSelected} of {totalStars} stars</p>
        </div>
    )
  }
})

render(
    <StarRating totalStars={7} starsSelected={3} />,
    document.getElementById('react-container')
)
```

componentWillMount is a part of the component lifecycle. It can be used to help you initialize state based on property values in components created with createClass or ES6 class components. We will dive deeper into the component lifecycle in the next chapter.

There is an easier way to initialize state within an ES6 class component. The constructor receives properties as an argument, so you can simply use the props argument passed to the constructor:

```
constructor(props) {
    super(props)
    this.state = {
        starsSelected: props.starsSelected || 0
    }
    this.change = this.change.bind(this)
}
```

For the most part, you'll want to avoid setting state variables from properties. Only use these patterns when they are absolutely required. You should find this goal easy to accomplish because when working with React components, you want to limit the number of components that have state.[3]

Updating Component Properties

When initializing state variables from component properties, you may need to reinitialize component state when a parent component changes those properties. The componentWillRecieveProps lifecycle method can be used to solve this issue. Chapter 7 goes into greater detail on this issue and the available methods of the component lifecycle.

---

3 React Docs, "Lifting State Up" (*http://bit.ly/2o6ob0z*).

State Within the Component Tree

All of your React components can have their own state, but should they? The joy of using React does not come from chasing down state variables all over your application. The joy of using React comes from building scalable applications that are easy to understand. The most important thing that you can do to make your application easy to understand is limit the number of components that use state as much as possible.

In many React applications, it is possible to group all state data in the root component. State data can be passed down the component tree via properties, and data can be passed back up the tree to the root via two-way function binding. The result is that all of the state for your entire application exists in one place. This is often referred to as having a "single source of truth."[4]

Next, we will look at how to architect presentation layers where all of the state is stored in one place, the root component.

Color Organizer App Overview

The color organizer allows users to add, name, rate, and remove colors in their customized lists. The entire state of the color organizer can be represented with a single array:

```
{
    colors: [
        {
            "id": "0175d1f0-a8c6-41bf-8d02-df5734d829a4",
            "title": "ocean at dusk",
            "color": "#00c4e2",
            "rating": 5
        },
        {
            "id": "83c7ba2f-7392-4d7d-9e23-35adbe186046",
            "title": "lawn",
            "color": "#26ac56",
            "rating": 3
        },
        {
            "id": "a11e3995-b0bd-4d58-8c48-5e49ae7f7f23",
            "title": "bright red",
            "color": "#ff0000",
            "rating": 0
        }
    ]
}
```

---

4 Paul Hudson, "State and the Single Source of Truth" (*http://bit.ly/2ne6BdY*), Chapter 12 of *Hacking with React*.

The array tells us that we need to display three colors: ocean at dusk, lawn, and bright red (Figure 6-8). It gives us the colors' hex values and the current rating for each color in the display. It also provides a way to uniquely identify each color.

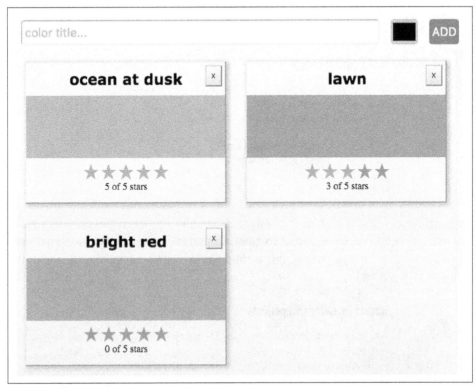

Figure 6-8. Color organizer with three colors in state

This state data will drive our application. It will be used to construct the UI every time this object changes. When users add or remove colors, they will be added to or removed from this array. When users rate colors, their ratings will change in the array.

Passing Properties Down the Component Tree

Earlier in this chapter, we created a StarRating component that saved the rating in the state. In the color organizer, the rating is stored in each color object. It makes more sense to treat the StarRating as a *presentational component*[5] and declare it as a stateless functional component. Presentational components are only concerned with

---

5 Dan Abramov, "Presentational and Container Components" (*http://bit.ly/2ndQ9u0*), Medium, March 23, 2015.

how things look in the application. They only render DOM elements or other presentational components. All data is sent to these components via properties and passed out of these components via callback functions.

In order to make the StarRating component purely presentational, we need to remove state. Presentational components only use props. Since we are removing state from this component, when a user changes the rating, that data will be passed out of this component via a callback function:

```
const StarRating = ({starsSelected=0, totalStars=5, onRate=f=>f}) =>
    <div className="star-rating">
        {[...Array(totalStars)].map((n, i) =>
            <Star key={i}
                selected={i<starsSelected}
                onClick={() => onRate(i+1)}/>
        )}
        <p>{starsSelected} of {totalStars} stars</p>
    </div>
```

First, starsSelected is no longer a state variable; it is a property. Second, an onRate callback property has been added to this component. Instead of calling setState when the user changes the rating, this component now invokes onRate and sends the rating as an argument.

State in Reusable Components

You may need to create stateful UI components for distribution and reuse across many different applications. It is not absolutely required that you remove every last state variable from components that are only used for presentation. It is a good rule to follow, but sometimes it may make sense to keep state in a presentation component.

Restricting state to a single location, the root component, means that all of the data must be passed down to child components as properties (Figure 6-9).

In the color organizer, state consists of an array of colors that is declared in the App component. Those colors are passed down to the ColorList component as a property:

```
class App extends Component {

    constructor(props) {
        super(props)
        this.state = {
            colors: []
        }
    }
```

```
render() {
    const { colors } = this.state
    return (
        <div className="app">
            <AddColorForm />
            <ColorList colors={colors} />
        </div>
    )
}

}
```

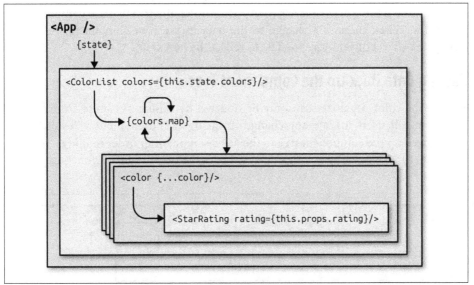

Figure 6-9. State is passed from the App component to child components as properties

Initially the `colors` array is empty, so the `ColorList` component will display a message instead of each color. When there are colors in the array, data for each individual color is passed to the `Color` component as properties:

```
const ColorList = ({ colors=[] }) =>
    <div className="color-list">
        {(colors.length === 0) ?
            <p>No Colors Listed. (Add a Color)</p> :
            colors.map(color =>
                <Color key={color.id} {...color} />
            )
        }
    </div>
```

Now the `Color` component can display the color's title and hex value and pass the color's rating down to the `StarRating` component as a property:

```
const Color = ({ title, color, rating=0 }) =>
    <section className="color">
        <h1>{title}</h1>
        <div className="color"
            style={{ backgroundColor: color }}>
        </div>
        <div>
            <StarRating starsSelected={rating} />
        </div>
    </section>
```

The number of starsSelected in the star rating comes from each color's rating. All of the state data for every color has been passed down the tree to child components as properties. When there is a change to the data in the root component, React will change the UI as efficiently as possible to reflect the new state.

Passing Data Back Up the Component Tree

State in the color organizer can only be updated by calling setState from the App component. If users initiate any changes from the UI, their input will need to be passed back up the component tree to the App component in order to update the state (Figure 6-10). This can be accomplished through the use of callback function properties.

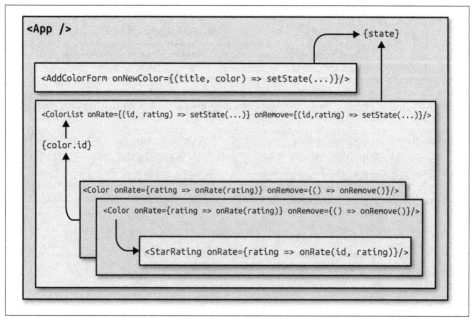

Figure 6-10. Passing data back up to the root component when there are UI events

In order to add new colors, we need a way to uniquely identify each color. This identifier will be used to locate colors within the state array. We can use the uuid library to create absolutely unique IDs:

```
npm install uuid --save
```

All new colors will be added to the color organizer from the AddColorForm component that we constructed in "Refs" on page 119. That component has an optional callback function property called onNewColor. When the user adds a new color and submits the form, the onNewColor callback function is invoked with the new title and color hex value obtained from the user:

```
import { Component } from 'react'
import { v4 } from 'uuid'
import AddColorForm from './AddColorForm'
import ColorList from './ColorList'

export class App extends Component {

    constructor(props) {
        super(props)
        this.state = {
            colors: []
        }
        this.addColor = this.addColor.bind(this)
    }

    addColor(title, color) {
        const colors = [
            ...this.state.colors,
            {
                id: v4(),
                title,
                color,
                rating: 0
            }
        ]
        this.setState({colors})
    }

    render() {
        const { addColor } = this
        const { colors } = this.state
        return (
            <div className="app">
                <AddColorForm onNewColor={addColor} />
                <ColorList colors={colors} />
            </div>
        )
    }
}
```

```
    }
```

All new colors can be added from the addColor method in the App component. This function is bound to the component in the constructor, which means that it has access to this.state and this.setState.

New colors are added by concatenating the current colors array with a new color object. The ID for the new color object is set using uuid's v4 function. This creates a unique identifier for each color. The title and color are passed to the addColor method from the AddColorForm component. Finally, the initial value for each color's rating will be 0.

When the user adds a color with the AddColorForm component, the addColor method updates the state with a new list of colors. Once the state has been updated, the App component rerenders the component tree with the new list of colors. The render method is invoked after every setState call. The new data is passed down the tree as properties and is used to construct the UI.

If the user wishes to rate or remove a color, we need to collect information about that color. Each color will have a remove button: if the user clicks the remove button, we'll know they wish to remove that color. Also, if the user changes the color's rating with the StarRating component, we want to change the rating of that color:

```
const Color = ({title,color,rating=0,onRemove=f=>f,onRate=f=>f}) =>
    <section className="color">
        <h1>{title}</h1>
        <button onClick={onRemove}>X</button>
        <div className="color"
            style={{ backgroundColor: color }}>
        </div>
        <div>
            <StarRating starsSelected={rating} onRate={onRate} />
        </div>
    </section>
```

The information that will change in this app is stored in the list of colors. Therefore, onRemove and onRate callback properties will have to be added to each color to pass those events back up the tree. The Color component will also have onRate and onRemove callback function properties. When colors are rated or removed, the ColorList component will need to notify its parent, the App component, that the color should be rated or removed:

```
const ColorList = ({ colors=[], onRate=f=>f, onRemove=f=>f }) =>
    <div className="color-list">
        {(colors.length === 0) ?
            <p>No Colors Listed. (Add a Color)</p> :
            colors.map(color =>
                <Color key={color.id}
```

```
                    {...color}
                    onRate={(rating) => onRate(color.id, rating)}
                    onRemove={() => onRemove(color.id)} />
            )
        }
    </div>
```

The ColorList component will invoke onRate if any colors are rated and onRemove if any colors are removed. This component manages the collection of colors by mapping them to individual Color components. When individual colors are rated or removed the ColorList identifies which color was rated or removed and passes that info to its parent via callback function properties.

ColorList's parent is App. In the App component, rateColor and removeColor methods can be added and bound to the component instance in the constructor. Any time a color needs to be rated or removed, these methods will update the state. They are added to the ColorList component as callback function properties:

```
class App extends Component {

    constructor(props) {
        super(props)
        this.state = {
            colors: []
        }
        this.addColor = this.addColor.bind(this)
        this.rateColor = this.rateColor.bind(this)
        this.removeColor = this.removeColor.bind(this)
    }

    addColor(title, color) {
        const colors = [
            ...this.state.colors,
            {
                id: v4(),
                title,
                color,
                rating: 0
            }
        ]
        this.setState({colors})
    }

    rateColor(id, rating) {
        const colors = this.state.colors.map(color =>
            (color.id !== id) ?
                color :
                {
                    ...color,
                    rating
                }
```

```
            )
            this.setState({colors})
        }

        removeColor(id) {
            const colors = this.state.colors.filter(
                color => color.id !== id
            )
            this.setState({colors})
        }

        render() {
            const { addColor, rateColor, removeColor } = this
            const { colors } = this.state
            return (
                <div className="app">
                    <AddColorForm onNewColor={addColor} />
                    <ColorList colors={colors}
                            onRate={rateColor}
                            onRemove={removeColor} />
                </div>
            )
        }

    }
```

Both `rateColor` and `removeColor` expect the ID of the color to rate or remove. The ID is captured in the `ColorList` component and passed as an argument to `rateColor` or `removeColor`. The `rateColor` method finds the color to rate and changes its rating in the state. The `removeColor` method uses `Array.filter` to create a new state array without the removed color.

Once `setState` is called, the UI is rerendered with the new state data. All data that changes in this app is managed from a single component, `App`. This approach makes it much easier to understand what data the application uses to create state and how that data will change.

React components are quite robust. They provide us with a clean way to manage and validate properties, communicate with child elements, and manage state data from within a component. These features make it possible to construct beautifully scalable presentation layers.

We have mentioned many times that state is for data that changes. You can also use state to cache data in your application. For instance, if you had a list of records that the user could search, the records list could be stored in state until they are searched.

Reducing state to root components is often recommended. You will encounter this approach in many React applications. Once your application reaches a certain size, two-way data binding and explicitly passing properties can become quite a nuisance.

The Flux design pattern and Flux libraries like Redux can be used to manage state and reduce boilerplate in these situations.

React is a relatively small library, and thus far we've reviewed much of its functionality. The major features of React components that we have yet to discuss include the component lifecycle and higher-order components, which we will cover in the next chapter.

CHAPTER 7

Enhancing Components

So far we've learned how to mount and compose components to create application presentation layers with React. It is possible to build quite a few applications using only the React component's render method. However, the world of JavaScript is complex. There is asynchronicity everywhere. We have latency to deal with when we load our data. We have delays to work with when we create animations. It is highly likely that you have preferred JavaScript libraries to help you navigate the complexity of real-world JavaScript.

Before we can enhance our applications with third-party JavaScript libraries or back-end data requests, we must first understand how to work with the *component lifecycle*: a series of methods that can be invoked every time we mount or update a component.

We will start this chapter by exploring the component lifecycle. After we introduce the lifecycle, we will review how we can use it to load data, incorporate third-party JavaScript, and even improve our component's performance. Next, we will explore how to reuse functionality across our applications with *higher-order components*. We will wrap up this chapter by looking at alternative application architectures that manage state entirely outside of React.

Component Lifecycles

The component lifecycle consists of methods that are invoked in series when a component is mounted or updated. These methods are invoked either before or after the component renders the UI. In fact, the render method itself is a part of the component lifecycle. There are two primary lifecycles: the mounting lifecycle and the updating lifecycle.

Mounting Lifecycle

The *mounting lifecycle* consists of methods that are invoked when a component is mounted or unmounted. In other words, these methods allow you to initially set up state, make API calls, start and stop timers, manipulate the rendered DOM, initialize third-party libraries, and more. These methods allow you to incorporate JavaScript to assist in the initialization and destruction of a component.

The mounting lifecycle is slightly different depending upon whether you use ES6 class syntax or `React.createClass` to create components. When you use `createClass`, `getDefaultProps` is invoked first to obtain the component's properties. Next, `getInitialState` is invoked to initialize the state.

ES6 classes do not have these methods. Instead, default props are obtained and sent to the constructor as an argument. The constructor is where the state is initialized. Both ES6 class constructors and `getInitialState` have access to the properties and, if required, can use them to help define the initial state.

Table 7-1 lists the methods of the component mounting lifecycle.

Table 7-1. The component mounting lifecycle

ES6 class	React.createClass()
	`getDefaultProps()`
`constructor(props)`	`getInitialState()`
`componentWillMount()`	`componentWillMount()`
`render()`	`render()`
`componentDidMount()`	`componentDidMount()`
`componentWillUnmount()`	`componentWillUnmount()`

Class Constructors

Technically, the constructor is not a lifecycle method. We include it because it is used for component initialization (this is where the state is initialized). Also, the constructor is always the first function invoked when a component is mounted.

Once the properties are obtained and state is initialized, the `componentWillMount` method is invoked. This method is invoked before the DOM is rendered and can be used to initialize third-party libraries, start animations, request data, or perform any additional setup that may be required before a component is rendered. It is possible to invoke `setState` from this method to change the component state just before the component is initially rendered.

Let's use the `componentWillMount` method to initialize a request for some members. When we get a successful response, we will update the state. Remember the `getFakeMembers` promise that we created in Chapter 2? We will use that to load a random list of members from *randomuser.me*:

```
const getFakeMembers = count => new Promise((resolves, rejects) => {
    const api = `https://api.randomuser.me/?nat=US&results=${count}`
    const request = new XMLHttpRequest()
    request.open('GET', api)
    request.onload = () => (request.status == 200) ?
        resolves(JSON.parse(request.response).results) :
        reject(Error(request.statusText))
    request.onerror = err => rejects(err)
    request.send()
})
```

We will use this promise in the `componentWillMount` method in a `MemberList` component. This component will use a `Member` component to display each user's picture, name, email address, and location:

```
const Member = ({ email, picture, name, location }) =>
    <div className="member">
        <img src={picture.thumbnail} alt="" />
        <h1>{name.first} {name.last}</h1>
        <p><a href={"mailto:" + email}>{email}</a></p>
        <p>{location.city}, {location.state}</p>
    </div>

class MemberList extends Component {

    constructor() {
        super()
        this.state = {
            members: [],
            loading: false,
            error: null
        }
    }

    componentWillMount() {
        this.setState({loading: true})
        getFakeMembers(this.props.count).then(
            members => {
                this.setState({members, loading: false})
            },
            error => {
                this.setState({error, loading: false})
            }
        )
    }

    componentWillUpdate() {
```

```
            console.log('updating lifecycle')
        }

        render() {
            const { members, loading, error } = this.state
            return (
                <div className="member-list">
                    {(loading) ?
                        <span>Loading Members</span> :
                        (members.length) ?
                            members.map((user, i) =>
                                <Member key={i} {...user} />
                            ) :
                            <span>0 members loaded...</span>
                    }
                    {(error) ? <p>Error Loading Members: error</p> : ""}
                </div>
            )
        }
    }
```

Initially, when the component is mounted, `MemberList` has an empty array for `mem bers` and `loading` is `false`. In the `componentWillMount` method, the state is changed to reflect the fact that a request was made to load some users. Next, while waiting for the request to complete, the component is rendered. Because `loading` is now `true`, a message will be displayed alerting the user to the latency. When the promise passes or fails, the loading state is returned to `false` and either the members have been loaded or an error has been returned. Calling `setState` at this point will rerender our UI with either some members or an error.

Using setState in componentWillMount

Calling `setState` before the component has rendered will not kick off the updating lifecycle. Calling `setState` after the component has been rendered will kick off the updating lifecycle. If you call `setState` inside an asynchronous callback defined within the `componentWillMount` method, it will be invoked after the component has rendered and will trigger the updating lifecycle.

The other methods of the component mounting lifecycle include `componentDidMount` and `componentWillUnmount`. `componentDidMount` is invoked just after the component has rendered, and `componentWillUnmount` is invoked just before the component is unmounted.

`componentDidMount` is another good place to make API requests. This method is invoked after the component has rendered, so any `setState` calls from this method will kick off the updating lifecycle and rerender the component.

---

componentDidMount is also a good place to initialize any third-party JavaScript that requires a DOM. For instance, you may want to incorporate a drag-and-drop library or a library that handles touch events. Typically, these libraries require a DOM before they can be initialized.

Another good use for componentDidMount is to start background processes like intervals or timers. Any processes started in componentDidMount or componentWillMount can be cleaned up in componentWillUnmount. You don't want to leave background processes running when they are not needed.

Components are unmounted when their parents remove them or they have been unmounted with the unmountComponentAtNode function found in react-dom. This method is used to unmount the root component. When a root component is unmounted, its children are unmounted first.

Let's take a look at a clock example. When the Clock component has mounted, a timer will be started. When the user clicks on the close button, the clock will be unmounted with unmountComponentAtNode and the timer stopped:

```
import React from 'react'
import { render, unmountComponentAtNode } from 'react-dom'
import { getClockTime } from './lib'
const { Component } = React
const target = document.getElementById('react-container')

class Clock extends Component {

    constructor() {
        super()
        this.state = getClockTime()
    }

    componentDidMount() {
        console.log("Starting Clock")
        this.ticking = setInterval(() =>
                this.setState(getClockTime())
            , 1000)
    }

    componentWillUnmount() {
        clearInterval(this.ticking)
        console.log("Stopping Clock")
    }

    render() {
        const { hours, minutes, seconds, ampm } = this.state
        return (
            <div className="clock">
                <span>{hours}</span>
                <span>:</span>
```

```
            <span>{minutes}</span>
            <span>:</span>
            <span>{seconds}</span>
            <span>{ampm}</span>
            <button onClick={this.props.onClose}>x</button>
        </div>
    )
  }

}

render(
    <Clock onClose={() => unmountComponentAtNode(target) }/>,
    target
)
```

In Chapter 3, we created a serializeTime function that abstracts civilian time with leading zeros from the data object. Every time serializeTime is invoked, the current time is returned in an object that contains hours, minutes, seconds, and the a.m. or p.m. indicator. Initially, we call serializeTime to get the initial state for our clock.

After the component has mounted, we start an interval called ticking. It invokes set State with a new time every second. The UI for the clock changes its value to the updated time every second.

When the close button is clicked, the Clock component is unmounted. Just before the clock is removed from the DOM, the ticking interval is cleared so that it no longer runs in the background.

Updating Lifecycle

The *updating lifecycle* is a series of methods that are invoked when a component's state changes or when new properties are received from the parent. This lifecycle can be used to incorporate JavaScript before the component updates or to interact with the DOM after the update. Additionally, it can be used to improve the performance of an application because it gives you the ability to cancel unnecessary updates.

The updating lifecycle kicks off every time setState is called. Calling setState within the updating lifecycle will cause an infinite recursive loop that results in a stack overflow error. Therefore, setState can only be called in componentWillRecei veProps, which allows the component to update state when its properties are upda‐ ted.

The updating lifecycle methods include:

componentWillReceiveProps(nextProps)
   Only invoked if new properties have been passed to the component. This is the only method where setState can be called.

shouldComponentUpdate(nextProps, nextState)

The update lifecycle's gatekeeper—a predicate that can call off the update. This method can be used to improve performance by only allowing necessary updates.

componentWillUpdate(nextProps, nextState)

Invoked just before the component updates. Similar to componentWillMount, only it is invoked before each update occurs.

componentDidUpdate(prevProps, prevState)

Invoked just after the update takes place, after the call to render. Similar to componentDidMount, but it is invoked after each update.

Let's modify the color organizer application that we created in the last chapter. Specifically, we'll add some updating lifecycle functions to the Color component that will allow us to see how the updating lifecycle works. Let's assume that we already have four colors in the state array: Ocean Blue, Tomato, Lawn, and Party Pink. First, we will use the componentWillMount method to initialize color objects with a style, and set all four Color elements to have grey backgrounds:

```
import { Star, StarRating } from '../components'

export class Color extends Component {

    componentWillMount() {
        this.style = { backgroundColor: "#CCC" }
    }

    render() {
        const { title, rating, color, onRate } = this.props
        return
            <section className="color" style={this.style}>
                <h1 ref="title">{title}</h1>
                <div className="color"
                    style={{ backgroundColor: color }}>
                </div>
                <StarRating starsSelected={rating}
                            onRate={onRate} />
            </section>
    }

}

Color.propTypes = {
  title: PropTypes.string,
  rating: PropTypes.number,
  color: PropTypes.string,
  onRate: PropTypes.func
}

Color.defaultProps = {
```

```
      title: undefined,
      rating: 0,
      color: "#000000",
      onRate: f=>f
    }
```

When the color list originally mounts, each color background will be grey (Figure 7-1).

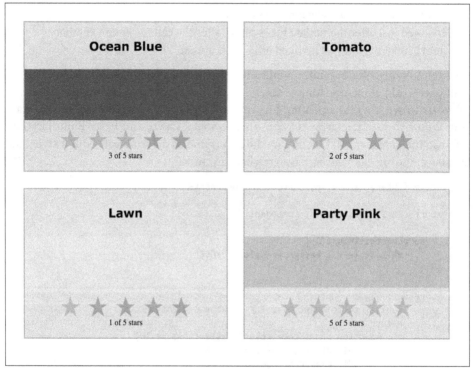

Figure 7-1. Mounted colors with grey background

We can add `componentWillUpdate` to the `Color` component in order to remove the grey background from each color just before the color updates:

```
componentWillMount() {
  this.style = { backgroundColor: "#CCC" }
}

componentWillUpdate() {
    this.style = null
}
```

Adding these lifecycle functions allows us to see when a component has mounted and when that component is updating. Initially, mounted components will have a grey background. Once each color is updated, the background will return to white.

If you run this code and rate any color, you will notice that all four colors update even though you have only changed the rating of a single color (see Figure 7-2).

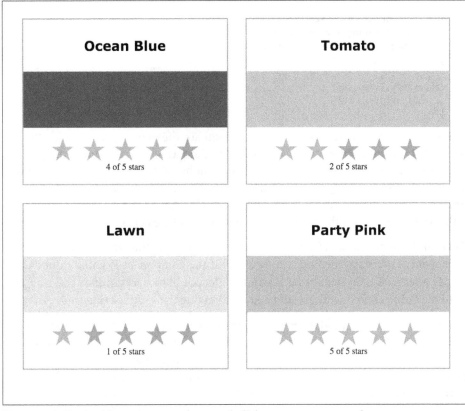

Figure 7-2. Rating blue triggers update, and all four components update

Here, changing the rating of Ocean Blue from three to four stars caused all four colors to update because when the parent, the ColorList, updates state, it rerenders each Color component. Components that are rerendered are not re-mounted; if they are already there, an update occurs instead. When a component is updated, all of its children are also updated. When a single color is rated, all four colors are updated, all four StarRating components are updated, and all five stars on each component are updated.

We can improve the performance of our application by preventing colors from being updated when their property values have not changed. Adding the lifecycle function shouldComponentUpdate prevents unnecessary updates from occurring. This method returns either true or false (true when the component should update and false when updating should be skipped):

```
componentWillMount() {
  this.style = { backgroundColor: "#CCC" }
}

shouldComponentUpdate(nextProps) {
    const { rating } = this.props
    return rating !== nextProps.rating
}

componentWillUpdate() {
    this.style = null
}
```

The shouldComponentUpdate method can compare the new properties with the old ones. The new properties are passed to this method as an argument, the old properties are still the current props, and the component has not updated. If the rating is the same in the current properties and the new ones, there is no need for the color to update. If the color does not update, none of its children will update either. When the rating does not change, the entire component tree under each Color will not update.

This can be demonstrated by running this code and updating any of the colors. The componentWillUpdate method is only called if the component is going to update. It comes after shouldComponentUpdate in the lifecycle. The backgrounds will stay grey until the Color components are updated by changing their ratings (Figure 7-3).

If the shouldComponentUpdate method returns true, the rest of the updating lifecycle will get to it. The rest of the lifecycle functions also receive the new props and new state as arguments. (The componentDidUpdate method receives the previous props and the previous state because once this method is reached, the update already has occurred and the props have been changed.)

Let's log a message after the component updates. In the componentDidUpdate function, we'll compare the current properties to the old ones to see if the rating got better or worse:

```
componentWillMount() {
    this.style = { backgroundColor: "#CCC" }
}

shouldComponentUpdate(nextProps) {
    const { rating } = this.props
    return rating !== nextProps.rating
}

componentWillUpdate() {
    this.style = null
}

componentDidUpdate(prevProps) {
    const { title, rating } = this.props
```

```
    const status = (rating > prevProps.rating) ? 'better' : 'worse'
    console.log(`${title} is getting ${status}`)
}
```

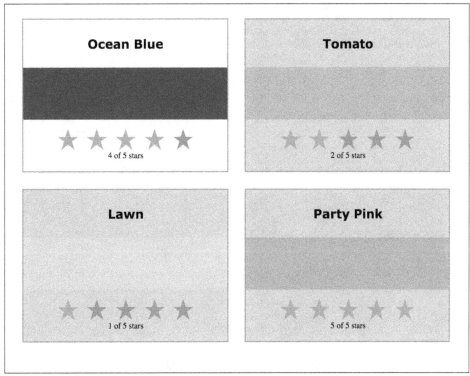

Figure 7-3. One update at a time with shouldComponentUpdate

The updating lifecycle methods componentWillUpdate and componentDidUpdate are
great places to interact with DOM elements before or after updates. In this next sample, the updating process will be paused with an alert in componentWillUpdate:

```
componentWillMount() {
    this.style = { backgroundColor: "#CCC" }
}

shouldComponentUpdate(nextProps) {
    return this.props.rating !== nextProps.rating
}

componentWillUpdate(nextProps) {
    const { title, rating } = this.props
    this.style = null
    this.refs.title.style.backgroundColor = "red"
    this.refs.title.style.color = "white"
    alert(`${title}: rating ${rating} -> ${nextProps.rating}`)
```

```
  }

  componentDidUpdate(prevProps) {
    const { title, rating } = this.props
    const status = (rating > prevProps.rating) ? 'better' : 'worse'
    this.refs.title.style.backgroundColor = ""
    this.refs.title.style.color = "black"
  }
```

If change the rating of Tomato from two to four stars, the updating process will be paused by an alert (Figure 7-4). The current DOM element for the color's title is given a different background and text color.

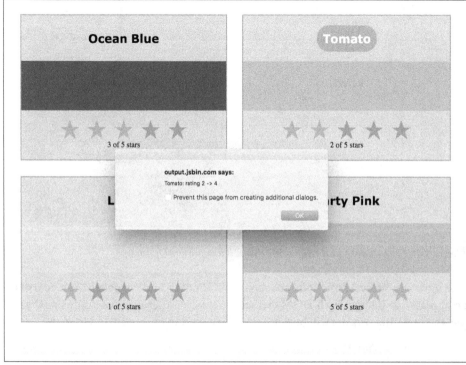

Figure 7-4. Updating paused with alert

As soon as we clear the alert, the component updates and `componentDidUpdate` is invoked, clearing the title's background color (Figure 7-5).

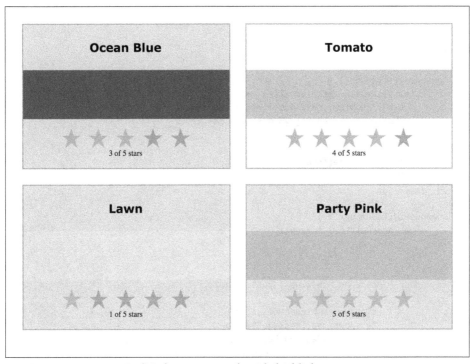

Figure 7-5. componentDidUpdate removes the title highlight

Sometimes our components hold state that is originally set based upon properties. We can set the initial state of our component classes in the constructor or the componentWillMount lifecycle method. When those properties change, we will need to update the state using the componentWillReceiveProps method.

In Example 7-1, we have a parent component that holds state, HiddenMessages. This component holds three messages in state and shows only one message at a time. When HiddenMessages mounts, an interval is added to cycle through the messages, only displaying one at a time.

Example 7-1. HiddenMessages component

```
class HiddenMessages extends Component {

    constructor(props) {
        super(props)
        this.state = {
            messages: [
                "The crow crows after midnight",
                "Bring a watch and dark clothes to the spot",
                "Jericho Jericho Go"
```

```
        ],
        showing: -1
    }
}

componentWillMount() {
    this.interval = setInterval(() => {
        let { showing, messages } = this.state
        showing = (++showing >= messages.length) ?
            -1 :
            showing
        this.setState({showing})
    }, 1000)
}

componentWillUnmount() {
    clearInterval(this.interval)
}

render() {
    const { messages, showing } = this.state
    return (
        <div className="hidden-messages">
            {messages.map((message, i) =>
                <HiddenMessage key={i}
                               hide={(i!==showing)}>
                    {message}
                </HiddenMessage>
            )}
        </div>
    )
}
}
```

The HiddenMessages component cycles through each of the messages in the state array and shows one at a time. The logic for this is set up in componentWillMount. When the component mounts, an interval is added that updates the index for the message that should be showing. The component renders all of the messages using the HiddenMessage component and only sets the hide property on one of them to true on each cycle. The rest of the properties are set to false, and the hidden message changes every second.

Take a look at the HiddenMessage component, the one used for each message (Example 7-2). When this component is originally mounted, the hide property is used to determine its state. However, when the parent updates this component's properties, nothing happens. This component will not know about it.

Example 7-2. HiddenMessage component

```
class HiddenMessage extends Component {

    constructor(props) {
        super(props)
        this.state = {
            hidden: (props.hide) ? props.hide : true
        }
    }

    render() {
        const { children } = this.props
        const { hidden } = this.state
        return (
            <p>
                {(hidden) ?
                    children.replace(/[a-zA-Z0-9]/g, "x") :
                    children
                }
            </p>
        )
    }

}
```

The problem occurs when the parent component changes the `hide` property. That change does not automatically cause the state of `HiddenMessage` to change.

The `componentWillReceiveProps` lifecycle method was created for these scenarios. It will be invoked when the properties have been changed by the parent, and those changed properties can be used to modify the state internally:

```
class HiddenMessage extends Component {

    constructor(props) {
        super(props)
        this.state = {
            hidden: (props.hide) ? props.hide : true
        }
    }

    componentWillReceiveProps(nextProps) {
        this.setState({hidden: nextProps.hide})
    }

    render() {
        const { children } = this.props
        const { hidden } = this.state
        return (
            <p>
                {(hidden) ?
```

```
                        children.replace(/[a-zA-Z0-9]/g, "x") :
                        children
                }
            </p>
        )
    }

}
```

When the parent component, `HiddenMessages`, changes the property for `hide`, `componentWillReceiveProps` allows us to update the state.

Setting State from Props

The previous code sample has been reduced to demonstrate the use of `componentWill ReceiveProps`. If this is all we are doing with `HiddenMessage`, then we should use a stateless functional component instead. The only reason we would ever add state to a child component is when we want that component to change things about itself internally.

For example, using `componentWillReceiveProps` to modify state would be warranted if the component required a `setState` call:

```
hide() {
    const hidden = true
    this.setState({hidden})
}

show() {
    const hidden = false
    this.setState({hidden})
}

return
    <p onMouseEnter={this.show}
       onMouseLeave={this.hide}>
        {(hidden) ?
            children.replace(/[a-zA-Z0-9]/g, "x") :
            children
        }
    </p>
```

In this case, it would be appropriate to store state in the `HiddenMessage` component. If the component is not going to change itself, keep it stateless and manage the state from the parent only.

The component lifecycle methods give us much more control over how a component should be rendered or updated. They provide hooks for us to add functionality before or after both mounting and updating have occurred. Next, we will explore how these lifecycle methods can be used to incorporate third-party JavaScript libraries. First, however, we'll take a brief look at the "React.Children" API.

React.Children

React.Children provides a way of working with the children of a particular component. It allows you to count, map, loopover, or convert props.children to an array. It also allows you to verify that you are displaying a single child with React.Children.only:

```
import { Children, PropTypes } from 'react'
import { render } from 'react-dom'

const Display = ({ ifTruthy=true, children }) =>
    (ifTruthy) ?
        Children.only(children) :
        null

const age = 22

render(
    <Display ifTruthy={age >= 21}>
        <h1>You can enter</h1>
    </Display>,
    document.getElementById('react-container')
)
```

In this example, the Display component will display only a single child, the h1 element. If the Display component contained multiple children, React would throw an error: "onlyChild must be passed a children with exactly one child."

We can also use React.Children to convert the children property to an array. This next sample extends the Display component to additionally handle else cases:

```
const { Children, PropTypes } = React
const { render } = ReactDOM

const findChild = (children, child) =>
  Children.toArray(children)
        .filter(c => c.type === child )[0]

const WhenTruthy = ({children}) =>
    Children.only(children)

const WhenFalsy = ({children}) =>
    Children.only(children)

const Display = ({ ifTruthy=true, children }) =>
    (ifTruthy) ?
        findChild(children, WhenTruthy) :
        findChild(children, WhenFalsy)
```

```
const age = 19

render(
    <Display ifTruthy={age >= 21}>
        <WhenTruthy>
            <h1>You can Enter</h1>
        </WhenTruthy>
        <WhenFalsy>
            <h1>Beat it Kid</h1>
        </WhenFalsy>
    </Display>,
    document.getElementById('react-container')
)
```

The `Display` component will display a single child when a condition is true or another when the condition is false. To accomplish this, we create `WhenTruthy` and `WhenFalsy` components and use them as children in the `Display` component. The `findChild` function uses `React.Children` to convert the children into an array. We can filter that array to locate and return an individual child by component type.

JavaScript Library Integration

Frameworks such as Angular and jQuery come with their own tools for accessing data, rendering the UI, modeling state, handling routing, and more. React, on the other hand, is simply a library for creating views, so we may need to work with other JavaScript libraries. If we understand how the lifecycle functions operate, we can make React play nice with just about any JavaScript library.

React with jQuery

Using jQuery with React is generally frowned upon by the community. It is possible to integrate jQuery and React, and the integration could be a good choice for learning React or migrating legacy code to React. However, applications perform much better if we incorporate smaller libraries with React, as opposed to large frameworks. Additionally, using jQuery to manipulate the DOM directly bypasses the virtual DOM, which can lead to strange errors.

In this section, we'll incorporate a couple of different JavaScript libraries into React components. Specifically, we'll look at ways to make API calls and visualize data with the support of other JavaScript libraries.

Making Requests with Fetch

Fetch is a polyfill created by the WHATWG group that allows us to easily make API calls using promises. In this section we will introduce `isomorphic-fetch`, a version of Fetch that works nicely with React. Let's install `isomorphic-fetch`:

```
npm install isomorphic-fetch --save
```

The component lifecycle functions provide us a place to integrate JavaScript. In this case, they are where we will make an API call. Components that make API calls have to handle *latency*, the delay that the user experiences while waiting for a response. We can address these issues in our state by including variables that tell the component whether a request is pending or not.

In the following example, the `CountryList` component creates an ordered list of country names. Once mounted, the component makes an API call and changes the state to reflect that it is loading data. The loading state remains `true` until there is a response from this API call:

```
import { Component } from 'react'
import { render } from 'react-dom'
import fetch from 'isomorphic-fetch'

class CountryList extends Component {

    constructor(props) {
        super(props)
        this.state = {
            countryNames: [],
            loading: false
        }
    }

    componentDidMount() {
        this.setState({loading: true})
        fetch('https://restcountries.eu/rest/v1/all')
            .then(response => response.json())
            .then(json => json.map(country => country.name))
            .then(countryNames =>
                this.setState({countryNames, loading: false})
            )
    }

    render() {
        const { countryNames, loading } = this.state
        return (loading) ?
            <div>Loading Country Names...</div> :
            (!countryNames.length) ?
                <div>No country Names</div> :
                <ul>
                    {countryNames.map(
```

```
                    (x,i) => <li key={i}>{x}</li>
                )}
            </ul>
    }

}

render(
    <CountryList />,
    document.getElementById('react-container')
)
```

When the component mounts, just before the `fetch` call, we set the loading state to `true`. This tells our component, and ultimately our users, that we are in the process of retrieving the data. When we get a response from our `fetch` call, we obtain the JSON object and map it to an array of country names. Finally, the country names are added to the state and the DOM updated.

Incorporating a D3 Timeline

Data Driven Documents (D3) is a JavaScript framework that can be used to construct data visualizations for the browser. D3 provides a rich set of tools that allow us to scale and interpolate data. Additionally, D3 is functional. You compose D3 applications by chaining function calls together to produce a DOM visualization from an array of data.

A timeline is an example of a data visualization. A timeline takes event dates as data and represents that information visually with graphics. Historic events that occurred earlier are represented to the left of those events that occurred later. The space between each event on a timeline in pixels represents the time that has elapsed between the events (Figure 7-6).

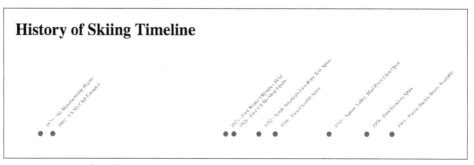

Figure 7-6. Timeline data visualization

This timeline visualizes almost 100 years' worth of events in just 500 pixels. The process of converting year values to their corresponding pixel values is called *interpola-*

tion. D3 provides all of the tools necessary for interpolating data ranges from one measurement to another.

Let's take a look at how to incorporate D3 with React to build this timeline. First, we'll need to install D3:

```
npm install d3@3.5.6 --save
```

D3 takes data, typically arrays of objects, and develops visualizations based upon that data. Take a look at the array of historic ski dates. This is the data for our timeline:

```
const historicDatesForSkiing = [
    {
        year: 1879,
        event: "Ski Manufacturing Begins"
    },
    {
        year: 1882,
        event: "US Ski Club Founded"
    },
    {
        year: 1924,
        event: "First Winter Olympics Held"
    },
    {
        year: 1926,
        event: "First US Ski Shop Opens"
    },
    {
        year: 1932,
        event: "North America's First Rope Tow Spins"
    },
    {
        year: 1936,
        event: "First Chairlift Spins"
    },
    {
        year: 1949,
        event: "Squaw Valley, Mad River Glen Open"
    },
    {
        year: 1958,
        event: "First Gondola Spins"
    },
    {
        year: 1964,
        event: "Plastic Buckle Boots Available"
    }
]
```

The easiest way to incorporate D3 into a React component is to let React render the UI, then have D3 create and add the visualization. In the following example, D3 is incorporated into a React component. Once the component renders, D3 builds the visualization and adds it to the DOM:

```
import d3 from 'd3'
import { Component } from 'react'
import { render } from 'react-dom'
class Timeline extends Component {

    constructor({data=[]}) {
        const times = d3.extent(data.map(d => d.year))
        const range = [50, 450]
        super({data})
        this.state = {data, times, range}
    }

    componentDidMount() {
        let group
        const { data, times, range } = this.state
        const { target } = this.refs
        const scale = d3.time.scale().domain(times).range(range)

        d3.select(target)
            .append('svg')
            .attr('height', 200)
            .attr('width', 500)

        group = d3.select(target.children[0])
            .selectAll('g')
            .data(data)
            .enter()
            .append('g')
            .attr(
                'transform',
                (d, i) => 'translate(' + scale(d.year) + ', 0)'
            )

        group.append('circle')
            .attr('cy', 160)
            .attr('r', 5)
            .style('fill', 'blue')

        group.append('text')
            .text(d => d.year + " - " + d.event)
            .style('font-size', 10)
            .attr('y', 115)
            .attr('x', -95)
            .attr('transform', 'rotate(-45)')
    }

    render() {
        return (
            <div className="timeline">
```

```
                <h1>{this.props.name} Timeline</h1>
                <div ref="target"></div>
            </div>
        )
    }

}

render(
    <Timeline name="History of Skiing"
              data={historicDatesForSkiing} />,
    document.getElementById('react-container')
)
```

In this example, some of the D3 setup occurs in the constructor, but most of the heavy lifting is done by D3 in the componentDidMount function. Once the DOM is rendered, D3 builds the visualization using Scalable Vector Graphics (SVG). This approach will work and is a good way to quickly incorporate existing D3 visualizations into React components.

We can, however, take this integration one step further by letting React manage the DOM and D3 do the math. Take a look at these three lines of code:

```
const times = d3.extent(data.map(d => d.year))
const range = [50, 450]

const scale = d3.time.scale().domain(times).range(range)
```

Both times and range are set up in the constructor and added to the component state. times represents our domain. It contains the values for the earliest year and the latest year. It is calculated by using D3's extent function to find the minimum and maximum values in an array of numeric values. range represents the range in pixels for the timeline. The first date, 1879, will be placed at 0 px on the x-scale and the last date, 1964, will be placed at 450 px on the x-scale.

The next line creates the scale, which is a function that can be used to interpolate the pixel value for any year on our time scale. The scale is created by sending the domain and the range to the D3 time.scale function. The scale function is used in the visualization to get the *x* position for every date that falls between 1879 and 1964.

Instead of creating the scale in componentDidMount, we can add it to the component in the constructor after we have the domain and range. Now the scale can be accessed anywhere in the component using this.scale(year):

```
constructor({data=[]}) {
    const times = d3.extent(data.map(d => d.year))
    const range = [50, 450]
    super({data})
    this.scale = d3.time.scale().domain(times).range(range)
```

```
        this.state = {data, times, range}
    }
```

Within `componentDidMount`, D3 first creates an SVG element and adds it to the target ref:

```
d3.select(target)
    .append('svg')
    .attr('height', 200)
    .attr('width', 500)
```

Constructing a UI is a task for React. Instead of using D3 for this task, let's create a `Canvas` component that returns an SVG element:

```
const Canvas = ({children}) =>
    <svg height="200" width="500">
        {children}
    </svg>
```

Next, D3 selects the `svg` element, the first child under the target, and adds a `group` element for every data point in our timeline array. After it is added, the `group` element is positioned by transforming the x-axis value using the `scale` function:

```
group = d3.select(target.children[0])
    .selectAll('g')
    .data(data)
    .enter()
    .append('g')
    .attr(
        'transform',
        (d, i) => 'translate(' + scale(d.year) + ', 0)'
    )
```

The `group` element is a DOM element, so we can let React handle this task too. Here is a `TimelineDot` component that can be used to set up `group` elements and position them along the x-axis:

```
const TimelineDot = ({position}) =>
    <g transform={`translate(${position},0)`}></g>
```

Next, D3 adds a `circle` element and some "style" to the group. The `text` element gets its value by concatenating the event year with the event title. It then positions and rotates that text around the blue circle:

```
group.append('circle')
    .attr('cy', 160)
    .attr('r', 5)
    .style('fill', 'blue')

group.append('text')
    .text(d => d.year + " - " + d.event)
    .style('font-size', 10)
    .attr('y', 115)
```

```
.attr('x', -95)
.attr('transform', 'rotate(-45)')
```

All we need to do is modify our `TimelineDot` component to include a `circle` element and a `text` element that retrieves the text from the properties:

```
const TimelineDot = ({position, txt}) =>
    <g transform={`translate(${position},0)`}>

        <circle cy={160}
                r={5}
                style={{fill: 'blue'}} />

        <text y={115}
              x={-95}
              transform="rotate(-45)"
              style={{fontSize: '10px'}}>{txt}</text>

    </g>
```

React is now responsible for managing the UI using the virtual DOM. The role of D3 has been reduced, but it still provides some essential functionality that React does not. It helps create the domain and range and constructs a `scale` function that we can use to interpolate pixel values from years. This is what our refactored `Timeline` component might look like:

```
class Timeline extends Component {

    constructor({data=[]}) {
        const times = d3.extent(data.map(d => d.year))
        const range = [50, 450]
        super({data})
        this.scale = d3.time.scale().domain(times).range(range)
        this.state = {data, times, range}
    }

    render() {
        const { data } = this.state
        const { scale } = this
        return (
            <div className="timeline">
                <h1>{this.props.name} Timeline</h1>
                <Canvas>
                    {data.map((d, i) =>
                        <TimelineDot position={scale(d.year)}
                                     txt={`${d.year} - ${d.event}`}
                        />
                    )}
                </Canvas>
            </div>
        )
    }
}
```

```
        }
```

We can integrate just about any JavaScript library with React. The lifecycle functions are the place where other JavaScript can pick up where React leaves off. However, we should avoid adding libraries that manage the UI: that's React's job.

Higher-Order Components

A *higher-order component*, or HOC, is a simply a function that takes a React component as an argument and returns another React component. Typically, HOCs wrap the incoming component with a class that maintains state or has functionality. Higher-order components are the best way to reuse functionality across React components.

Mixins Not Supported

Until React v0.13, the best way to incorporate functionality in a React component was to use a *mixin*. Mixins can be added directly to components created with create Class as a configuration property. You can still use mixins with React.createClass, but they are not supported in ES6 classes or stateless functional components. They will also not be supported by future versions of React.

An HOC allows us to wrap a component with another component. The parent component can hold state or contain functionality that can be passed down to the composed component as properties. The composed component does not need to know anything about the implementation of an HOC other than the names of the properties and methods that it makes available.

Take a look at this `PeopleList` component. It loads random users from an API and renders a list of member names. While the users are loading, a loading message is displayed. Once they have loaded, they are displayed on the DOM:

```
import { Component } from 'react'
import { render } from 'react-dom'
import fetch from 'isomorphic-fetch'

class PeopleList extends Component {

    constructor(props) {
        super(props)
        this.state = {
            data: [],
            loaded: false,
            loading: false
        }
```

```
    }

    componentWillMount() {
        this.setState({loading:true})
        fetch('https://randomuser.me/api/?results=10')
            .then(response => response.json())
            .then(obj => obj.results)
            .then(data => this.setState({
                loaded: true,
                loading: false,
                data
            }))
    }

    render() {
        const { data, loading, loaded } = this.state
        return (loading) ?
            <div>Loading...</div> :
            <ol className="people-list">
                {data.map((person, i) => {
                    const {first, last} = person.name
                    return <li key={i}>{first} {last}</li>
                })}
            </ol>
    }
}

render(
    <PeopleList />,
    document.getElementById('react-container')
)
```

PeopleList incorporates a getJSON call from jQuery to load people from a JSON API. When the component is rendered, it displays a loading message or renders a list of names based upon whether or not the loading state is true.

If we harness this loading functionality, we can reuse it across components. We could create a higher-order component, the DataComponent, that can be used to create React components that load data. To use the DataComponent, we strip the PeopleList of state and create a stateless functional component that receives data via props:

```
import { render } from 'react-dom'

const PeopleList = ({data}) =>
    <ol className="people-list">
        {data.results.map((person, i) => {
            const {first, last} = person.name
            return <li key={i}>{first} {last}</li>
        })}
    </ol>

const RandomMeUsers = DataComponent(
```

```
                PeopleList,
                "https://randomuser.me/api/"
        )

    render(
        <RandomMeUsers count={10} />,
        document.getElementById('react-container')
    )
```

Now we are able to create a RandomMeUsers component that always loads and displays
users from the same source, *randomuser.me*. All we have to do is provide the count of
how many users we wish to load. The data handling has been moved into the HOC,
and the UI is handled by the PeopleList component. The HOC provides the state for
loading and the mechanism to load data and change its own state. While data is loading, the HOC displays a loading message. Once the data has loaded, the HOC handles
mounting the PeopleList and passing it people as the data property:

```
    const DataComponent = (ComposedComponent, url) =>
        class DataComponent extends Component {
            constructor(props) {
                super(props)
                this.state = {
                    data: [],
                    loading: false,
                    loaded: false
                }
            }

            componentWillMount() {
                this.setState({loading:true})
                fetch(url)
                    .then(response => response.json())
                    .then(data => this.setState({
                        loaded: true,
                        loading: false,
                        data
                    }))
            }

            render() {
                return (
                    <div className="data-component">
                        {(this.state.loading) ?
                            <div>Loading...</div> :
                            <ComposedComponent {...this.state} />}
                    </div>
                )
            }
        }
```

Notice that `DataComponent` is actually a function. All higher-order components are functions. `ComposedComponent` is the component that we will wrap. The returned class, `DataComponent`, stores and manages the state. When that state changes and the data has loaded, the `ComposedComponent` is rendered and that data is passed to it as a property.

This HOC can be used to create any type of data component. Let's take a look at how `DataComponent` can be reused to create a `CountryDropDown` that is populated with a country name for every country in the world delivered from the *restcountries.eu* API:

```
import { render } from 'react-dom'

const CountryNames = ({data, selected=""}) =>
    <select className="people-list" defaultValue={selected}>
        {data.map(({name}, i) =>
            <option key={i} value={name}>{name}</option>
        )}
    </select>

const CountryDropDown =
    DataComponent(
        CountryNames,
        "https://restcountries.eu/rest/v1/all"
    )

render(
    <CountryDropDown selected="United States" />,
    document.getElementById('react-container')
)
```

The `CountryNames` component obtains the country names via props. `DataComponent` handles loading and passing information about each country.

Notice that the `CountryNames` component also has a `selected` property. This property should cause the component to select "United States" by default. However, at present, it is not working. We did not pass the properties to the composed component from our HOC.

Let's modify our HOC to pass any properties that it receives down to the composed component:

```
render() {
    return (
        <div className="data-component">
            {(this.state.loading) ?
                <div>Loading...</div> :
                <ComposedComponent {...this.state}
                                   {...this.props} />
            }
        </div>
```

```
        )
    }
```

Now the HOC passes state and props down to the composed component. If we run this code now, we will see that the `CountryDropDown` preselects "United States".

Let's take a look at another HOC. We developed a `HiddenMessage` component earlier in this chapter. The ability to show or hide content is something that can be reused. In this next example, we have an `Expandable` HOC that functions similarly to the `HiddenMessage` component. You can show or hide content based upon the Boolean property `collapsed`. This HOC also provides a mechanism for toggling the `collapsed` property (Example 7-3).

Example 7-3. ./components/hoc/Expandable.js

```
import { Component } from 'react'

const Expandable = ComposedComponent =>
    class Expandable extends Component {

        constructor(props) {
            super(props)
            const collapsed =
                (props.hidden && props.hidden === true) ?
                    true :
                    false
            this.state = {collapsed}
            this.expandCollapse = this.expandCollapse.bind(this)
        }

        expandCollapse() {
            let collapsed = !this.state.collapsed
            this.setState({collapsed})
        }

        render() {
            return <ComposedComponent
                        expandCollapse={this.expandCollapse}
                        {...this.state}
                        {...this.props} />
        }
    }
```

The `Expandable` HOC takes a `ComposedComponent` and wraps it with state and functionality that allows it to show or hide content. Initially, the collapsed state is set using incoming properties, or it defaults to `false`. The collapsed state is passed down to the `ComposedComponent` as a property.

This component also has a method for toggling the collapsed state called `expandCol` `lapse`. This method is also passed down to the `ComposedComponent`. Once invoked, it will change the collapsed state and update the `ComposedComponent` with the new state.

If the properties of the `DataComponent` are changed by a parent, the component will update the collapsed state and pass the new state down to the `ComposedComponent` as a property.

Finally, all state and props are passed down to the `ComposedComponent`. Now we can use this HOC to create several new components. First, let's use it to create the `Hidden` `Message` component that we defined earlier in this chapter:

```
const ShowHideMessage = ({children, collapsed, expandCollapse}) =>
    <p onClick={expandCollapse}>
        {(collapsed) ?
            children.replace(/[a-zA-Z0-9]/g, "x") :
            children}
    </p>

const HiddenMessage = Expandable(ShowHideMessage)
```

Here we create a `HiddenMessage` component that will replace every letter or number in a string with an "x" when the `collapsed` property is `true`. When the `collapsed` property is `false`, the message will be shown. Try this `HiddenMessage` component out in the `HiddenMessages` component that we defined earlier in this chapter.

Let's use this same HOC to create a button that shows and hides hidden content in a div. In the following example, the `MenuButton` can be used to create `PopUpButton`, a component that toggles content display:

```
class MenuButton extends Component {

    componentWillReceiveProps(nextProps) {
        const collapsed =
            (nextProps.collapsed && nextProps.collapsed === true) ?
                true :
                false
        this.setState({collapsed})
    }

    render() {
        const {children, collapsed, txt, expandCollapse} = this.props
        return (
            <div className="pop-button">
                <button onClick={expandCollapse}>{txt}</button>
                {(!collapsed) ?
                    <div className="pop-up">
                        {children}
                    </div> :
                    ""
```

```
            }
          </div>
        )
      }
    }

    const PopUpButton = Expandable(MenuButton)

    render(
        <PopUpButton hidden={true} txt="toggle popup">
            <h1>Hidden Content</h1>
            <p>This content will start off hidden</p>
        </PopUpButton>,
        document.getElementById('react-container')
        )
```

The PopUpButton is created with the MenuButton component. It will pass the collapsed state along with the function to change that state to the MenuButton as properties. When users click on the button, it will invoke expandCollapse and toggle the collapsed state. When the state is collapsed, we only see a button. When it is expanded we see a button and a div with the hidden content.

Higher-order components are a great way to reuse functionality and abstract away the details of how component state or lifecycle are managed. They will allow you to produce more stateless functional components that are solely responsible for the UI.

Managing State Outside of React

State management in React is great. We could build a lot of applications using React's built-in state management system. However, when our applications get larger, state becomes a little bit harder for us to wrap our heads around. Keeping state in one place at the root of your component tree will help make this task easier, but even then, your application may grow to a point where it makes the most sense to isolate state data in its own layer, independent of the UI.

One of the benefits of managing state outside of React is that it will reduce the need for many, if any, class components. If you are not using state, it is easier to keep most of your components stateless. You should only need to create a class when you need lifecycle functions, and even then you can isolate class functionality to HOCs and keep components that only contain UI stateless. Stateless functional components are easier to understand and easier to test. They are pure functions, so they fit into strictly functional applications quite nicely.

Managing state outside of React could mean a lot of different things. You can use React with Backbone Models, or with any other MVC library that models state. You can create your own system for managing state. You can manage state using global variables or localStorage and plain JavaScript. Managing state outside of React simply means not using React state or setState in your applications.

Rendering a Clock

Back in Chapter 3, we created a ticking clock that followed the rules of functional programming. The entire application consists of functions and higher-order functions that are composed into larger functions that compose a startTicking function that starts the clock and displays the time in the console:

```
const startTicking = () =>
    setInterval(
        compose(
            clear,
            getCurrentTime,
            abstractClockTime,
            convertToCivilianTime,
            doubleDigits,
            formatClock("hh:mm:ss tt"),
            display(log)
        ),
        oneSecond()
    )

startTicking()
```

But instead of displaying the clock in the console, what if we displayed it in the browser? We could build a React component to display the clock time in a div:

```
const AlarmClockDisplay = ({hours, minutes, seconds, ampm}) =>
    <div className="clock">
        <span>{hours}</span>
        <span>:</span>
        <span>{minutes}</span>
        <span>:</span>
        <span>{seconds}</span>
        <span>{ampm}</span>
    </div>
```

This component takes in properties for hours, minutes, seconds, and time of day. It then creates a DOM where those properties can be displayed.

We could replace the log method with a render method and send our component to be used to render the civilian time, with leading zeros added to values less than 10:

```
const startTicking = () =>
    setInterval(
        compose(
            getCurrentTime,
            abstractClockTime,
            convertToCivilianTime,
```

```
            doubleDigits,
            render(AlarmClockDisplay)
        ),
        oneSecond()
    )

    startTicking()
```

The `render` method will need to be a higher-order function. It will need to take the `AlarmClockDisplay` as a property initially when the `startTicking` method is composed and hang on to it. Eventually, it will need to use that component to render the display with the formatted time every second:

```
const render = Component => civilianTime =>
    ReactDOM.render(
        <Component {...civilianTime} />,
        document.getElementById('react-container')
    )
```

The higher-order function for `render` invokes `ReactDOM.render` every second and updates the DOM. This approach takes advantage of React's speedy DOM rendering, but does not require a component class with state.

The state of this application is managed outside of React. React allowed us to keep our functional architecture in place by providing our own higher-order function that renders a component with `ReactDOM.render`. Managing state outside of React is not a requirement, it is simply another option. React is a library, and it is up to you to decide how best to use it in your applications.

Next, we will introduce Flux, a design pattern that was created as an alternative to state management in React.

Flux

Flux is a design pattern developed at Facebook that was designed to keep data flowing in one direction. Before Flux was introduced, web development architecture was dominated by variations of the MVC design pattern. Flux is an alternative to MVC, an entirely different design pattern that complements the functional approach.

What does React or Flux have to do with functional JavaScript? For starters, a stateless functional component is a pure function. It takes in instructions as props and returns UI elements. A React class uses state or props as input and also will produce UI elements. React components are composed into a single component. Immutable data provides the component with input and output as UI elements are returned:

```
const Countdown = ({count}) => <h1>{count}</h1>
```

Flux provides us with a way to architect web applications that complements how React works. Specifically, Flux provides a way to provide the data that React will use to create the UI.

In Flux, application state data is managed outside of React components in *stores*. Stores hold and change the data, and are the only thing that can update a view in Flux. If a user were to interact with a web page—say, click a button or submit a form —then an *action* would be created to represent the user's request. An action provides the instructions and data required to make a change. Actions are dispatched using a central control component called the *dispatcher*. The dispatcher is designed to queue up our actions and dispatch them to the appropriate store. Once a store receives an action, it will use it as instructions to modify state and update the view. Data flows in one direction: action to a dispatcher to the store and finally to the view (Figure 7-7).

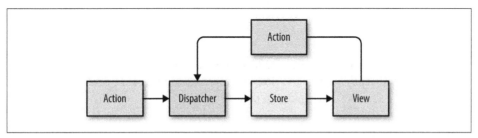

Figure 7-7. Facebook's Flux Design Pattern

Actions and state data are immutable in Flux. Actions can be dispatched from a view, or they can come from other sources, typically a web server.

Every change requires an action. Every action provides the instructions to make the change. Actions also serve as receipts that tell us what has changed, what data was used to make the change, and where the action originated. This pattern causes no side effects. The only thing that can make a change is a store. Stores update the data, views render those updates in the UI, and actions tell us how and why the changes have occurred.

Restricting the data flow of your application to this design pattern will make your application much easier to fix and scale. Take a look at the application in Figure 7-8. We can see that every dispatched action has been logged to the console. These actions tell us about how we got to the current UI that is displaying a giant number 3.

As we can see, the last state change that occurred was a TICK. It changed the count to 3 from the count before that, which looks to have been a 4. The actions tell us how the state has been changing. We can trace the actions back to the source to see that first change was to a 9, so presumably this app is counting down from 10.

Figure 7-8. Countdown app with Flux

Let's take a look at how this countdown is constructed using the Flux design pattern. We will introduce each part of the design pattern and discuss its contribution to the unidirectional data flow that makes up this countdown.

Views

Let's begin by looking at the view, a React stateless component. Flux will manage our application state, so unless you need a lifecycle function you will not need class components.

The countdown view takes in the count to display as a property. It also receives a couple of functions, `tick` and `reset`:

```
const Countdown = ({count, tick, reset}) => {

  if (count) {
    setTimeout(() => tick(), 1000)
  }

  return (count) ?
      <h1>{count}</h1> :
      <div onClick={() => reset(10)}>
          <span>CELEBRATE!!!</span>
          <span>(click to start over)</span>
      </div>

}
```

When this view renders it will display the count, unless the count is 0, in which case it will display a message instructing the user to "CELEBRATE!!!" If the count is not 0, then the view sets a timeout, waits for a second, and invokes a TICK.

When the count is 0, this view will not invoke any other action creators until a user clicks the main div and triggers a reset. This resets the count to 10 and starts the whole countdown process over again.

State in Components

Using Flux does not mean that you cannot have state in any of your view components. It means that application state is not managed in your view components. For example, Flux can manage the dates and times that make up timelines. It would not be off-limits to use a timeline component that has internal state to visualize your application's timelines.

State should be used sparingly—only when needed, from reusable components that internally manage their own state. The rest of the application does not need to be "aware" of a child component's state.

Actions and Action Creators

Actions provide the instructions and data that the store will use to modify the state. *Action creators* are functions that can be used to abstract away the nitty-gritty details required to build an action. Actions themselves are objects that at minimum contain a type field. The action type is typically an uppercase string that describes the action. Additionally, actions may package any data required by the store. For example:

```
const countdownActions = dispatcher =>
  ({
     tick(currentCount) {
        dispatcher.handleAction({
          type: 'TICK',
          count: count - 1
        })
     },
     reset(count) {
        dispatcher.handleAction({
          type: 'RESET',
          count
        })
     }
  })
```

When countdown action creators are loaded, the dispatcher is sent as an argument. Every time a TICK or a RESET is invoked, the dispatcher's handleAction method is invoked, which "dispatches" the action object.

Dispatcher

There is only ever one dispatcher, and it represents the air traffic control part of this design pattern. The dispatcher takes the action, packages it with some information about where the action was generated, and sends it on to the appropriate store or stores that will handle the action.

Although Flux is not a framework, Facebook does open source a `Dispatcher` class that you can use. How dispatchers are implemented is typically standard, so it is better to use Facebook's dispatcher rather than coding your own:

```
import Dispatcher from 'flux'

class CountdownDispatcher extends Dispatcher {

    handleAction(action) {
        console.log('dispatching action:', action)
        this.dispatch({
            source: 'VIEW_ACTION',
            action
        })
    }

}
```

When `handleAction` is invoked with an action, it is dispatched along with some data about where the action originated. When a store is created, it is registered with the dispatcher and starts listening for actions. When an action is dispatched it is handled in the order that it was received and sent to the appropriate stores.

Stores

Stores are objects that hold the application's logic and state data. Stores are similar to models in the MVC pattern, but stores are not restricted to managing data in a single object. It is possible to build Flux applications that consist of a single store that manages many different data types.

Current state data can be obtained from a store via properties. Everything a store needs to change state data is provided in the action. A store will handle actions by type and change their data accordingly. Once data is changed, the store will emit an event and notify any views that have subscribed to the store that their data has changed. Let's take a look at an example:

```
import { EventEmitter } from 'events'

class CountdownStore extends EventEmitter {

    constructor(count=5, dispatcher) {
        super()
```

```
            this._count = count
            this.dispatcherIndex = dispatcher.register(
                this.dispatch.bind(this)
            )
        }

        get count() {
            return this._count
        }

        dispatch(payload) {
            const { type, count } = payload.action
            switch(type) {

                case "TICK":
                    this._count = this._count - 1
                    this.emit("TICK", this._count)
                    return true

                case "RESET":
                    this._count = count
                    this.emit("RESET", this._count)
                    return true

            }
        }

    }
```

This store holds the countdown application's state, the count. The count can be accessed through a read-only property. When actions are dispatched, the store uses them to change the count. A TICK action decrements the count. A RESET action resets the count entirely with data that is included with the action.

Once the state has changed, the store emits an event to any views that may be listening.

Putting It All Together

Now that you understand how data flows through each part of a Flux application, let's take a look at how all these parts get connected:

```
const appDispatcher = new CountdownDispatcher()
const actions = countdownActions(appDispatcher)
const store = new CountdownStore(10, appDispatcher)

const render = count => ReactDOM.render(
    <Countdown count={count} {...actions} />,
    document.getElementById('react-container')
)
```

```
store.on("TICK", () => render(store.count))
store.on("RESET", () => render(store.count))
render(store.count)
```

First, we create the `appDispatcher`. Next, we use the `appDispatcher` to generate our action creators. Finally, the `appDispatcher` is registered with our store, and the store sets the initial count to 10.

The `render` method is used to render the view with a count that it receives as an argument. It also passes the action creators to the view as properties.

Finally, some listeners are added to the store, which completes the circle. When the store emits a `TICK` or a `RESET`, it yields a new count, which is immediately rendered in the view. After that, the initial view is rendered with the store's count. Every time the view emits a `TICK` or `RESET`, the action is sent through this circle and eventually comes back to the view as data that is ready to be rendered.

Flux Implementations

There are different approaches to the implementation of Flux. A few libraries have been open-sourced based upon specific implementations of this design pattern. Here are a few approaches to Flux worth mentioning:

Flux (https://facebook.github.io/flux/)
Facebook's Flux is the design pattern that we just covered. The Flux library includes an implementation of a dispatcher.

Reflux (https://github.com/reflux/refluxjs)
A simplified approach to unidirectional data flow that focuses on actions, stores, and views.

Flummox (http://acdlite.github.io/flummox)
A Flux implementation that allows you to build Flux modules through extending JavaScript classes.

Fluxible (http://fluxible.io)
A Flux framework created by Yahoo for working with isomorphic Flux applications. Isomorphic applications will be discussed in Chapter 12.

Redux (http://redux.js.org)
A Flux-like library that achieves modularity through functions instead of objects.

MobX (https://mobx.js.org/getting-started.html)
A state management library that uses observables to respond to changes in state.

All of these implementations have stores, actions, and a dispatch mechanism, and favor React components as the view layer. They are all variations of the Flux design pattern, which at its core is all about unidirectional data flow.

Redux has quickly become one of the more popular Flux frameworks. The next chapter covers how to use Redux to construct functional data architectures for your client applications.

CHAPTER 8

Redux

Redux (*http://redux.js.org*) has emerged as one of the clear winners in the field of Flux or Flux-like libraries. Redux is based on Flux, and it was designed to tackle the challenge of understanding how data changes flow through your application. Redux was developed by Dan Abramov (*https://github.com/gaearon*) and Andrew Clark. Since creating Redux, both have been hired by Facebook to work on the React team.

Andrew Clark was working on version 4 of Flummox, another Flux-based library, when he started assisting Dan with the task of completing Redux. The message on the npm page for Flummox (*https://www.npmjs.com/package/flummox*) reads:

> Eventually 4.x should be the last major release but it never happened. If you want the latest features, then use Redux instead. It's really great.[1]

Redux is surprisingly small, only 99 lines of code (*http://bit.ly/2nawjzD*).

We have mentioned that Redux is Flux-like, but it is not exactly Flux. It has actions, action creators, a store, and action objects that are used to change state. Redux simplifies the concepts of Flux a bit by removing the dispatcher, and representing application state with a single immutable object. Redux also introduces *reducers*, which are not a part of the Flux pattern. Reducers are pure functions that return a new state based on the current state and an action: `(state, action) => newState`.

---

1 Flummox documentation (*https://github.com/acdlite/flummox*)

State

The idea of storing state in one place isn't so crazy. In fact, we did it in the last chapter. We stored it in the root of our application. In pure React or Flux apps, storing state in as few objects as possible is recommended. In Redux, it's a rule.[2]

When you hear that you have to store state in one place, it might seem like an unreasonable requirement, especially when you have different types of data. Let's consider how this can be achieved with an application that has many different types of data. We'll look at a social media app that has state spread out across different components (Figure 8-1). The app itself has user state. All of the messages are stored in state under that. Each message has its own state, and all of the posts are stored under the posts component.

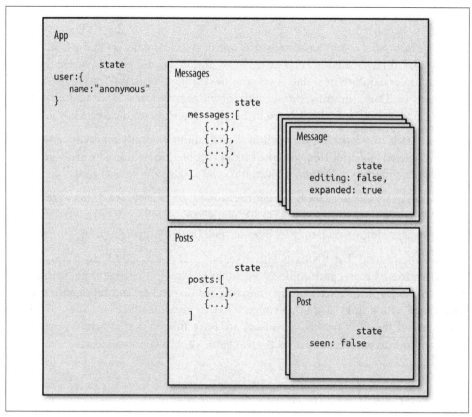

Figure 8-1. React app where components hold their own state

---

2 Redux Docs, "Three Principles" (*http://bit.ly/2mJ0U4Y*).

An app structured like this may work well, but as it grows it may be hard to determine the overall state of the application. It may also become cumbersome to understand where updates are coming from, considering that each component will mutate its own state with internal `setState` calls.

What messages are expanded? What posts have been read? In order to figure out these details, we must dive into the component tree and track down the state inside of individual components.

Redux simplifies the way we view state in our application by requiring us to store all state data in a single object. Everything we need to know about the application is in one place: a single source of truth. We could construct the same application with Redux by moving all of the state data into a single location (see Figure 8-2).

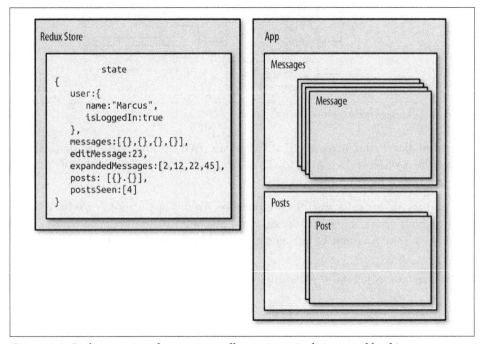

Figure 8-2. Redux requires that we store all state in a single immutable object

In the social media app, we can see that we are managing the state of the current user, messages, and posts from the same object: the Redux store. This object even stores information about the message that is being edited, which messages are expanded, and which posts have been seen. This information is captured in arrays containing IDs that reference specific records. All of the messages and posts are cached in this state object, so that data is there.

With Redux, we pull state management away from React entirely. Redux will manage the state.

In Figure 8-3, we can see the state tree for the social media app. In it, we have the messages in an array. The same is true for the posts. Everything we need is rooted in one object: the state tree. Each key in this single object represents a branch of the state tree.

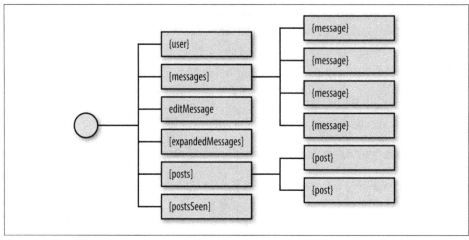

Figure 8-3. Sample state tree

When building Redux apps, the first thing you need to think about is state. Try to define it in a single object. It is usually a good idea to draft a JSON sample of your state tree with some placeholder data.

Let's go back to our color organizer application. In this application, we'll have information about each color stored in an array, and information about how the colors should be sorted. A sample of our state data would look like Example 8-1.

Example 8-1. Color organizer sample application state

```
{
    colors: [
        {
            "id": "8658c1d0-9eda-4a90-95e1-8001e8eb6036",
            "title": "Ocean Blue",
            "color": "#0070ff",
            "rating": 3,
            "timestamp": "Sat Mar 12 2016 16:12:09 GMT-0800 (PST)"
        },
        {
            "id": "f9005b4e-975e-433d-a646-79df172e1dbb",
            "title": "Tomato",
            "color": "#d10012",
            "rating": 2,
            "timestamp": "Fri Mar 11 2016 12:00:00 GMT-0800 (PST)"
```

```
    },
    {
        "id": "58d9caee-6ea6-4d7b-9984-65b145031979",
        "title": "Lawn",
        "color": "#67bf4f",
        "rating": 1,
        "timestamp": "Thu Mar 10 2016 01:11:12 GMT-0800 (PST)"
    },
    {
        "id": "a5685c39-6bdc-4727-9188-6c9a00bf7f95",
        "title": "Party Pink",
        "color": "#ff00f7",
        "rating": 5,
        "timestamp": "Wed Mar 9 2016 03:26:00 GMT-0800 (PST)"
    }
  ],
  sort: "SORTED_BY_DATE"
}
```

Now that we have identified the basic structure of our application's state, let's see how we update and change this state via actions.

Actions

In the last section, we introduced an important Redux rule: application state should be stored in a single immutable object. *Immutable* means this state object doesn't change. We will eventually update this state object by replacing it entirely. In order to do this, we will need instructions about what changes. That's what *actions* provide: instructions about what should change in the application state along with the necessary data to make those changes.[3]

Actions are the only way to update the state of a Redux application. Actions provide us with instructions about what should change, but we can also look at them like receipts about the history of what has changed over time. If users were to remove three colors, add four colors, and then rate five colors, they would leave a trail of information, as shown in Figure 8-4.

_____

3 Redux Docs, "Actions" (*http://bit.ly/2m09uit*).

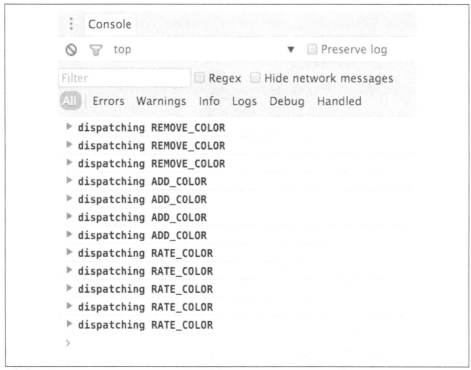

Figure 8-4. Actions being logged to the console as they are dispatched

Usually, when we sit down to construct an object-oriented application, we start by identifying the objects, their properties, and how they work together. Our thinking, in this case, is *noun-oriented*. When building a Redux application, we want to shift our thinking into being *verb-oriented*. How will the actions affect the state data? Once you identify the actions, you can list them in a file called *constants.js* (Example 8-2).

Example 8-2. Constants listed in ./constants.js

```
const constants = {
    SORT_COLORS: "SORT_COLORS",
    ADD_COLOR: "ADD_COLOR",
    RATE_COLOR: "RATE_COLOR",
    REMOVE_COLOR: "REMOVE_COLOR"
}
export default constants
```

In the case of the color organizer, users will need to be able to add a color, rate a color, remove a color, or sort the color list. Here we have defined a string value for each of these action types. An action is a JavaScript object that has at minimum a field for type:

```
{ type: "ADD_COLOR" }
```

The *action type* is a string that defines what should happen. ADD_COLOR is the action that will add a new color to our list of colors in the application state.

It is pretty easy to make typos when creating actions using strings:

```
{ type: "ADD_COOLOR" }
```

This typo would cause a bug in our application. This type of error usually does not trigger any warnings; you simply will not see the expected change of your state data. If you make these errors, they can be tough to find. This is where *constants* can save you:

```
import C from "./constants"
```

```
{ type: C.ADD_COLOR }
```

This specifies the same action, but with a JavaScript constant instead of a string. A typo in a JavaScript variable will cause the browser to throw an error. Defining actions as constants also lets you tap into the benefits of IntelliSense and code completion in your IDE. When you type the first letter or two of a constant, the IDE will autocomplete it for you. Using constants is not required, but it is not a bad idea to get into the habit of incorporating them.

Action Type Naming Conventions

Action types, like ADD_COLOR or RATE_COLOR, are just strings, so technically you could call an action anything. Typically, action types are capitalized and use underscores instead of spaces. You should also aim to clearly state the action's intended purpose.

Action Payload Data

Actions are JavaScript literals that provide the instructions necessary to make a state change. Most state changes also require some data. Which record should I remove? What new information should I provide in a new record?

We refer to this data as the action's *payload*. For example, when we dispatch an action like RATE_COLOR, we will need to know what color to rate and what rating to apply to that color. This information can be passed directly with the action in the same JavaScript literal (see Example 8-3).

Example 8-3. RATE_COLOR action

```
{
  type: "RATE_COLOR",
  id: "a5685c39-6bdc-4727-9188-6c9a00bf7f95",
```

```
    rating: 4
}
```

Example 8-3 contains the action type, RATE_COLOR, and the data necessary to change the specified color's rating to 4.

When we add new colors, we will need details about the color to add (Example 8-4).

Example 8-4. ADD_COLOR action

```
{
    type: "ADD_COLOR",
    color: "#FFFFFF",
    title: "Bright White",
    rating: 0,
    id: "b5685c39-3bdc-4727-9188-6c9a33df7f52",
    timestamp: "Sat Mar 12 2016 16:12:09 GMT-0800 (PST)"
}
```

This action tells Redux to add a new color called Bright White to the state. All of the information for the new color is included in the action. Actions are nice little packages that tell Redux how state should be changed. They also include any associated data that Redux will need to make the change.

Reducers

Our entire state tree is stored in a single object. A potential complaint might be that it's not modular enough, possibly because you're considering modularity as describing objects. Redux achieves modularity via functions. Functions are used to update parts of the state tree. These functions are called *reducers*.[4]

Reducers are functions that take the current state along with an action as arguments and use them to create and return a new state. Reducers are designed to update specific parts of the state tree, either leaves or branches. We can then compose reducers into one reducer that can handle updating the entire state of our app given any action.

The color organizer stores all of the state data in a single tree (see Example 8-5). If we want to use Redux for this app, we can create several reducers that each target specific leaves and branches on our state tree.

Example 8-5. Color organizer sample application state

```
{
    colors: [
```

---

4 Redux Docs, "Reducers" (*http://redux.js.org/docs/basics/Reducers.html*).

```
{
    "id": "8658c1d0-9eda-4a90-95e1-8001e8eb6036",
    "title": "Ocean Blue",
    "color": "#0070ff",
    "rating": 3,
    "timestamp": "Sat Mar 12 2016 16:12:09 GMT-0800 (PST)"
},
{
    "id": "f9005b4e-975e-433d-a646-79df172e1dbb",
    "title": "Tomato",
    "color": "#d10012",
    "rating": 2,
    "timestamp": "Fri Mar 11 2016 12:00:00 GMT-0800 (PST)"
},
{
    "id": "58d9caee-6ea6-4d7b-9984-65b145031979",
    "title": "Lawn",
    "color": "#67bf4f",
    "rating": 1,
    "timestamp": "Thu Mar 10 2016 01:11:12 GMT-0800 (PST)"
},
{
    "id": "a5685c39-6bdc-4727-9188-6c9a00bf7f95",
    "title": "Party Pink",
    "color": "#ff00f7",
    "rating": 5,
    "timestamp": "Wed Mar 9 2016 03:26:00 GMT-0800 (PST)"
}
],
sort: "SORTED_BY_DATE"
}
```

This state data has two main branches: colors and sort. The sort branch is a leaf. It doesn't contain any child nodes. The colors branch stores multiple colors. Each color object represents a leaf (Figure 8-5).

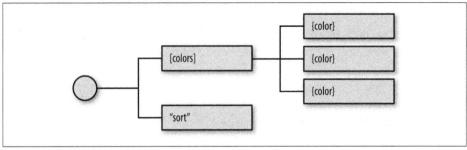

Figure 8-5. Color organizer state tree

A separate reducer will be used to handle each part of this state tree. Each reducer is simply a function, so we can stub them all at once with the code in Example 8-6.

Example 8-6. Color organizer stubbed reducers

```
import C from '../constants'

export const color = (state={}, action) => {
   return {}
}

export const colors = (state=[], action) => {
   return []
}

export const sort = (state="SORTED_BY_DATE", action) => {
  return ""
}
```

Notice that the color reducer expects `state` to be an object and returns an object. The colors reducer takes in `state` as an array and returns an array. The sort reducer takes in a string and returns a string. Each function is focused on a specific part of our state tree. The returned value and initial state for each function correspond to their data type in the state tree. Colors are being stored in n array. Each color is an object. The `sort` property is a string.

Each reducer is designed to handle only the actions necessary to update its part of the state tree. The color reducer will handle only actions that require a new or changed color object: `ADD_COLOR` and `RATE_COLOR`. The colors reducer will focus on those actions necessary for managing the `colors` array: `ADD_COLOR`, `REMOVE_COLOR`, `RATE_COLOR`. Finally, the sort reducer will handle the `SORT_COLORS` action.

Each reducer is composed or combined into a single reducer function that will use the store. The colors reducer is composed with the color reducer to manage individual colors within the array. The sort reducer will then be combined with the colors reducer to create a single reducer function. This can update our entire state tree and handle any action sent to it (see Figure 8-6).

Both the colors and color reducers will handle `ADD_COLOR` and `RATE_COLOR`. But remember, each reducer focuses on a specific part of the state tree. `RATE_COLOR` in the color reducer will handle the task of changing an individual color's rating value; `RATE_COLOR` in the colors reducer will focus on locating the color that needs to be rated in the array. `ADD_COLOR` in the color reducer will result in a new color object with the correct properties; `ADD_COLOR` in the colors reducer will return an array that has an additional color object. They are meant to work together. Each reducer focuses on what a specific action means for its branch in the state tree.

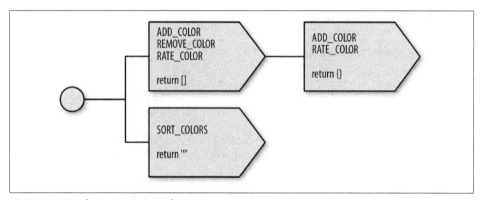

Figure 8-6. Color organizer reducer tree

Reducer Composition Is Not Required, Just Recommended

Redux does not require that we create smaller, more focused reducers and compose them into a single reducer. We could create one reducer function to handle every action in our app. In doing so, we would lose the benefits of modularity and functional programming.

The Color Reducer

Reducers can be coded in a number of different ways. Switch statements are a popular choice because they can process the different types of actions that reducers must handle. The color reducer tests the `action.type` in a switch statement and then handles each action type with a switch case:

```
export const color = (state = {}, action) => {
    switch (action.type) {
        case C.ADD_COLOR:
            return {
                id: action.id,
                title: action.title,
                color: action.color,
                timestamp: action.timestamp,
                rating: 0
            }
        case C.RATE_COLOR:
            return (state.id !== action.id) ?
                state :
                {
                    ...state,
                    rating: action.rating
                }
        default :
            return state
```

```
    }
}
```

Here are the actions for the color reducer:

ADD_COLOR
Returns a new color object constructed from the action's payload data.

RATE_COLOR
Returns a new color object with the desired rating. The ES7 object spread operator allows us to assign the value of the current state to a new object.

Reducers should always return something. If for some reason this reducer is invoked with an unrecognized action, we will return the current state: the default case.

Now that we have a color reducer, we can use it to return new colors or rate existing colors. For example:

```
// Adding a new color

const action = {
    type: "ADD_COLOR",
    id: "4243e1p0-9abl-4e90-95p4-8001l8yf3036",
    color: "#0000FF",
    title: "Big Blue",
    timestamp: "Thu Mar 10 2016 01:11:12 GMT-0800 (PST)"
}

console.log( color({}, action) )

// Console Output

// {
//    id: "4243e1p0-9abl-4e90-95p4-8001l8yf3036",
//    color: "#0000FF",
//    title: "Big Blue",
//    timestamp: "Thu Mar 10 2016 01:11:12 GMT-0800 (PST)",
//    rating: "0"
// }
```

The new color object is returned with all fields represented, including the default rating of 0. To change an existing color, we can send the RATE_COLOR action with the ID and new rating:

```
const existingColor = {
    id: "4243e1p0-9abl-4e90-95p4-8001l8yf3036",
    title: "Big Blue",
    color: "#0000FF",
    timestamp: "Thu Mar 10 2016 01:11:12 GMT-0800 (PST)",
    rating: 0
}
```

```
const action =  {
    type: "RATE_COLOR",
    id: "4243e1p0-9abl-4e90-95p4-8001l8yf3036",
    rating: 4
}

console.log( color(existingColor, action) )

// Console Output

// {
//    id: "4243e1p0-9abl-4e90-95p4-8001l8yf3036",
//    title: "Big Blue",
//    color: "#0000FF",
//    timestamp: "Thu Mar 10 2016 01:11:12 GMT-0800 (PST)",
//    rating: 4
// }
```

The color reducer is a function that creates a new object or rates an existing one. You'll notice that the RATE_COLOR action passes an ID that's not used by the color reducer. That's because the ID of this action is used to locate the color in an entirely different reducer. One action object can impact several reducers.

The Colors Reducer

The color reducer is designed to manage leaves on the colors branch of our state tree. The colors reducer will be used to manage the entire colors branch:

```
export const colors = (state = [], action) => {
    switch (action.type) {
        case C.ADD_COLOR :
            return [
                ...state,
                color({}, action)
            ]
        case C.RATE_COLOR :
            return state.map(
                c => color(c, action)
            )
        case C.REMOVE_COLOR :
            return state.filter(
                c => c.id !== action.id
            )
        default:
            return state
    }
}
```

The colors reducer will handle any actions for adding, rating, and removing colors.

ADD_COLOR

Creates a new array by concatenating all of the values of the existing state array with a new color object. The new color is created by passing a blank state object and the action to the color reducer.

RATE_COLOR

Returns a new array of colors with the desired color rated. The colors reducer locates the color to be rated within the current state array. It then uses the color reducer to obtain the newly rated color object and replaces it in the array.

REMOVE_COLOR

Creates a new array by filtering out the desired color to remove.

The colors reducer is concerned with the array of colors. It uses the color reducer to focus on the individual color objects.

Treat State as an Immutable Object

In all of these reducers, we need to treat state as an immutable object. Although it may be tempting to use `state.push({})` or `state[index].rating`, we should resist the urge to do so.

Now colors can be added, rated, or removed from the `colors` array with this pure function:

```
const currentColors = [
  {
    id: "9813e2p4-3abl-2e44-95p4-8001l8yf3036",
    title: "Berry Blue",
    color: "#000066",
    rating: 0,
    timestamp: "Thu Mar 10 2016 01:11:12 GMT-0800 (PST)"
  }
]

const action = {
    type: "ADD_COLOR",
    id: "5523e7p8-3ab2-1e35-95p4-8001l8yf3036",
    title: "Party Pink",
    color: "#F142FF",
    timestamp: "Thu Mar 10 2016 01:11:12 GMT-0800 (PST)"
}

console.log( colors(currentColors, action) )


// Console Output

// [{
```

```
//    id: "9813e2p4-3abl-2e44-95p4-8001l8yf3036",
//    title: "Berry Blue",
//    color: "#000066",
//    timestamp: "Thu Mar 10 2016 01:11:12 GMT-0800 (PST)",
//    rating: 0
// },
// {
//    id: "5523e7p8-3ab2-1e35-95p4-8001l8yf3036",
//    title: "Party Pink",
//    color: "#F142FF",
//    timestamp: "Thu Mar 10 2016 01:11:12 GMT-0800 (PST)",
//    rating: 0
// }]
```

No Side Effects in Reducers

Reducers should be predictable. They are used to simply manage the state data. In the previous example, notice that the timestamp and IDs are generated prior to sending the action to the reducer. Generating random data, calling APIs, and other asynchronous processes should be handled outside of reducers. Avoiding state mutations and side effects is always recommended.

We can also remove a color from state or rate an individual color in state by sending the appropriate action to the colors reducer.

The Sort Reducer

The sort reducer is an entire function designed to manage one string variable in our state:

```
export const sort = (state = "SORTED_BY_DATE", action) => {
    switch (action.type) {
        case C.SORT_COLORS:
            return action.sortBy
        default :
            return state
    }
}
```

The sort reducer is used to change the sort state variable. It sets the sort state to the value of the action's sortBy field (if this is not a state provided, it will return SOR TED_BY_DATE):

```
const state = "SORTED_BY_DATE"

const action =  {
    type: C.SORT_COLORS,
    sortBy: "SORTED_BY_TITLE"
}
```

```
console.log( sort(state, action) )      // "SORTED_BY_TITLE"
```

To recap, state updates are handled by reducers. Reducers are pure functions that take in state as the first argument and an action as the second argument. Reducers do not cause side effects and should treat their arguments as immutable data. In Redux, modularity is achieved through reducers. Eventually, reducers are combined into a single reducer, a function that can update the entire state tree.

In this section, we saw how reducers can be composed. We saw how the colors reducer uses the color reducer to assist in color management. In the next section, we will look at how the colors reducer can be combined with the sort reducer to update state.

The Store

In Redux, the store is what holds the application's state data and handles all state updates.[5] While the Flux design pattern allows for many stores that each focus on a specific set of data, Redux only has one store.

The store handles state updates by passing the current state and action through a single reducer. We will create this single reducer by combining and composing all of our reducers.

If we create a store using the colors reducer, then our state object will be an array— the array of colors. The getState method of the store will return the present application state. In Example 8-7, we create a store with the color reducer, proving that you can use any reducer to create a store.

Example 8-7. Store with color reducer

```
import { createStore } from 'redux'
import { color } from './reducers'

const store = createStore(color)

console.log( store.getState() )          // {}
```

In order to create a single reducer tree that looks like Figure 8-6 from the previous section, we must combine the colors and sort reducers. Redux has a function for doing just that, combineReducers, which combines all of the reducers into a single reducer. These reducers are used to build your state tree. The names of the fields match the names of the reducers that are passed in.

---

5 Redux Docs, "Store" (*http://bit.ly/2m0iGDG*).

A store can also be created with initial data. Invoking the colors reducer without state returns an empty array:

```
import { createStore, combineReducers } from 'redux'
import { colors, sort } from './reducers'

const store = createStore(
    combineReducers({ colors, sort })
)

console.log( store.getState() )

// Console Output

//{
//   colors: [],
//   sort: "SORTED_BY_DATE"
//}
```

In Example 8-8, the store was created with three colors and a sort value of SOR TED_BY_TITLE.

Example 8-8. Initial state data

```
import { createStore, combineReducers } from 'redux'
import { colors, sort } from './reducers'

const initialState = {
    colors: [
        {
            id: "3315e1p5-3abl-0p523-30e4-8001l8yf3036",
            title: "Rad Red",
            color: "#FF0000",
            rating: 3,
            timestamp: "Sat Mar 12 2016 16:12:09 GMT-0800 (PST)"
        },
        {
            id: "3315e1p5-3abl-0p523-30e4-8001l8yf4457",
            title: "Crazy Green",
            color: "#00FF00",
            rating: 0,
            timestamp: "Fri Mar 11 2016 12:00:00 GMT-0800 (PST)"
        },
        {
            id: "3315e1p5-3abl-0p523-30e4-8001l8yf2412",
            title: "Big Blue",
            color: "#0000FF",
            rating: 5,
            timestamp: "Thu Mar 10 2016 01:11:12 GMT-0800 (PST)"
        }
    ],
```

```
    sort: "SORTED_BY_TITLE"
}

const store = createStore(
    combineReducers({ colors, sort }),
    initialState
)

console.log( store.getState().colors.length ) // 3
console.log( store.getState().sort )          // "SORTED_BY_TITLE"
```

The only way to change the state of your application is by dispatching actions through the store. The store has a `dispatch` method that is ready to take actions as an argument. When you dispatch an action through the store, the action is sent through the reducers and the state is updated:

```
console.log(
    "Length of colors array before ADD_COLOR",
    store.getState().colors.length
)

// Length of colors array before ADD_COLOR 3

store.dispatch({
  type: "ADD_COLOR",
  id: "2222e1p5-3abl-0p523-30e4-8001l8yf2222",
  title: "Party Pink",
  color: "#F142FF",
  timestamp: "Thu Mar 10 2016 01:11:12 GMT-0800 (PST)"
})

console.log(
    "Length of colors array after ADD_COLOR",
    store.getState().colors.length
)

// Length of colors array after ADD_COLOR 4

console.log(
    "Color rating before RATE_COLOR",
    store.getState().colors[3].rating
)

// Color rating before RATE_COLOR 0

store.dispatch({
  type: "RATE_COLOR",
  id: "2222e1p5-3abl-0p523-30e4-8001l8yf2222",
  rating: 5
})

console.log(
```

```
        "Color rating after RATE_COLOR",
        store.getState().colors[3].rating
)

// Color rating after RATE_COLOR 5
```

Here, we created a store and dispatched an action that added a new color followed by an action that changed the color's rating. The console output shows us that dispatching the actions did in fact change our state.

Originally, we had three colors in the array. We added a color, and now there are four. Our new color had an original rating of zero. Dispatching an action changed it to five. The only way to change data is to dispatch actions to the store.

Subscribing to Stores

Stores allow you to subscribe handler functions that are invoked every time the store completes dispatching an action. In the following example, we will log the count of colors in the state:

```
store.subscribe(() =>
    console.log('color count:', store.getState().colors.length)
)

store.dispatch({
    type: "ADD_COLOR",
    id: "2222e1p5-3abl-0p523-30e4-8001l8yf2222",
    title: "Party Pink",
    color: "#F142FF",
    timestamp: "Thu Mar 10 2016 01:11:12 GMT-0800 (PST)"
})

store.dispatch({
    type: "ADD_COLOR",
    id: "3315e1p5-3abl-0p523-30e4-8001l8yf2412",
    title: "Big Blue",
    color: "#0000FF",
    timestamp: "Thu Mar 10 2016 01:11:12 GMT-0800 (PST)"
})

store.dispatch({
    type: "RATE_COLOR",
    id: "2222e1p5-3abl-0p523-30e4-8001l8yf2222",
    rating: 5
})

store.dispatch({
    type: "REMOVE_COLOR",
    id: "3315e1p5-3abl-0p523-30e4-8001l8yf2412"
})
```

```
// Console Output

// color count: 1
// color count: 2
// color count: 2
// color count: 1
```

Subscribing this listener to the store will log the color count to the console every time we submit an action. In the preceding example we see four logs: the first two for ADD_COLOR, the third for RATE_COLOR, and the fourth for REMOVE_COLOR.

The store's subscribe method returns a function that you can use later to unsubscribe the listener:

```
const logState = () => console.log('next state', store.getState())

const unsubscribeLogger = store.subscribe(logState)

// Invoke when ready to unsubscribe the listener
unsubscribeLogger()
```

Saving to localStorage

Using the store's subscribe function, we will listen for state changes and save those changes to localStorage under the key 'redux-store'. When we create the store we can check to see if any data has been saved under this key and, if so, load that data as our initial state. With just a few lines of code, we can have persistent state data in the browser:

```
const store = createStore(
    combineReducers({ colors, sort }),
    (localStorage['redux-store']) ?
        JSON.parse(localStorage['redux-store']) :
        {}
)

store.subscribe(() => {
  localStorage['redux-store'] = JSON.stringify(store.getState())
})

console.log('current color count', store.getState().colors.length)
console.log('current state', store.getState())

store.dispatch({
    type: "ADD_COLOR",
    id: uuid.v4(),
    title: "Party Pink",
    color: "#F142FF",
    timestamp: new Date().toString()
})
```

Every time we refresh this code, our colors list gets larger by one color. First, within the createStore function call, we see if the redux-store key exists. If it exists, we'll parse the JSON. If it doesn't exist, we'll return an empty object. Next, we subscribe a listener to the store that saves the store's state every time an action is dispatched. Refreshing the page would continue to add the same color.

To recap, stores hold and manage state data in Redux applications, and the only way to change state data is by dispatching actions through the store. The store holds application state as a single object. State mutations are managed through reducers. Stores are created by supplying a reducer along with optional data for the initial state. Also, we can subscribe listeners to our store (and unsubscribe them later), and they will be invoked every time the store finishes dispatching an action.

Action Creators

Action objects are simply JavaScript literals. Action *creators* are functions that create and return these literals. Let's consider the following actions:

```
{
  type: "REMOVE_COLOR",
  id: "3315e1p5-3abl-0p523-30e4-8001l8yf2412"
}

{
  type: "RATE_COLOR",
  id: "441e0p2-9ab4-0p523-30e4-8001l8yf2412",
  rating: 5
}
```

We can simplify the logic involved with generating an action by adding an action creators for each of these action types:

```
import C from './constants'

export const removeColor = id =>
    ({
        type: C.REMOVE_COLOR,
        id
    })

export const rateColor = (id, rating) =>
    ({
        type: C.RATE_COLOR,
        id,
        rating
    })
```

Now whenever we need to dispatch a RATE_COLOR or a REMOVE_COLOR, we can use the action creator and send the necessary data as function arguments:

```
store.dispatch( removeColor("3315e1p5-3abl-0p523-30e4-8001l8yf2412") )
store.dispatch( rateColor("441e0p2-9ab4-0p523-30e4-8001l8yf2412", 5) )
```

Action creators simplify the task of dispatching actions; we only need to call a function and send it the necessary data. Action creators can abstract away details of how an action is created, which can greatly simplify the process of creating an action. For example, if we create an action called sortBy, it can decide the appropriate action to take:

```
import C from './constants'

export const sortColors = sortedBy =>
    (sortedBy === "rating") ?
        ({
            type: C.SORT_COLORS,
            sortBy: "SORTED_BY_RATING"
        }) :
        (sortedBy === "title") ?
            ({
                type: C.SORT_COLORS,
                sortBy: "SORTED_BY_TITLE"
            }) :
            ({
                type: C.SORT_COLORS,
                sortBy: "SORTED_BY_DATE"
            })
```

The sortColors action creator checks sortedBy for "rating", "title", and the default. Now there is considerably less typing involved whenever you want to dispatch a sortColors action:

```
store.dispatch( sortColors("title") )
```

Action creators can have logic. They also can help abstract away unnecessary details when creating an action. For example, take a look at the action for adding a color:

```
{
    type: "ADD_COLOR",
    id: uuid.v4(),
    title: "Party Pink",
    color: "#F142FF",
    timestamp: new Date().toString()
}
```

So far, the IDs and timestamps have been generated when the actions are dispatched. Moving this logic into an action creator would abstract the details away from the process of dispatching actions:

```
import C from './constants'
import { v4 } from 'uuid'

export const addColor = (title, color) =>
```

```
({
    type: C.ADD_COLOR,
    id: v4(),
    title,
    color,
    timestamp: new Date().toString()
})
```

The addColor action creator will generate a unique ID and will provide a timestamp. Now it's much easier to create new colors—we provide a unique ID by creating a variable that we can increment, and the timestamp is automatically set using the client's present time:

```
store.dispatch( addColor("#F142FF", "Party Pink") )
```

The really nice thing about action creators is that they provide a place to encapsulate all of the logic required to successfully create an action. The addColor action creator handles everything associated with adding new colors, including providing unique IDs and timestamping the action. It is all in one place, which makes debugging our application much easier.

Action creators are where we should put any logic for communicating with backend APIs. With an action creator, we can perform asynchronous logic like requesting data or making an API call. We will cover this in Chapter 12 when we introduce the server.

---

compose

Redux also comes with a compose function that you can use to compose several functions into a single function. It is similar to the compose function that we created in Chapter 3, but is more robust. It also composes functions from right to left as opposed to from left to right.

If we just wanted to get a comma-delimited list of color titles, we could use this one crazy line of code:

```
console.log(store.getState().colors.map(c=>c.title).join(", "))
```

A more functional approach would be to break this down into smaller functions and compose them into a single function:

```
import { compose } from 'redux'

const print = compose(
    list => console.log(list),
    titles => titles.join(", "),
    map => map(c=>c.title),
    colors => colors.map.bind(colors),
    state => state.colors
)
```

```
    print(store.getState())
```
The compose function takes in functions as arguments and invokes the rightmost first. First it obtains the colors from state, then it returns a bound map function, followed by an array of color titles, which are joined as a comma-delimited list and finally logged to the console.

Middleware

If you ever used a server-side framework such as Express, Sinatra, Django, KOA, or ASP.NET, then you are probably already familiar with the concept of *middleware*. (In case you're not, middleware serves as the glue between two different layers or different pieces of software.)

Redux also has middleware. It acts on the store's dispatch pipeline. In Redux, middleware consists of a series of functions that are executed in a row in the process of dispatching an action, as shown in Figure 8-7.

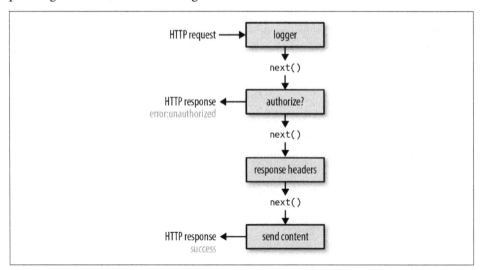

Figure 8-7. HTTP request middleware pipeline

These higher-order functions allow you to insert functionality before or after actions are dispatched and state is updated. Each middleware function is executed sequentially (Figure 8-8).

Each piece of middleware is a function that has access to the action, a dispatch function, and a function that will call next. next causes the update to occur. Before next is called, you can modify the action. After next, the state will have changed.

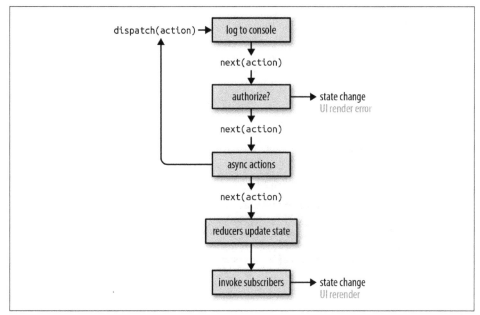

Figure 8-8. Middleware functions execute sequentially

Applying Middleware to the Store

In this section, we are going to create a `storeFactory`. A *factory* is a function that manages the process of creating stores. In this case, the factory will create a store that has middleware for logging and saving data. The `storeFactory` will be one file that contains one function that groups everything needed to create the store. Whenever we need a store, we can invoke this function:

```
const store = storeFactory(initialData)
```

When we create the store, we create two pieces of middleware: the *logger* and the *saver* (Example 8-9). The data is saved to `localStorage` with middleware instead of the `store` method.

Example 8-9. storeFactory: ./store/index.js

```
import { createStore,
         combineReducers,
         applyMiddleware } from 'redux'
import { colors, sort } from './reducers'
import stateData from './initialState'

const logger = store => next => action => {
    let result
    console.groupCollapsed("dispatching", action.type)
```

```
        console.log('prev state', store.getState())
        console.log('action', action)
        result = next(action)
        console.log('next state', store.getState())
        console.groupEnd()
        return result
}

const saver = store => next => action => {
    let result = next(action)
    localStorage['redux-store'] = JSON.stringify(store.getState())
    return result
}

const storeFactory = (initialState=stateData) =>
    applyMiddleware(logger, saver)(createStore)(
        combineReducers({colors, sort}),
        (localStorage['redux-store']) ?
            JSON.parse(localStorage['redux-store']) :
            initialState
    )

export default storeFactory
```

Both the logger and the saver are middleware functions. In Redux, middleware is defined as a higher-order function: it's a function that returns a function that returns a function. The last function returned is invoked every time an action is dispatched. When this function is invoked, you have access to the action, the store, and the function for sending the action to the next middleware.

Instead of exporting the store directly, we export a function, a factory that can be used to create stores. If this factory is invoked, then it will create and return a store that incorporates logging and saving.

In the logger, before the action is dispatched, we open a new console group and log the current state and the current action. Invoking next pipes the action on to the next piece of middleware and eventually the reducers. The state at this point has been updated, so we log the changed state and end the console group.

In the saver, we invoke next with the action, which will cause the state to change. Then we save the new state in localStorage and return the result, as in Example 8-9.

In Example 8-10 we create a store instance using the storeFactory. Since we do not send any arguments to this store, the initial state will come from state data.

Example 8-10. Creating a store using the factory

```
import storeFactory from "./store"
```

```
const store = storeFactory(true)

store.dispatch( addColor("#FFFFFF","Bright White") )
store.dispatch( addColor("#00FF00","Lawn") )
store.dispatch( addColor("#0000FF","Big Blue") )
```

Every action dispatched from this store will add a new group of logs to the console, and the new state will be saved in localStorage.

In this chapter, we looked at all of the key features of Redux: state, actions, reducers, stores, action creators, and middleware. We handled all of the state for our application with Redux, and now we can wire it up to the user interface.

In the next chapter we will take a look at the react-redux framework, a tool used to efficiently connect our Redux store to the React UI.

CHAPTER 9

React Redux

In Chapter 6, we learned how to construct React components. We built the color organizer app using React's state management system. In the last chapter, we learned how to use Redux to manage our application's state data. We completed building a store for our color organizer app that is ready to dispatch actions. In this chapter, we are going to combine the UI that we created in Chapter 6 with the store that we created in the last chapter.

The app that we developed in Chapter 6 stores state in a single object in a single location—the App component.

```
export default class App extends Component {

    constructor(props) {
        super(props)
        this.state = {
            colors: [
                {
                    "id": "8658c1d0-9eda-4a90-95e1-8001e8eb6036",
                    "title": "Ocean Blue",
                    "color": "#0070ff",
                    "rating": 3
                },
                {
                    "id": "f9005b4e-975e-433d-a646-79df172e1dbb",
                    "title": "Tomato",
                    "color": "#d10012",
                    "rating": 2
                },
                {
                    "id": "58d9caee-6ea6-4d7b-9984-65b145031979",
                    "title": "Lawn",
                    "color": "#67bf4f",
                    "rating": 1
```

```
            },
            {
                "id": "a5685c39-6bdc-4727-9188-6c9a00bf7f95",
                "title": "Party Pink",
                "color": "#ff00f7",
                "rating": 5
            }
        ]
    }
    this.addColor = this.addColor.bind(this)
    this.rateColor = this.rateColor.bind(this)
    this.removeColor = this.removeColor.bind(this)
}

addColor(title, color) {
    ...
}

rateColor(id, rating) {
    ...
}

removeColor(id) {
    ...
}

render() {
    const { addColor, rateColor, removeColor } = this
    const { colors } = this.state
    return (
        <div className="app">
            <AddColorForm onNewColor={addColor} />
            <ColorList colors={colors}
                        onRate={rateColor}
                        onRemove={removeColor} />
        </div>
    )
}

}
```

The App component is the component that holds state. State is passed down to child components as properties. Specifically, the colors are passed from the App component's state to the ColorList component as a property. When events occur, data is passed back up the component tree to the App component via callback function properties (Figure 9-1).

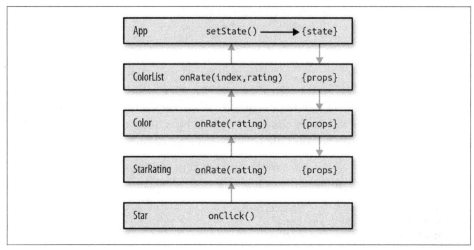

Figure 9-1. Data flow through the component tree

The process of passing data all the way down and back up the tree introduces complexity that libraries like Redux are designed to alleviate. Instead of passing data up the tree through two-way function binding, we can dispatch actions directly from child components to update application state.

In this chapter, we'll take a look at various ways to incorporate the Redux store. We will first look at how the store can be used without any additional frameworks. After that, we will explore react-redux, a framework that can be used to integrate a Redux store with React components.

Explicitly Passing the Store

The first, and most logical, way to incorporate the store into your UI is to pass it down the component tree explicitly as a property. This approach is simple and works very well for smaller apps that only have a few nested components.

Let's take a look at how we can incorporate the store into the color organizer. In the *./ index.js* file, we will render an App component and pass it the store:

```
import React from 'react'
import ReactDOM from 'react-dom'
import App from './components/App'
import storeFactory from './store'

const store = storeFactory()

const render = () =>
    ReactDOM.render(
        <App store={store}/>,
```

```
            document.getElementById('react-container')
    )

    store.subscribe(render)
    render()
```

This is the *./index.js* file. In this file, we create the store with the `storeFactory` and render the `App` component into the document. When the `App` is rendered the store is passed to it as a property. Every time the store changes, the `render` function will be invoked, which efficiently updates the UI with new state data.

Now that we have passed the store to the `App`, we have to continue to pass it down to the child components that need it:

```
    import AddColorForm from './AddColorForm'
    import SortMenu from './SortMenu'
    import ColorList from './ColorList'

    const App = ({ store }) =>
        <div className="app">
            <SortMenu store={store} />
            <AddColorForm store={store} />
            <ColorList store={store} />
        </div>

    export default App
```

The `App` component is our root component. It captures the store from props and explicitly passes it down to its child components. The store is passed to the `SortMenu`, `AddColorForm`, and `ColorList` components as a property.

Now that we have passed the store from the `App`, we can use it inside the child components. Remember we can read state from the store with `store.getState`, and we can dispatch actions to the store with `store.dispatch`.

From the `AddColorForm` component, we can use the store to dispatch `ADD_COLOR` actions. When the user submits the form, we collect the color and the title from refs and use that data to create and dispatch a new `ADD_COLOR` action:

```
    import { PropTypes, Component } from 'react'
    import { addColor } from '../actions'

    const AddColorForm = ({store}) => {

        let _title, _color

        const submit = e => {
            e.preventDefault()
            store.dispatch( addColor(_title.value, _color.value) )
            _title.value = ''
            _color.value = '#000000'
```

```
            _title.focus()
    }

    return (
        <form className="add-color" onSubmit={submit}>
            <input ref={input => _title = input}
                    type="text"
                    placeholder="color title..." required/>
            <input ref={input => _color = input}
                    type="color" required/>
            <button>ADD</button>
        </form>
    )

}

AddColorForm.propTypes = {
    store: PropTypes.object
}

export default AddColorForm
```

From this component, we import the necessary action creator, addColor. When the user submits the form, we'll dispatch a new ADD_COLOR action directly to the store using this action creator.

The ColorList component can use the store's getState method to obtain the original colors and sort them appropriately. It can also dispatch RATE_COLOR and REMOVE_COLOR actions directly as they occur:

```
import { PropTypes } from 'react'
import Color from './Color'
import { rateColor, removeColor } from '../actions'
import { sortFunction } from '../lib/array-helpers'

const ColorList = ({ store }) => {
    const { colors, sort } = store.getState()
    const sortedColors = [...colors].sort(sortFunction(sort))
    return (
        <div className="color-list">
            {(colors.length === 0) ?
                <p>No Colors Listed. (Add a Color)</p> :
                sortedColors.map(color =>
                    <Color key={color.id}
                        {...color}
                        onRate={(rating) =>
                            store.dispatch(
                                rateColor(color.id, rating)
                            )
                        }
                        onRemove={() =>
                            store.dispatch(
```

```
                              removeColor(color.id)
                        )
                    } />
            )
        }
        </div>
    )
}

ColorList.propTypes = {
    store: PropTypes.object
}

export default ColorList
```

The store has been passed all the way down the component tree to the `ColorList` component. This component interacts with the store directly. When colors are rated or removed, those actions are dispatched to the store.

The store is also used to obtain the original colors. Those colors are duplicated and sorted according to the store's `sort` property and saved as `sortedColors`. `sortedColors` is then used to create the UI.

This approach is great if your component tree is rather small, like this color organizer. The drawback of using this approach is that we have to explicitly pass the store to child components, which means slightly more code and slightly more headaches than with other approaches. Additionally, the `SortMenu`, `AddColorForm`, and `ColorList` components require this specific store. It would be hard to reuse them in another application.

In the next couple of sections, we will look at other ways to get the store to the components that need it.

Passing the Store via Context

In the last section, we created a store and passed it all the way down the component tree from the `App` component to the `ColorList` component. This approach required that we pass the store through every component that comes between the `App` and the `ColorList`.

Let's say we have some cargo to move from Washington, DC, to San Francisco, CA. We could use a train, but that would require that we lay tracks through at least nine states so that our cargo can travel to California. This is like explicitly passing the store down the component tree from the root to the leaves. You have to "lay tracks" through every component that comes between the origin and the destination. If using a train is like explicitly passing the store through props, then implicitly passing the store via context is like using a jet airliner. When a jet flies from DC to San Francisco, it flies over at least nine states—no tracks required.

Similarly, we can take advantage of a React feature called *context* that allows us to pass variables to components without having to explicitly pass them down through the tree as properties.[1] Any child component can access these context variables.

If we were to pass the store using context in our color organizer app, the first step would be to refactor the App component to hold context. The App component will also need to listen to the store so that it can trigger a UI update every time the state changes:

```
import { PropTypes, Component } from 'react'
import SortMenu from './SortMenu'
import ColorList from './ColorList'
import AddColorForm from './AddColorForm'
import { sortFunction } from '../lib/array-helpers'

class App extends Component {

    getChildContext() {
        return {
            store: this.props.store
        }
    }

    componentWillMount() {
        this.unsubscribe = store.subscribe(
            () => this.forceUpdate()
        )
    }

    componentWillUnmount() {
        this.unsubscribe()
    }

    render() {
        const { colors, sort } = store.getState()
        const sortedColors = [...colors].sort(sortFunction(sort))
        return (
            <div className="app">
                <SortMenu />
                <AddColorForm />
                <ColorList colors={sortedColors} />
            </div>
        )
    }
}
```

---

1 Dan Abramov, "Redux: Extracting Container Components" (*http://bit.ly/2mJaTr9*), Egghead.io.

```
}

App.propTypes = {
    store: PropTypes.object.isRequired
}

App.childContextTypes = {
    store: PropTypes.object.isRequired
}

export default App
```

First, adding context to a component requires that you use the getChildContext life-cycle function. It will return the object that defines the context. In this case, we add the store to the context, which we can access through props.

Next, you will need to specify childContextTypes on the component instance and define your context object. This is similar to adding propTypes or defaultProps to a component instance. However, for context to work, you must take this step.

At this point, any children of the App component will have access to the store via the context. They can invoke store.getState and store.dispatch directly. The final step is to subscribe to the store and update the component tree every time the store updates state. This can be achieved with the mounting lifecycle functions (see "Mounting Lifecycle" on page 142). In componentWillMount, we can subscribe to the store and use this.forceUpdate to trigger the updating lifecycle, which will re-render our UI. In componentWillUnmount, we can invoke the unsubscribe function and stop listening to the store. Because the App component itself triggers the UI update, there is no longer a need to subscribe to the store from the entry ./index.js file; we are listening to store changes from the same component that adds the store to the context, App.

Let's refactor the AddColorForm component to retrieve the store and dispatch the ADD_COLOR action directly:

```
const AddColorForm = (props, { store }) => {

    let _title, _color

    const submit = e => {
        e.preventDefault()
        store.dispatch(addColor(_title.value, _color.value))
        _title.value = ''
        _color.value = '#000000'
        _title.focus()
    }

    return (
        <form className="add-color" onSubmit={submit}>
```

```
                <input ref={input => _title = input}
                        type="text"
                        placeholder="color title..." required/>
                <input ref={input => _color = input}
                        type="color" required/>
                <button>ADD</button>
        </form>
    )

}

AddColorForm.contextTypes = {
    store: PropTypes.object
}
```

The context object is passed to stateless functional components as the second argument, after props. We can use object destructuring to obtain the store from this object
directly in the arguments. In order to use the store, we must define contextTypes on
the AddColorForm instance. This is where we tell React which context variables this
component will use. This is a required step. Without it, the store cannot be retrieved
from the context.

Let's take a look at how to use context in a component class. The Color component
can retrieve the store and dispatch RATE_COLOR and REMOVE_COLOR actions directly:

```
import { PropTypes, Component } from 'react'
import StarRating from './StarRating'
import TimeAgo from './TimeAgo'
import FaTrash from 'react-icons/lib/fa/trash-o'
import { rateColor, removeColor } from '../actions'

class Color extends Component {

    render() {
        const { id, title, color, rating, timestamp } = this.props
        const { store } = this.context
        return (
            <section className="color" style={this.style}>
                <h1 ref="title">{title}</h1>
                <button onClick={() =>
                    store.dispatch(
                        removeColor(id)
                    )
                }>
                    <FaTrash />
                </button>
                <div className="color"
                        style={{ backgroundColor: color }}>
                </div>
                <TimeAgo timestamp={timestamp} />
                <div>
```

```
                    <StarRating starsSelected={rating}
                          onRate={rating =>
                              store.dispatch(
                                  rateColor(id, rating)
                              )
                          } />
                </div>
            </section>
        )
    }

}

Color.contextTypes = {
    store: PropTypes.object
}

Color.propTypes = {
    id: PropTypes.string.isRequired,
    title: PropTypes.string.isRequired,
    color: PropTypes.string.isRequired,
    rating: PropTypes.number
}

Color.defaultProps = {
    rating: 0
}

export default Color
```

Color is now a component class, and can access context via this.context. Colors are now read directly from the store via store.getState. The same rules apply that do for stateless functional components. contextTypes must be defined on the instance.

Retrieving the store from the context is a nice way to reduce your boilerplate, but this is not something that is required for every application. Dan Abramov, the creator of Redux, even suggests that these patterns do not need to be religiously followed:

> Separating the container and presentational components is often a good idea, but you shouldn't take it as dogma. Only do this when it truly reduces the complexity of your codebase.[2]

Presentational Versus Container Components

In the last example, the Color component retrieved the store via context and used it to dispatch RATE_COLOR and REMOVE_COLOR actions directly. Before that, the Color

---

2 React Docs, "Context" (*https://facebook.github.io/react/docs/context.html*).

List component retrieved the store via context to read the current list of colors from state. In both examples, these components rendered UI elements by interacting directly with the Redux store. We can improve the architecture of our application by decoupling the store from components that render the UI.[3]

Presentational components are components that only render UI elements.[4] They do not tightly couple with any data architecture. Instead, they receive data as props and send data to their parent component via callback function properties. They are purely concerned with the UI and can be reused across applications that contain different data. Every component that we created in Chapter 6, with the exception of the App component, is a presentational component.

Container components are components that connect presentational components to the data. In our case, container components will retrieve the store via context and manage any interactions with the store. They render presentational components by mapping properties to state and callback function properties to the store's dispatch method. Container components are not concerned with UI elements; they are used to connect presentational components to data.

There are many benefits to this architecture. Presentational components are reusable. They are easy to swap out and easy to test. They can be composed to create the UI. Presentational components can be reused across browser applications that may use different data libraries.

Container components are not concerned with the UI at all. Their main focus is connecting the presentation components to the data architecture. Container components can be reused across device platforms to connect native presentational components to the data.

The AddColorForm, ColorList, Color, StarRating, and Star components that we created in Chapter 6 are examples of presentational components. They receive data via props, and when events occur, they invoke callback function properties. We are already pretty familiar with presentation components, so let's see how we can use them to create container components.

The App component will mostly remain the same. It still defines the store in the context so that it can be retrieved by child components. Instead of rendering the Sort Menu, AddColorForm, and ColorList components, however, it will render containers for those items. The Menu container will connect the SortMenu, NewColor will connect the AddColorForm, and Colors will connect the ColorList:

---

3 Redux Docs, "Presentational and Container Components" (*http://bit.ly/2mJ92Co*).

4 Dan Abramov, "Presentational and Container Components" (*http://bit.ly/2mJfLw4*), Medium, March 23, 2015.

```
render() {
    return (
        <div className="app">
            <Menu />
            <NewColor />
            <Colors />
        </div>
    )
}
```

Any time you want to connect a presentational component to some data, you can wrap that component in a container that controls the properties and connects them to data. The NewColor container, Menu container, and Colors container can all be defined in the same file:

```
import { PropTypes } from 'react'
import AddColorForm from './ui/AddColorForm'
import SortMenu from './ui/SortMenu'
import ColorList from './ui/ColorList'
import { addColor,
         sortColors,
         rateColor,
         removeColor } from '../actions'
import { sortFunction } from '../lib/array-helpers'

export const NewColor = (props, { store }) =>
    <AddColorForm onNewColor={(title, color) =>
                    store.dispatch(addColor(title,color))
                } />

NewColor.contextTypes = {
    store: PropTypes.object
}

export const Menu = (props, { store }) =>
    <SortMenu sort={store.getState().sort}
            onSelect={sortBy =>
                store.dispatch(sortColors(sortBy))
            } />

Menu.contextTypes = {
    store: PropTypes.object
}

export const Colors = (props, { store }) => {
    const { colors, sort } = store.getState()
    const sortedColors = [...colors].sort(sortFunction(sort))
    return (
        <ColorList colors={sortedColors}
                onRemove={id =>
                    store.dispatch( removeColor(id) )
                }
```

```
                onRate={(id, rating) =>
                    store.dispatch( rateColor(id, rating) )
                }/>
        )
    }

    Colors.contextTypes = {
        store: PropTypes.object
    }
```

The NewColor container does not render UI. Instead, it renders the AddColorForm component and handles onNewColor events from this component. This container component retrieves the store from the context and uses it to dispatch ADD_COLOR actions. It *contains* the AddColorForm component and connects it to the Redux store.

The Menu container renders the SortMenu component. It passes the current sort property from the store's state and dispatches sort actions when the user selects a different menu item.

The Colors container retrieves the store via context and renders a ColorList component with colors from the store's current state. It also handles onRate and onRemove events invoked from the ColorList component. When these events occur, the Colors container dispatches the appropriate actions.

All of the Redux functionality is connected here in this file. Notice that all of the action creators are being imported and used in one place. This is the only file that invokes store.getState or store.dispatch.

This approach of separating UI components from containers that connect them to data is generally a good approach. However, this could be overkill for a small project, proof of concept, or prototype.

In the next section, we introduce a new library, React Redux. This library can be used to quickly add the Redux store to context and create container components.

The React Redux Provider

React Redux is a library that contains some tools to help ease the complexity involved with implicitly passing the store via context. This library is also brought to you by Dan Abramov, the creator of Redux. Redux does not require that you use this library. However, using React Redux reduces your code's complexity and may help you build apps a bit faster.

In order to use React Redux, we must first install it. It can be installed via npm (*https://www.npmjs.com/package/react-redux*):

```
npm install react-redux --save
```

react-redux supplies us with a component that we can use to set up our store in the context, the *provider*. We can wrap any React element with the provider and that element's children will have access to the store via context.

Instead of setting up the store as a context variable in the App component, we can keep the App component stateless:

```
import { Menu, NewColor, Colors } from './containers'

const App = () =>
    <div className="app">
        <Menu />
        <NewColor />
        <Colors />
    </div>

export default App
```

The provider adds the store to the context and updates the App component when actions have been dispatched. The provider expects a single child component:

```
import React from 'react'
import { render } from 'react-dom'
import { Provider } from 'react-redux'
import App from './components/App'
import storeFactory from './store'

const store = storeFactory()

render(
    <Provider store={store}>
        <App />
    </Provider>,
    document.getElementById('react-container')
)
```

The provider requires that we pass the store as a property. It adds the store to the context so that it can be retrieved by any child of the App component. Simply using the provider can save us some time and simplify our code.

Once we've incorporated the provider, we can retrieve the store via context in child container components. However, React Redux provides us with another way to quickly create container components that work with the provider: the connect function.

React Redux connect

If we keep our UI components purely presentational, we can rely on React Redux to create the container components. React Redux helps us create container components through mapping the current state of the Redux store to the properties of a presentational component. It also maps the store's `dispatch` function to callback properties. This is all accomplished through a higher-order function called `connect`.

Let's create the `Colors` container component using `connect`. The `Colors` container connects the `ColorList` component to the store:

```
import ColorList from './ColorList'

const mapStateToProps = state =>
    ({
        colors: [...state.colors].sort(sortFunction(state.sort))
    })

const mapDispatchToProps = dispatch =>
    ({
        onRemove(id) {
            dispatch(removeColor(id))
        },
        onRate(id, rating) {
            dispatch(rateColor(id, rating))
        }
    })

export const Colors = connect(
    mapStateToProps,
    mapDispatchToProps
)(ColorList)
```

`connect` is a higher-order function that returns a function that returns a component. No, that's not a typo or a tongue-twister: it's functional JavaScript. `connect` expects two arguments: `mapStateToProps` and `mapDispatchToProps`. Both are functions. It returns a function that expects a presentational component, and wraps it with a container that sends it data via props.

The first function, `mapStateToProps`, injects state as an argument and returns an object that will be mapped to props. We set the `colors` property of the `ColorList` component to an array of sorted colors from state.

The second function, `mapDispatchToProps`, injects the store's `dispatch` function as an argument that can be used when the `ColorList` component invokes callback function properties. When the `ColorList` raises `onRate` or `onRemove` events, data about the color to rate or remove is obtained and dispatched.

`connect` works in conjunction with the provider. The provider adds the store to the context and `connect` creates components that retrieve the store. When using `connect`, you do not have to worry about context.

All of our containers can be created using the React Redux connect function in a single file:

```
import { connect } from 'react-redux'
import AddColorForm from './ui/AddColorForm'
import SortMenu from './ui/SortMenu'
import ColorList from './ui/ColorList'
import { addColor,
         sortColors,
         rateColor,
         removeColor } from '../actions'
import { sortFunction } from '../lib/array-helpers'

export const NewColor = connect(
    null,
    dispatch =>
        ({
            onNewColor(title, color) {
                dispatch(addColor(title,color))
            }
        })
)(AddColorForm)

export const Menu = connect(
    state =>
        ({
            sort: state.sort
        }),
    dispatch =>
        ({
            onSelect(sortBy) {
                dispatch(sortColors(sortBy))
            }
        })
)(SortMenu)

export const Colors = connect(
    state =>
        ({
            colors: [...state.colors].sort(sortFunction(state.sort))
        }),
    dispatch =>
        ({
            onRemove(id) {
                dispatch(removeColor(id))
            },
            onRate(id, rating) {
                dispatch(rateColor(id, rating))
            }
        })
)(ColorList)
```

In this example, each of our containers are defined using React Redux's connect function. The connect function connects Redux to purely presentational components. The first argument is a function that maps state variables to properties. The second argument is a function that dispatches actions when events are raised. If you only want to map callback function properties to dispatch you can provide null as a placeholder for the first argument, as we have in the definition of the NewColor container.

In this chapter, we looked at various ways to connect Redux to React. We explicitly passed the store down the component tree to children as a property. We implicitly passed the store directly to the components that need to use it via context. We decoupled the store's functionality from our presentation through the use of container components. And finally, we used react-redux to help us rapidly connect the store to presentation using context and container components.

At this point we have a working app that uses React and Redux together. In the next chapter, we will look at how we can write unit tests for all of the various parts of this application.

CHAPTER 10

Testing

In order to keep up with our competitors, we must move quickly while ensuring quality. One vital tool that allows us to do this is *unit testing*. Unit testing makes it possible to verify that every piece, or unit, of our application functions as intended.[1]

One benefit of practicing functional techniques is that they lend themselves to writing testable code. Pure functions are naturally testable. Immutability is easily testable. Composing applications out of small functions designed for specific tasks produces testable functions or units of code.

In this section, we will demonstrate techniques that can be used to unit test React Redux applications. This chapter will not only cover testing, but also tools that can be used to help evaluate and improve your code and your tests.

ESLint

In most programming languages, code needs to be compiled before you can run anything. Programming languages have pretty strict rules about coding style and will not compile until the code is formatted appropriately. JavaScript does not have those rules and does not come with a compiler. We write code, cross our fingers, and run it in the browser to see if it works or not. The good news is that there are tools that we can use to analyze our code and make us stick to specific formatting guidelines.

The process of analyzing JavaScript code is called *hinting* or *linting*. JSHint and JSLint are the original tools used to analyze JavaScript and provide feedback about formatting. ESLint (*http://eslint.org*) is the latest code linter that supports emerging Java-

---

1 For a brief introduction to unit testing, see Martin Fowler's article, "Unit Testing" (*http://martinfowler.com/bliki/UnitTest.html*).

Script syntax. Additionally, ESLint is pluggable. This means that we can create and share plugins that can be added to ESLint configurations to extend its capabilities.

We will be working with a plugin called `eslint-plugin-react` (*http://bit.ly/2kuEylV*). This plugin will analyze our JSX and React syntax in addition to our JavaScript.

Let's install `eslint` globally. You can install `eslint` with npm:

```
sudo npm install -g eslint
```

Before we use ESLint, we'll need to define some configuration rules that we can agree to follow. We'll define these in a configuration file that is located in our project root. This file can be formatted as JSON or YAML. YAML (*http://yaml.org*) is a data serialization formation like JSON but with less syntax, making it a little easier for humans to read.

ESLint comes with a tool that helps us set up configuration. There are several companies that have created ESLint config files that we can use as a starting point, or we can create our own.

We can create an ESLint configuration by running `eslint --init` and answering some questions about our coding style:

```
$ eslint --init

? How would you like to configure ESLint?
Answer questions about your style

? Are you using ECMAScript 6 features? Yes
? Are you using ES6 modules? Yes
? Where will your code run? Browser
? Do you use CommonJS? Yes
? Do you use JSX? Yes
? Do you use React? Yes
? What style of indentation do you use? Spaces
? What quotes do you use for strings? Single
? What line endings do you use? Unix
? Do you require semicolons? No
? What format do you want your config file to be in? YAML

Local ESLint installation not found.
Installing eslint, eslint-plugin-react
```

After `eslint --init` runs, three things happen:

1. ESLint and `eslint-plugin-react` are installed locally to the *./node_modules* folder.

2. These dependencies are automatically added to the *package.json* file.

3. A configuration file, *.eslintrc.yml*, is created and added to the root of our project.

Let's test our ESLint configuration out by creating a *sample.js* file:

```
const gnar ="gnarly";

const info = ({file=__filename, dir=__dirname}) =>
  <p>{dir}: {file}</p>

switch(gnar) {
    default :
        console.log('gnarley')
        break
}
```

This file has some issues, but nothing that would cause errors in the browser. Technically, this code works just fine. Let's run ESLint on this file and see what feedback we get based upon our customized rules:

```
$ ./node_modules/.bin/eslint sample.js

/Users/alexbanks/Desktop/eslint-learn/sample.js
  1:20  error  Strings must use singlequote          quotes
  1:28  error  Extra semicolon                       semi
  3:7   error  'info' is defined but never used      no-unused-vars
  3:28  error  '__filename' is not defined           no-undef
  3:44  error  '__dirname' is not defined            no-undef
  7:5   error  Expected indentation of 0 space ch... indent
  8:9   error  Expected indentation of 4 space ch... indent
  8:9   error  Unexpected console statement          no-console
  9:9   error  Expected indentation of 4 space ch... indent

✖ 9 problems (9 errors, 0 warnings)
```

ESLint has analyzed our sample and is reporting some issues based upon our configuration choices. We see here that ESLint is complaining about the use of double quotes and a semicolon on line 1 because we have specified single quotes only and no semicolons in our *.eslintrc.yml* configuration file. Next, ESLint complains about the info function being defined but never used; ESLint hates that. ESLint also complains about __filename and __dirname because it does not automatically include Node.js globals. And finally, ESLint does not like the indentation of our switch statement or the use of a console statement.

We can modify our ESLint configuration, *.eslintrc.yml*, to make it less strict:

```
env:
  browser: true
  commonjs: true
  es6: true
extends: 'eslint:recommended'
parserOptions:
  ecmaFeatures:
    experimentalObjectRestSpread: true
    jsx: true
```

```yaml
        sourceType: module
    plugins:
      - react
    rules:
      indent:
        - error
        - 4
        - SwitchCase: 1
      quotes:
        - error
        - single
      semi:
        - error
        - never
      linebreak-style:
        - error
        - unix
      no-console: 0
    globals:
        __filename: true
        __dirname: true
```

Upon opening *.eslintrc.yml*, you'll first notice that the file is readable and approacha-ble—that is the goal of YAML. Here, we've modified the indentation rules to allow for the indentation of switch statements. Next we've added a no-console rule, which will prevent ESLint from complaining about the console.log statement. Finally, we've added a couple of global variables for ESLint to ignore.

We'll still need to make a couple of changes to our file in order to follow our style guide:

```javascript
const gnar = 'gnarly'

export const info = ({file=__filename, dir=__dirname}) =>
  <p>{dir}: {file}</p>

switch(gnar) {
    default :
        console.log('gnarly')
        break
}
```

We've removed the semicolon and double quotes from line 1. Also, exporting the info function means ESLint will no longer complain about it being unused. Between modifying the ESLint configuration and making some changes to our code, we have a file that passes the code-formatting test.

The command eslint . will lint your entire directory. In order to do this, you will most likely require that ESLint ignore some JavaScript files. The *.eslintignore* file is where you can add files or directories for ESLint to ignore:

```
dist/assets/
sample.js
```

This *.eslintignore* file tells ESLint to ignore our new *sample.js* file, as well as anything in the *dist/assets* folder. If we do not ignore the *assets* folder, ESLint will analyze the client *bundle.js* file and it will find a lot to complain about in that file.

Let's add a script to our *package.json* file for running lint:

```
"scripts": {
    "lint": "./node_modules/.bin/eslint ."
}
```

Now ESLint can be run any time we want with `npm run lint`, and it will analyze all of the files in our project except the ones we have ignored.

Testing Redux

Testing is essential for Redux because it only works with data—it does not have a UI. Redux is naturally testable because its reducers are pure functions, and it is easy to inject state into a store. Writing a reducer test first makes it easy to understand how the reducer is supposed to work. And writing tests for your store and your action creators will give you confidence that your client data layer is working as intended.

In this section, we will write some unit tests for the Redux components of the color organizer.

Test-Driven Development

Test-driven development, or TDD, is a practice—not a technology. It does not mean that you simply have tests for your application. Rather, it is the practice of letting the tests drive the development process. In order to practice TDD, you must follow these steps:

Write the tests first
> This is the most critical step. You declare what you are building and how it should work first in a test.

Run the tests and watch them fail (red)
> Run your tests and watch them fail before you write the code.

Write the minimal amount of code required to make the tests pass (green)
> Now all you have to do is make the tests pass. Focus specifically on making each test pass; do not add any functionality beyond the scope of the test.

Refactor both the code and the tests (gold)
> Once the tests pass, it is time to take a closer look at your code and your tests. Try to express your code as simply and as beautifully as possible.[2]

TDD is an excellent way to approach a Redux application. It is typically easier to reason about how a reducer should work before actually writing the reducer. Practicing TDD will allow you to build and certify the entire data structure for a feature or application independent of the UI.

TDD and Learning

If you are new to TDD, or new to the language that you are testing, you may find it challenging to write a test before writing code. This is to be expected, and it is OK to write the code before the test until you get the hang of it. Try to work in small batches: a little bit of code, a few tests, and so on. Once you get the hang of how to write a test, it will be easier to write the tests first.

For the remainder of this chapter, we will be writing tests for code that already exists. Technically, we are not practicing TDD. However, in the next section we will pretend that our code does not already exist so we can get a feel for the TDD workflow.

Testing Reducers

Reducers (*http://bit.ly/2kuCR82*) are pure functions that calculate and return results based upon the input arguments. In a test, we get to control the input, the current state, and the action. Given a current state and an action, we should be able to predict a reducer's output.

Before we can get started writing tests, we will need to install a testing framework. You can write tests for React and Redux with any JavaScript testing framework. We'll use Jest, a JavaScript testing framework that was designed with React in mind:

```
sudo npm install -g jest
```

This command installs Jest and the Jest CLI globally. You can now run the `jest` command from any folder to run the tests.

Since we are using emerging JavaScript and React, we will need to transpile our code and our tests before they can run. Just install the `babel-jest` package to make that possible:

```
npm install --save-dev babel-jest
```

---

2 For more on this development pattern, see Jeff McWherter and James Bender, "Red, Green, Refactor" (*http://bit.ly/2kXvDN3*).

With `babel-jest` installed, all of your code and tests will be transpiled with Babel before the tests run. A *.babelrc* file is required for this to work, but we should already have one in the root of our project.

create-react-app

Projects that were initialized with `create-react-app` already come with the `jest` and `babel-jest` packages installed. They also create a *__tests__* directory in the root of the project.

Jest has two important functions for setting up tests: `describe` and `it`. `describe` is used to create a suite of tests, and `it` is used for each test. Both functions expect the name of the test or suite and a callback function that contains the test or suite of tests.

Let's create a test file and stub our tests. Create a folder called *./__tests__/store/reducers*, and in it create a new JavaScript file called *color.test.js*:

```
describe("color Reducer", () => {

    it("ADD_COLOR success")

    it("RATE_COLOR success")

})
```

In this example, we create a suite of tests for the color reducer by stubbing a test for each action that affects the reducer. Each test is defined with the `it` function. You can set up a pending test by only sending a single argument to the `it` function.

Run this test with the `jest` command. Jest will run and report that it has skipped our two pending tests:

```
$ jest

Test Suites: 1 skipped, 0 of 1 total
Tests:       2 skipped, 2 total
Snapshots:   0 total
Time:        0.863s

Ran all test suites.
```

Test Files

Jest will run any tests found in the *__tests__* directory, and any JavaScript files in your project whose names end with *.test.js*. Some developers prefer to place their tests directly next to the files they are testing, while others prefer to group their tests in a single folder.

It is now time to write both of these tests. Since we are testing the color reducer, we will import that function specifically. The color reducer function is referred to as our *system under test* (SUT). We will import this function, send it an action, and verify the results.

Jest "matchers" are returned by the expect function and used to verify results. To test the color reducer we will use the .toEqual matcher. This verifies that the resulting object matches the argument sent to .toEqual:

```
import C from '../../../src/constants'
import { color } from '../../../src/store/reducers'

describe("color Reducer", () => {

    it("ADD_COLOR success", () => {
        const state = {}
        const action = {
            type: C.ADD_COLOR,
            id: 0,
            title: 'Test Teal',
            color: '#90C3D4',
            timestamp: new Date().toString()
        }
        const results = color(state, action)
        expect(results)
            .toEqual({
                id: 0,
                title: 'Test Teal',
                color: '#90C3D4',
                timestamp: action.timestamp,
                rating: 0
            })
    })

    it("RATE_COLOR success", () => {
        const state = {
            id: 0,
            title: 'Test Teal',
            color: '#90C3D4',
            timestamp: 'Sat Mar 12 2016 16:12:09 GMT-0800 (PST)',
            rating: undefined
        }
        const action = {
            type: C.RATE_COLOR,
            id: 0,
            rating: 3
        }
        const results = color(state, action)
        expect(results)
            .toEqual({
                id: 0,
```

```
                title: 'Test Teal',
                color: '#90C3D4',
                timestamp: 'Sat Mar 12 2016 16:12:09 GMT-0800 (PST)',
                rating: 3
            })
        })

    })
```

To test a reducer, we need a state and a sample action. We obtain the result by invoking our SUT, the color function, with these sample objects. Finally, we check the result to make sure the appropriate state was returned using the .toEqual matcher.

To test ADD_COLOR, the initial state doesn't matter much. However, when we send the color reducer an ADD_COLOR action, it should return a new color object.

To test RATE_COLOR, we'll provide an initial color object with a rating of 0 for the assumed state. Sending this state object along with a RATE_COLOR action should result in a color object that has our new rating.

Now that we have written our tests, if we are pretending that we do not already have the code for the color reducer, we need to stub that function. We can stub the color reducer by adding a function called color to our */src/store/reducers.js* file. This will allow our tests to find the empty reducer and import it:

```
import C from '../constants'

export const color = (state={}, action=) => {
    return state
}
```

Why Stub the Reducer First?

Without a SUT in place, we would get an error in the test:

```
TypeError: (0 , _reducers.color) is not a function
```

This error occurs when the function that we are testing, color, is not defined. Simply adding the definition for the function that you wish to test will provide more detailed test failure feedback.

Let's run the tests and watch them fail. Jest will provide specific details on each failure, including a stack trace:

```
$ jest

 FAIL  __tests__/store/reducers/color.test.js
  ● color Reducer › ADD_COLOR success

    expect(received).toEqual(expected)
```

```
Expected value to equal:
  {"color": "#90C3D4", "id": 0, "rating": 0, "timestamp":
  "Mon Mar 13 2017 12:29:12 GMT-0700 (PDT)", "title": "Test Teal"}

Received:
  {}

Difference:

- Expected
+ Received

@@ -1,7 +1,1 @@
-Object {
-  "color": "#90C3D4",
-  "id": 0,
-  "rating": 0,
-  "timestamp": "Mon Mar 13 2017 12:29:12 GMT-0700 (PDT)",
-  "title": "Test Teal",
-}

+Object {}

  at Object.<anonymous> (__tests__/store/reducers/color.test.js:19:9)
  at process._tickCallback (internal/process/next_tick.js:103:7)
```

● color Reducer › RATE_COLOR success

```
  expect(received).toEqual(expected)

  Expected value to equal:
    {"color": "#90C3D4", "id": 0, "rating": 3, "timestamp":
    "Sat Mar 12 2016 16:12:09 GMT-0800 (PST)", "title": "Test Teal"}

  Received:
    {"color": "#90C3D4", "id": 0, "rating": undefined, "timestamp":
    "Sat Mar 12 2016 16:12:09 GMT-0800 (PST)", "title": "Test Teal"}

  Difference:

  - Expected
  + Received

  @@ -1,7 +1,7 @@
   Object {
     "color": "#90C3D4",
     "id": 0,
  -  "rating": 3,
  +  "rating": undefined,
     "timestamp": "Sat Mar 12 2016 16:12:09 GMT-0800 (PST)",
     "title": "Test Teal",
   }
```

```
        at Object.<anonymous> (__tests__/store/reducers/color.test.js:44:9)
        at process._tickCallback (internal/process/next_tick.js:103:7)

  color Reducer

    × ADD_COLOR success (8ms)
    × RATE_COLOR success (1ms)

Test Suites: 1 failed, 1 total
Tests:       2 failed, 2 total
Snapshots:   0 total
Time:        0.861s, estimated 1s
Ran all test suites.
```

Taking the time to write the tests and run them to watch them fail shows us that our tests are working as intended. This failure feedback represents our to-do list. It is our job to make both of these tests pass.

It's time to open the */src/store/reducers.js* file and write the minimal code required to make our tests pass:

```
import C from '../constants'

export const color = (state={}, action=) => {
    switch (action.type) {
        case C.ADD_COLOR:
            return {
                id: action.id,
                title: action.title,
                color: action.color,
                timestamp: action.timestamp,
                rating: 0
            }
        case C.RATE_COLOR:
            state.rating = action.rating
            return state
        default :
            return state
    }
}
```

The next time we run the `jest` command our tests should pass:

```
$ jest

 PASS  __tests__/store/reducers/color.test.js
  color Reducer

    ✓ ADD_COLOR success (4ms)
    ✓ RATE_COLOR success

Test Suites: 1 passed, 1 total
```

```
Tests:       2 passed, 2 total
Snapshots:   0 total
Time:        0.513s, estimated 1s

Ran all test suites.
```

The tests passed, but we are not finished. It is time to refactor both our tests and the code. Take a look at the RATE_COLOR case in the reducer:

```
case 'RATE_COLOR':
  state.rating = action.rating
  return state
```

If you look closely, this code should seem a little off. State is supposed to be immutable, yet here we are clearly mutating the state by changing the value for rating in the state object. Our tests still pass because we are not making sure that our state object is immutable.

deep-freeze (*https://github.com/substack/deep-freeze*) can help us make sure our state and action objects stay immutable by preventing them from changing:

```
npm install deep-freeze --save-dev
```

When invoking the color reducer, we will deep-freeze both the state and the action object. Both objects should be immutable, and deep-freezing them will cause an error if any code does try to mutate these objects:

```
import C from '../../../src/constants'
import { color } from '../../../src/store/reducers'
import deepFreeze from 'deep-freeze'

describe("color Reducer", () => {

    it("ADD_COLOR success", () => {
        const state = {}
        const action = {
            type: C.ADD_COLOR,
            id: 0,
            title: 'Test Teal',
            color: '#90C3D4',
            timestamp: new Date().toString()
        }
        deepFreeze(state)
        deepFreeze(action)
        expect(color(state, action))
            .toEqual({
                id: 0,
                title: 'Test Teal',
                color: '#90C3D4',
                timestamp: action.timestamp,
                rating: 0
            })
```

```
    })

    it("RATE_COLOR success", () => {
        const state = {
            id: 0,
            title: 'Test Teal',
            color: '#90C3D4',
            timestamp: 'Sat Mar 12 2016 16:12:09 GMT-0800 (PST)',
            rating: undefined
        }
        const action = {
            type: C.RATE_COLOR,
            id: 0,
            rating: 3
        }
        deepFreeze(state)
        deepFreeze(action)
        expect(color(state, action))
            .toEqual({
                id: 0,
                title: 'Test Teal',
                color: '#90C3D4',
                timestamp: 'Sat Mar 12 2016 16:12:09 GMT-0800 (PST)',
                rating: 3
            })
    })

})
```

Now we can run our modified test on our current color reducer and watch it fail, because rating a color mutates the incoming state:

```
$ jest

  FAIL  __tests__/store/reducers/color.test.js
   ● color Reducer › RATE_COLOR success

     TypeError: Cannot assign to read only property 'rating' of object '#<Object>'
       at color (src/store/reducers.js:14:26)
       at Object.<anonymous> (__tests__/store/reducers/color.test.js:43:36)
       at process._tickCallback (internal/process/next_tick.js:103:7)

   color Reducer

     ✓ ADD_COLOR success (3ms)
     ✕ RATE_COLOR success (3ms)

Test Suites: 1 failed, 1 total
Tests:       1 failed, 1 passed, 2 total
Snapshots:   0 total
Time:        0.513s, estimated 1s

Ran all test suites.
```

Let's change the color reducer so that this test will pass. We will use the spread operator to make a copy of the state object before we overwrite the rating:

```
case 'RATE_COLOR':
    return {
        ...state,
        rating: action.rating
    }
```

Now that we are not mutating state, both tests should pass:

```
$ jest

 PASS  __tests__/store/reducers/color.test.js

  color Reducer

    ✓ ADD_COLOR success (3ms)
    ✓ RATE_COLOR success

Test Suites: 1 passed, 1 total
Tests:       2 passed, 2 total
Snapshots:   0 total
Time:        0.782s, estimated 1s

Ran all test suites.
```

This process represents a typical TDD cycle. We wrote the tests first, wrote code to make the tests pass, and refactored both the code and the tests. This approach is very effective when working with JavaScript, and especially Redux.

Testing the Store

If the store works, there is a good chance that your app is going to work. The process for testing the store involves creating a store with your reducers, injecting an assumed state, dispatching actions, and verifying the results.

While testing the store you can integrate your action creators and kill two birds with one stone, testing the store and the action creators together.

In Chapter 8, we created a `storeFactory`, a function that we can use to manage the store creation process in the color organizer app:

```
import { createStore,
         combineReducers,
         applyMiddleware } from 'redux'
import { colors, sort } from './reducers'
import stateData from '../../data/initialState'

const logger = store => next => action => {
    let result
    console.groupCollapsed("dispatching", action.type)
```

```
        console.log('prev state', store.getState())
        console.log('action', action)
        result = next(action)
        console.log('next state', store.getState())
        console.groupEnd()
        return result
}

const saver = store => next => action => {
    let result = next(action)
    localStorage['redux-store'] = JSON.stringify(store.getState())
    return result
}

const storeFactory = (initialState=stateData) =>
    applyMiddleware(logger, saver)(createStore)(
        combineReducers({colors, sort}),
        (localStorage['redux-store']) ?
            JSON.parse(localStorage['redux-store']) :
            initialState
    )

export default storeFactory
```

This module exports a function that we can use to create stores. It abstracts away the details of creating a store for the color organizer. This file contains the reducers, middleware, and default state necessary to create a store for our app. When creating a store with the storeFactory, we can optionally pass in an initial state for our new store, which will help us when it is time to test this store.

Jest has setup and teardown features that allow you to execute some code before and after executing each test or suite. beforeAll and afterAll are invoked before and after each test suite is executed, respectively. beforeEach and afterEach are invoked before or after each it statement is executed.

Setup and Teardown

A good practice to follow when writing tests is to allow only one assertion for each test.[3] This means that you want to avoid calling expect multiple times within a single it statement. This way, each assertion can be independently verified, making it easier to figure out what went wrong when tests fail.

Jest's setup and teardown features can be used to help you follow this practice. Execute your test code in a beforeAll statement and verify the results with multiple it statements.

---

3 See Jay Fields, "Testing: One Assertion per Test" (*http://bit.ly/2kuK2Nf*), June 6, 2007.

Let's see how we can test the store while testing the `addColor` action creator in the file *./__tests__/actions-spec.js*. The following example will test our store by dispatching an `addColor` action creator and verifying the results:

```
import C from '../src/constants'
import storeFactory from '../src/store'
import { addColor } from '../src/actions'

describe("addColor", () => {

    let store
    const colors = [
        {
            id: "8658c1d0-9eda-4a90-95e1-8001e8eb6036",
            title: "lawn",
            color: "#44ef37",
            timestamp: "Mon Apr 11 2016 12:54:19 GMT-0700 (PDT)",
            rating: 4
        },
        {
            id: "f9005b4e-975e-433d-a646-79df172e1dbb",
            title: "ocean blue",
            color: "#0061ff",
            timestamp: "Mon Apr 11 2016 12:54:31 GMT-0700 (PDT)",
            rating: 2
        },
        {
            id: "58d9caee-6ea6-4d7b-9984-65b145031979",
            title: "tomato",
            color: "#ff4b47",
            timestamp: "Mon Apr 11 2016 12:54:43 GMT-0700 (PDT)",
            rating: 0
        }
    ]

    beforeAll(() => {
        store = storeFactory({colors})
        store.dispatch(addColor("Dark Blue", "#000033"))
    })

    it("should add a new color", () =>
        expect(store.getState().colors.length).toBe(4))

    it("should add a unique guid id", () =>
        expect(store.getState().colors[3].id.length).toBe(36))

    it("should set the rating to 0", () =>
        expect(store.getState().colors[3].rating).toBe(0))

    it("should set timestamp", () =>
        expect(store.getState().colors[3].timestamp).toBeDefined())
```

```
})
```

We set up the test by using the `storeFactory` to create a new store instance that contains three sample colors in the state. Next, we dispatch our `addColor` action creator to add a fourth color to the state: Dark Blue.

Each test now verifies the results of the dispatched action. They each contain one `expect` statement. If any of these tests were to fail, we would know exactly what field of the new action was causing issues.

This time we used two new matchers: `.toBe` and `.toBeDefined`. The `.toBe` matcher compares the results using the `===` operator. This matcher can be used to compare primitives like numbers or strings, whereas the `.toEqual` matcher is used to deeply compare objects. The `.toBeDefined` matcher can be used to check for the existence of a variable or a function. In this test, we check for the existence of the timestamp.

These tests verify that our store can successfully add new colors using the action creator. This should give us some confidence in our store code: it's working.

Testing React Components

React components provide instructions for React to follow when creating and managing updates to the DOM. We can test these components by rendering them and checking the resulting DOM.

We are not running our tests in a browser; we are running them in the terminal with Node.js. Node.js does not have the DOM API that comes standard with each browser. Jest incorporates an npm package called `jsdom` that is used to simulate a browser environment in Node.js, which is essential for testing React components.

Setting Up the Jest Environment

Jest provides us with the ability to run a script before any tests are run where we can set up additional global variables that can be used in any of our tests.

For example, let's say we wanted to add React to the global scope along with some sample colors that can be accessed by any of our tests. We could create a file called /_tests_/global.js:

```
import React from 'react'
import deepFreeze from 'deep-freeze'

global.React = React
global._testColors = deepFreeze([
    {
        id: "8658c1d0-9eda-4a90-95e1-8001e8eb6036",
        title: "lawn",
```

```
            color: "#44ef37",
            timestamp: "Sun Apr 10 2016 12:54:19 GMT-0700 (PDT)",
            rating: 4
    },
    {
            id: "f9005b4e-975e-433d-a646-79df172e1dbb",
            title: "ocean blue",
            color: "#0061ff",
            timestamp: "Mon Apr 11 2016 12:54:31 GMT-0700 (PDT)",
            rating: 2
    },
    {
            id: "58d9caee-6ea6-4d7b-9984-65b145031979",
            title: "tomato",
            color: "#ff4b47",
            timestamp: "Fri Apr 15 2016 12:54:43 GMT-0700 (PDT)",
            rating: 0
    }
])
```

This file adds React and some immutable test colors to the global scope. Next, we have to tell Jest to run this file before running our tests. We can do this by adding a setupFiles field to the jest node in *package.json*:

```
"jest": {
    "setupFiles": ["./__tests__/global.js"],
    "modulePathIgnorePatterns": ["global.js"]
}
```

The setupFiles field is used to provide an array of files that Jest should run to set up the global environment before our tests. The modulePathIgnorePatterns field tells Jest to ignore the *global.js* file when running the tests because it does not contain a test suite; it is a setup file. This field is necessary because we'd prefer to add the *global.js* file to the *__tests__* folder even though it does not contain any tests.

Ignoring SCSS imports

If you import SCSS (or CSS or SASS) files directly into your components, you will need to ignore these imports while testing. If you do not ignore them, they will cause the tests to fail.

These files can be ignored by incorporating a module mapper that returns an empty string when *.css*, *.scss*, or *.less* files are imported. Let's install jest-css-modules:

```
npm install jest-css-modules --save-dev
```

Now that we have this package installed, we need to tell Jest to use this module in place of any *.scss* import. We need to add a moduleNameMapper field to the jest node in our *package.json* file:

```
"jest": {
    "setupFiles": ["./__tests__/global.js"],
    "modulePathIgnorePatterns": ["global.js"],
    "moduleNameMapper": {
      "\\.(scss)$": "<rootDir>/node_modules/jest-css-modules"
    }
}
```

This tells Jest to use the `jest-css-modules` module in place of any import that ends with *.scss*. Adding these lines of code to your *package.json* file will prevent your tests from failing due to *.scss* imports.

Enzyme

We are almost ready to begin testing our React components. We only have two more npm modules to install before we begin writing our first component test:

```
npm install enzyme react-addons-test-utils --save-dev
```

Enzyme (*http://airbnb.io/enzyme/*) is a testing utility for React components designed at Airbnb. Enzyme requires `react-addons-test-utils`, a set of tools that can be used to render and interact with components during a test. Additionally, `react-dom` is required, but we'll assume that you already have `react-dom` installed.

Enzyme makes it easier to render a component and traverse the rendered output. Enzyme is not a testing or assertion framework. It handles the task of rendering React components for testing and provides the necessary tools for traversing child elements, verifying props, verifying state, simulating events, and querying the DOM.

Enzyme has three main methods for rendering:

shallow

> `shallow` renders components one level deep for unit testing.

mount

> `mount` renders components using the browser DOM and is necessary when you need to test the full component lifecycle and the properties or state of child elements.

render

> `render` is used to render static HTML markup with a component. With `render`, you can verify that your component returns the appropriate HTML.

Consider the `Star` component:

```
const Star = ({ selected=false, onClick=f=>f }) =>
    <div className={(selected) ? "star selected" : "star"}
        onClick={onClick}>
    </div>
```

It should render a `div` element with a `className` that depends upon the selected property. It should also respond to click events.

Let's write a test for the `Star` component with Enzyme. We will use Enzyme to render the component and find specific DOM elements within the rendered `Star`. We can use the `shallow` method to render our component one level deep:

```
import { shallow } from 'enzyme'
import Star from '../../../src/components/ui/Star'

describe("<Star /> UI Component", () => {

    it("renders default star", () =>
        expect(
            shallow(<Star />)
                .find('div.star')
                .length
        ).toBe(1)
    )

    it("renders selected stars", () =>
        expect(
            shallow(<Star selected={true} />)
                .find('div.selected.star')
                .length
        ).toBe(1)
    )

})
```

Enzyme comes with functions that somewhat resemble jQuery's. We can use the `find` method to query the resulting DOM using selector syntax.

In the first test, a sample Star is rendered and we verify that it results in a DOM that contains a `div` element that has the `star` class. In the second test, a sample selected Star is rendered and we verify that the resulting DOM contains a `div` element with both the `star` class and the `selected` class. Checking the length assures us that only one `div` was rendered in each test.

Next, we'll need to test the click event. Enzyme comes with tools that allow us to simulate events and verify that those events have occurred. For this test, we need a function that we can use to verify that the `onClick` property is working. We need a mock function, and Jest has us covered:

```
it("invokes onClick", () => {

    const _click = jest.fn()

    shallow(<Star onClick={_click} />)
            .find('div.star')
```

```
        .simulate('click')

    expect(_click).toBeCalled()

  })
```

In this test a mock function, _click, is created using jest.fn. When we render the Star, we send our mock function as the onClick property. Next, we locate the rendered div element and simulate a click event on that element using Enzyme's simulate method. Clicking the Star should invoke the onClick property and, in turn, invoke our mock function. The .toBeCalled matcher can be used to verify that a mock function was invoked.

Enzyme can be used to help us render components, find rendered DOM elements or other components, and interact with them.

Mocking Components

The last test introduced the concept of mocking: we used a mock function to test the Star component. Jest is full of tools to help us create and inject all sorts of different mocks that can help us write better tests. Mocking is an important testing technique that can help focus unit tests. Mocks are objects that are used in place of real objects for the purposes of testing.[4]

Mocks are to the test world what stunt doubles are to Hollywood. Both mocks and stunt doubles are used in place of the real deal (component or movie star). In a film, the stunt double looks like the real actor. In a test, a mocked object looks like the real object.

The purpose of mocking is to allow you to focus your tests on the one component or object that you are trying to test, the SUT. Mocks are used in the place of objects, components, or functions that your SUT depends on. This allows you to certify that your SUT is working appropriately without any interference from its dependencies. Mocking allows you to isolate, build, and test functionality independently of other components.

Testing HOCs

One place where we will need to use mocks is when we are testing higher-order components. HOCs are responsible for adding functionality to injected components via properties. We can create a mock component and send it to an HOC to certify that the HOC adds the appropriate properties to our mock.

---

4 For a more in-depth look at mocks, see Martin Fowler's article, "Mocks Aren't Stubs" (*http://bit.ly/2kuR98s*).

Let's take a look at a test for `Expandable`, the HOC that we developed back in Chapter 7. In order to set up a test for the HOC, we must first create a mock component and send it to the HOC. The `MockComponent` will be the stunt double that is used in place of a real component:

```
import { mount } from 'enzyme'
import Expandable from '../../../src/components/HOC/Expandable'

describe("Expandable Higher-Order Component", () => {

    let props,
        wrapper,
        ComposedComponent,
        MockComponent = ({collapsed, expandCollapse}) =>
            <div onClick={expandCollapse}>
                {(collapsed) ? 'collapsed' : 'expanded'}
            </div>

    describe("Rendering UI", ... )

    describe("Expand Collapse Functionality", ... )

})
```

The `MockComponent` is simply a stateless functional component that we developed on the fly. It returns a `div` with an `onClick` handler that will be used to test the `expand Collapse` function. The state, expanded or collapsed, is displayed in the mock component as well. This component will not be used anywhere else but in this test.

The SUT is the `Expandable` HOC. Before our test, we will invoke the HOC using our mock and check the returned component to verify that the appropriate properties have been applied.

The `mount` function will be used instead of the `shallow` function so that we can check the properties and state of the returned component:

```
describe("Rendering UI", () => {

    beforeAll(() => {
        ComposedComponent = Expandable(MockComponent)
        wrapper = mount(<ComposedComponent foo="foo" gnar="gnar"/>)
        props = wrapper.find(MockComponent).props()
    })

    it("starts off collapsed", () =>
        expect(props.collapsed).toBe(true)
    )

    it("passes the expandCollapse function to composed component", () =>
        expect(typeof props.expandCollapse)
            .toBe("function")
```

```
    )

    it("passes additional foo prop to composed component", () =>
        expect(props.foo)
            .toBe("foo")
    )

    it("passes additional gnar prop to composed component", () =>
        expect(props.gnar)
            .toBe("gnar")
    )

})
```

Once we create a composed component using our HOC, we can verify that the composed component has added the appropriate properties to our mock component by mounting it and checking the properties object directly. This test makes sure that the HOC has added the collapsed property and the method for changing that property, expandCollapse. It also verifies that any properties added to the composed component, foo and gnar, make their way to the mock.

Next, let's verify that we can change the collapsed property of our composed component:

```
describe("Expand Collapse Functionality", () => {

    let instance

    beforeAll(() => {
        ComposedComponent = Expandable(MockComponent)
        wrapper = mount(<ComposedComponent collapsed={false}/>)
        instance = wrapper.instance()
    })

    it("renders the MockComponent as the root element", () => {
        expect(wrapper.first().is(MockComponent))
    })

    it("starts off expanded", () => {
        expect(instance.state.collapsed).toBe(false)
    })

    it("toggles the collapsed state", () => {
        instance.expandCollapse()
        expect(instance.state.collapsed).toBe(true)
    })

})
```

Once we mount a component, we can gather information about the rendered instance with wrapper.instance. In this case, we want the component to start off as collapsed. We can check both the properties and state of the instance to assure ourselves that it has in fact started off collapsed.

The wrapper also has some methods for traversing the DOM. In the first test case, we select the first child element using `wrapper.first` and verify that the element is an instance of our `MockComponent`.

HOCs are a great place to get introduced to mocks because the process of injecting the mock is easy: simply send it to the HOC as an argument. The concept of mocking private components is the same, but the injection process is a little bit trickier.

Jest mocks

Jest allows us to inject mocks into any of our components, not just HOCs. With Jest, you can mock any module that your SUT imports. Mocking allows us to focus testing on the SUT and not other modules that could potentially cause issues.

For example, let's take a look at the `ColorList` component, which imports the `Color` component:

```
import { PropTypes } from 'react'
import Color from './Color'
import '../../../stylesheets/ColorList.scss'

const ColorList = ({ colors=[], onRate=f=>f, onRemove=f=>f }) =>
    <div className="color-list">
        {(colors.length === 0) ?
            <p>No Colors Listed. (Add a Color)</p> :
            colors.map(color =>
                <Color key={color.id}
                    {...color}
                        onRate={(rating) => onRate(color.id, rating)}
                        onRemove={() => onRemove(color.id)} />
            )
        }
    </div>

ColorList.propTypes = {
    colors: PropTypes.array,
    onRate: PropTypes.func,
    onRemove: PropTypes.func
}

export default ColorList
```

We want to make sure the `ColorList` component functions appropriately. We are not concerned with the `Color` component; it should have its own unit test. We can write a test for `ColorList` that replaces the `Color` component with a mock:

```
import { mount } from 'enzyme'
import ColorList from '../../../src/components/ui/ColorList'
```

```
jest.mock('../../../src/components/ui/Color', () =>
  ({rating, onRate=f=>f}) =>
    <div className="mock-color">
      <button className="rate" onClick={() => onRate(rating)} />
    </div>
)

describe("<ColorList /> UI Component", () => {

    describe("Rating a Color", () => {

        let _rate = jest.fn()

        beforeAll(() =>
            mount(<ColorList colors={_testColors} onRate={_rate} />)
                .find('button.rate')
                .first()
                .simulate('click')
        )

        it("invokes onRate Handler", () =>
            expect(_rate).toBeCalled()
        )

        it("rates the correct color", () =>
            expect(_rate).toBeCalledWith(
                "8658c1d0-9eda-4a90-95e1-8001e8eb6036",
                4
            )
        )

    })

})
```

In this test, we used `jest.mock` to inject a mock in place of the actual `Color` component. The first argument sent to `jest.mock` is the module that we wish to mock, and the second argument is a function that returns the mocked component. In this case, the `Color` mock is a scaled-back version of the `Color` component. This test is only concerned with rating the color, so the mock only handles the properties related to rating a color.

When this test runs, Jest will replace the `Color` component with our mock. We are sending the global `_testColors` that we set up earlier in this chapter when we render the `ColorList`. When the `ColorList` renders each color, our mock will be rendered instead. When we simulate a click event on the first button, that event will happen on our first mock.

The rendered DOM for this component would look something like:

```
<ColorList>
  <div className="color-list">
    <MockColor onRate={[Function]} rating={4}>
      <div className="mock-color">
        <button id="rate" onClick={[Function]} />
      </div>
    </MockColor>
    <MockColor onRate={[Function]} rating={2}>
      <div className="mock-color">
        <button id="rate" onClick={[Function]} />
      </div>
    </MockColor>
    <MockColor onRate={[Function]} rating={0}>
      <div className="mock-color">
        <button id="rate" onClick={[Function]} />
      </div>
    </MockColor>
  </div>
</ColorList>
```

The real `Color` component would pass the selected rating to the `ColorList`, but our mock does not use the `StarRating` component. It doesn't rate colors; instead, it pretends to rate the color simply by passing the current rating back to the `ColorList`. We do not care about the `Color` component in this test; we only care about the `Color List`. The `ColorList` behaves as expected. Clicking on the first color passes the correct rating to the `onRate` property.

Manual mocks

Jest allows us to create modules to use for our mocks. Instead of adding the code for mocks directly to the test, place each mock in its own file in a _mocks_ folder where Jest will look for them.

Let's take a look at the */src/components/containers.js* file that we created in Chapter 9. This file contains three containers. For this next test, we will focus on the `Colors` container:

```
import ColorList from './ui/ColorList'

export const Colors = connect(
    state =>
        ({
            colors: [...state.colors].sort(sortFunction(state.sort))
        }),
    dispatch =>
        ({
            onRemove(id) {
                dispatch(removeColor(id))
            },
            onRate(id, rating) {
```

```
            dispatch(rateColor(id, rating))
        }
    })
)(ColorList)
```

The `Colors` container is used to connect data from the store to the `ColorList` component. It sorts the colors found in state and sends them to the `ColorList` as a property. It also handles the `onRate` and `onRemove` function properties found in the `ColorList`. Finally, this container depends on the `ColorList` module.

You create a manual mock by adding a *<Module>.js* file to a folder called *__mocks__*. The *__mocks__* folder contains the mocked modules that are used in place of the real modules during testing.

For example, we will add a `ColorList` mock to our current project by creating a *__mocks__* folder in the */src/components/ui* folder, at the same level as the `ColorList` component. We will then place our mock, *ColorList.js*, in that folder.

Our mock will simply render an empty `div` element. Take a look at the code for the *ColorList.js* mock:

```
const ColorListMock = () => <div className="color-list-mock"></div>

ColorListMock.displayName = "ColorListMock"

export default ColorListMock
```

Now, whenever we mock the */src/components/ui/ColorList* component with `jest.mock`, Jest will obtain the appropriate mock from the *__mocks__* folder. We do not have to define the mock directly in our test.

In addition to manually mocking the `ColorList`, we will also create a mock for the store. Stores have three important functions: `dispatch`, `subscribe`, and `getState`. Our mock store will also have these functions. The `getState` function provides an implementation for that mock function that returns a sample state using our global test colors.

We will use this mock store to test the container. We will render a `Provider` component with our mock store as the `store` property. Our container should obtain the colors from the store, sort them, and send them to our mock:

```
import { mount, shallow } from 'enzyme'
import { Provider } from 'react-redux'
import { Colors } from '../../../src/components/containers'

jest.mock('../../../src/components/ui/ColorList')

describe("<Colors /> Container ", () => {

    let wrapper
```

```
const _store = {
    dispatch: jest.fn(),
    subscribe: jest.fn(),
    getState: jest.fn(() =>
        ({
            sort: "SORTED_BY_DATE",
            colors: _testColors
        })
    )
}

beforeAll(() => wrapper = mount(
  <Provider store={_store}>
      <Colors />
  </Provider>
))

it("renders three colors", () => {
    expect(wrapper
        .find('ColorListMock')
        .props()
        .colors
        .length
    ).toBe(3)
})

it("sorts the colors by date", () => {
    expect(wrapper
        .find('ColorListMock')
        .props()
        .colors[0]
        .title
    ).toBe("tomato")
})

})
```

In this test we invoke jest.mock to mock the ColorList component, but we only
send it one argument: the path to the module to mock. Jest knows to look in the
__mocks__ folder to find the implementation for that mock. We are no longer using
the real ColorList; we are using our bare-bones mock component. Once rendered,
our DOM should look something like this:

```
<Provider>
  <Connect(ColorListMock)>
    <ColorListMock colors={[...]}
      onRate={[Function]}
      onRemove={[Function]}>
        <div className="color-list-mock" />
    </ColorListMock>
  </Connect(ColorListMock)>
</Provider>
```

If our container works, it will have sent three colors to our mock. The container should have sorted those colors by date. We can verify this by checking that "tomato" is the first color, because of the three colors in _testColors, it has the most recent timestamp.

Let's add a few more tests to make sure that onRate and onRemove are working appropriately:

```
afterEach(() => jest.resetAllMocks())

it("dispatches a REMOVE_COLOR action", () => {
    wrapper.find('ColorListMock')
        .props()
        .onRemove('f9005b4e-975e-433d-a646-79df172e1dbb')

    expect(_store.dispatch.mock.calls[0][0])
        .toEqual({
            id: 'f9005b4e-975e-433d-a646-79df172e1dbb',
            type: 'REMOVE_COLOR'
        })
})

it("dispatches a RATE_COLOR action", () => {
    wrapper.find('ColorListMock')
        .props()
        .onRate('58d9caee-6ea6-4d7b-9984-65b145031979', 5)

    expect(_store.dispatch.mock.calls[0][0])
        .toEqual({
            id: "58d9caee-6ea6-4d7b-9984-65b145031979",
            type: "RATE_COLOR",
            rating: 5
        })
})
```

To test onRate and onRemove, we do not have to actually simulate clicks. All we need to do is invoke those function properties with some information and verify that the store's dispatch method was called with the correct data. Invoking the onRemove property should cause the store to dispatch a REMOVE_COLOR action. Invoking the onRate property should cause the store to dispatch a RATE_COLOR action. Additionally, we need to make sure the dispatch mock has been reset after each test is complete.

The ability to easily inject mocks into the modules that we want to test is one of Jest's most powerful features. Mocking is a very effective technique for focusing your tests on the SUT.

Snapshot Testing

Test-driven development is a great way to approach testing helper functions, custom classes, and datasets. However, when it comes to testing the UI, TDD can be tricky and often impractical. The UI frequently changes, which makes maintaining UI tests a time-consuming practice. It is also pretty common to be tasked with the job of writing tests for UI components that already exist in production.

Snapshot testing provides us with a way to quickly test UI components to make sure that we have not caused any unexpected changes. Jest can save a snapshot of the rendered UI and compare it to the rendered output of future tests. This allows us to verify that our updates have not had any unexpected effects while still allowing us to move quickly and not get too bogged down with the practicalities of testing the UI. Additionally, snapshots can easily be updated when UI changes are expected.

Let's see how we can test the `Color` component with snapshot testing. First, let's take a look at the existing code for the `Color` component:

```
import { PropTypes, Component } from 'react'
import StarRating from './StarRating'
import TimeAgo from './TimeAgo'
import FaTrash from 'react-icons/lib/fa/trash-o'
import '../../../stylesheets/Color.scss'

class Color extends Component {

    render() {
        const {
            title, color, rating, timestamp, onRemove, onRate
        } = this.props

        return (
            <section className="color" style={this.style}>
                <h1 ref="title">{title}</h1>
                <button onClick={onRemove}>
                    <FaTrash />
                </button>
                <div className="color"
                    style={{ backgroundColor: color }}>
                </div>
                <TimeAgo timestamp={timestamp} />
                <div>
                    <StarRating starsSelected={rating} onRate={onRate}/>
                </div>
            </section>
        )
    }

}
```

```
export default Color
```

If we render this component with specific properties, we would expect a DOM that contains specific components based on the properties that we have sent:

```
shallow(
    <Color title="Test Color"
        color="#F0F0F0"
        rating={3}
        timestamp="Mon Apr 11 2016 12:54:19 GMT-0700 (PDT)"
    />
).html()
```

The resulting DOM should look something like:

```
<section class=\"color\">
  <h1>Test Color</h1>
  <button><svg /></button>
  <div class=\"color\" style=\"background-color:#F0F0F0;\"></div>
  <div class=\"time-ago\">4/11/2016</div>
  <div>
    <div class=\"star-rating\">
      <div class=\"star selected\"></div>
      <div class=\"star selected\"></div>
      <div class=\"star selected\"></div>
      <div class=\"star\"></div>
      <div class=\"star\"></div>
      <p>3 of 5 stars</p>
    </div>
  </div>
</section>
```

Snapshot testing will allow us to save a snapshot of this DOM the very first time we run the test. Then, we'll be able to compare future tests to that snapshot to make sure the resulting output is always the same.

Let's go ahead and write a snapshot test for the Color component:

```
import { shallow } from 'enzyme'
import Color from '../../../src/components/ui/Color'

describe("<Color /> UI Component", () => {

    it("Renders correct properties", () =>
        let output = shallow(
            <Color title="Test Color"
                color="#F0F0F0"
                rating={3}
                timestamp="Mon Apr 11 2016 12:54:19 GMT-0700 (PDT)"
            />
        ).html()

        expect(output).toMatchSnapshot()
```

```
        )

    })
```

In this test, we use Enzyme to render the component and collect the resulting output as a string of HTML. `.toMatchSnapshot` is the Jest matcher used for snapshot testing. The first time this test is run, Jest will save a copy of the resulting HTML in a snapshot file. This file will be added to a *__snapshots__* folder in the same directory as the test. Currently, the snapshot file would look like:

```
exports[`<Color /> UI Component Renders correct properties 1`] =
    `"<section class=\"color\"><h1>Test Color</h1><button><svg ...
```

Every other time the test is run, Jest will compare the output to the same snapshot. If anything at all is different about the resulting HTML, the test will fail.

Snapshot testing allows us to move quickly, but if we move too fast, we could end up writing *flaky tests*, or tests that pass when they should fail. Taking snapshots of HTML strings will work for testing, but it is hard for us to verify that the snapshot is actually correct. Let's improve our snapshot by saving the output as JSX.

For this, we'll need to install the `enzyme-to-json` module:

```
npm install enzyme-to-json --save-dev
```

This module provides a function that we can use to render Enzyme wrappers as JSX, which makes it easier to review the snapshot output for correctness.

To render our snapshot using `enzyme-to-json`, we would first shallow-render the `Color` component with Enzyme, then send that result to the `toJSON` function and the result of `toJSON` to the `expect` function. We may be tempted to write code that looks like:

```
expect(
  toJSON(
    shallow(
      <Color title="Test Color"
             color="#F0F0F0"
             rating={3}
             timestamp="Mon Apr 11 2016 12:54:19 GMT-0700 (PDT)"
        />
    )
  )
).toMatchSnapshot()
```

But this is a perfect place to use a little composition to improve our code. Remember composition? Smaller functions can be put together to make larger functions. We can use the `compose` function from Redux to make a single larger function out of `shallow`, `toJSON`, and `expect`:

```
import { shallow } from 'enzyme'
import toJSON from 'enzyme-to-json'
import { compose } from 'redux'
import Color from '../../../src/components/ui/Color'

describe("<Color /> UI Component", () => {

    const shallowExpect = compose(expect,toJSON,shallow)

    it("Renders correct properties", () =>
        shallowExpect(
          <Color title="Test Color"
             color="#F0F0F0"
             rating={3}
             timestamp="Mon Apr 11 2016 12:54:19 GMT-0700 (PDT)"
          />
        ).toMatchSnapshot()
    )

})
```

The shallowExpect function takes a component and shallow-renders it, converts the result to JSON, and then sends it to the expect method that returns all of the Jest matchers.

If we run this test, it should fail because the output is now JSX and not an HTML string. Our test no longer matches the snapshot. However, snapshots are easy to update. We can update the snapshot by running the test again with the updateSnapshot flag:

```
jest --updateSnapshot
```

If we run Jest with the watch flag:

```
jest --watch
```

Jest will continue to run in the terminal and listen for changes to our source code and tests. If we make any changes, Jest will rerun our tests. When you are watching tests, you can easily update the snapshot by pressing the u key:

```
Snapshot Summary
 › 1 snapshot test failed in 1 test suite. Inspect your code changes or press
 `u` to update them.

Test Suites: 1 failed, 6 passed, 7 total
Tests:       1 failed, 28 passed, 29 total
Snapshots:   1 failed, 1 total
Time:        1.407s
Ran all test suites.

Watch Usage
 › Press u to update failing snapshots.
```

> › Press p to filter by a filename regex pattern.
> › Press q to quit watch mode.
> › Press Enter to trigger a test run.

Once you update the snapshot, the test will pass. The snapshot file has now changed. Instead of one long HTML string, the snapshot now looks like:

```
exports[`<Color /> UI Component Renders correct properties 1`] = `
<section
  className="color">
  <h1>
    Test Color
  </h1>
  <button
    onClick={[Function]}>
    <FaTrashO />
  </button>
  <div
    className="color"
    style={
      Object {
        "backgroundColor": "#F0F0F0",
      }
    } />
  <TimeAgo
    timestamp="Mon Apr 11 2016 12:54:19 GMT-0700 (PDT)" />
  <div>
    <StarRating
      onRate={[Function]}
      starsSelected={3} />
  </div>
</section>
`;
```

This snapshot is much more readable. We can take a quick look at it to verify the results are correct before moving on to our next test. Snapshot testing can be a very effective way to quickly add testing to your applications.

Using Code Coverage

Code coverage is the process of reporting on how many lines of code have actually been tested. It provides a metric that can help you decide when you have written enough tests.

Jest ships with Istanbul, a JavaScript tool used to review your tests and to generate a report that describes how many statements, branches, functions, and lines have been covered.

To run Jest with code coverage, simply add the coverage flag when you run the jest command:

```
jest --coverage
```

A report on current code coverage will be generated and displayed in the terminal:

```
PASS  __tests__/components/ui/ColorList.test.js
PASS  __tests__/components/containers/Colors.test.js
PASS  __tests__/components/ui/Color.test.js
PASS  __tests__/components/ui/Star.test.js
PASS  __tests__/components/HOC/Expandable.test.js
PASS  __tests__/actions.test.js
PASS  __tests__/store/reducers/color.test.js
```

File	% Stmts	% Branch	% Funcs	% Lines	Uncov'd Lines
All files	68.42	43.33	45.59	72.39	
src	100	100	100	100	
actions.js	100	100	100	100	
constants.js	100	100	100	100	
src/components	58.33	100	40	58.33	
containers.js	58.33	100	40	58.33	11,13,20,24,26
src/components/HOC	100	100	100	100	
Expandable.js	100	100	100	100	
src/components/ui	45.65	35.29	24	50	
AddColorForm.js	16.67	0	0	18.18	... 13,16,18,21
Color.js	66.67	100	33.33	66.67	40,41
ColorList.js	62.5	40	50	83.33	13
SortMenu.js	37.5	0	0	42.86	11,14,18,19
Star.js	100	100	100	100	
StarRating.js	33.33	0	0	40	5,7,9
TimeAgo.js	50	100	0	50	4
src/lib	58.54	15	16.67	67.65	
array-helpers.js	60	33.33	60	71.43	6,8
time-helpers.js	58.06	0	0	66.67	... 43,45,49,54
src/store	97.14	70	100	96.77	
index.js	100	100	100	100	
reducers.js	94.12	64.71	100	94.12	21

```
Test Suites: 7 passed, 7 total
Tests:       29 passed, 29 total
Snapshots:   1 passed, 1 total
Time:        1.691s, estimated 2s

Ran all test suites.

Watch Usage
 › Press p to filter by a filename regex pattern.
 › Press q to quit watch mode.
 › Press Enter to trigger a test run.
```

This report tells us how much of our code in each file has been executed during the testing process and reports on all files that have been imported into tests.

Jest also generates a report that you can run in your browser, which provides more details about what code has been covered by tests. After running Jest with coverage reporting, you will notice that a *coverage* folder has been added to the root. In a web browser, open this file: */coverage/lcov-report/index.html*. It will show you your code coverage in an interactive report (Figure 10-1).

Figure 10-1. Code coverage report

This report tells you how much of the code has been covered, as well as the individual coverage based upon each subfolder. You can drill down into a subfolder to see how well the individual files within have been covered. If you select the *components/ui* folder, you will see how well your user interface components are covered by testing (Figure 10-2).

You can see what lines have been covered in an individual file by clicking on the file-name. Figure 10-3 shows the lines that have been covered in the ColorList component.

Figure 10-2. UI component test coverage

Figure 10-3. ColorList coverage

The ColorList component has been tested pretty well. In the column on the left of
the screen, you can see how many times each line has been executed in a test. The

lines that are highlighted yellow and red have not been executed. In this case, it looks like we have yet to test the onRemove property. Let's add a suite to *ColorList.test.js* to test the onRemove property and get line 13 covered:

```
jest.mock('../../../src/components/ui/Color', () =>
  ({rating, onRate=f=>f, onRemove=f=>f}) =>
    <div className="mockColor">
      <button className="rate" onClick={() => onRate(rating)} />
      <button className="remove" onClick={onRemove} />
    </div>
)

..

describe("Removing a Color", () => {

    let _remove = jest.fn()

    beforeAll(() =>
        mount(<ColorList colors={_testColors} onRemove={_remove} />)
            .find('button.remove')
            .last()
            .simulate('click')
    )

    it("invokes onRemove Handler", () =>
        expect(_remove).toBeCalled()
    )

    it("removes the correct color", () =>
        expect(_remove).toBeCalledWith(
            "58d9caee-6ea6-4d7b-9984-65b145031979"
        )
    )
})
```

The onRemove property has been added to the Color mock, as well as a button for triggering that property. When we render the ColorList, we will test the onRemove property the exact same way we tested the onRate property. We will render a Color List with our three test colors, click the last remove button, and make sure the correct ID is being passed to the mock function, _remove.

The next time we generate the coverage report we will see an improvement—line 13 is now covered (Figure 10-4).

Figure 10-4. Improved coverage by testing onRemove

It looks like line 8 is not being covered either. This is because we've never rendered the ColorList with an empty array of colors. Let's get line 8 covered by a test:

```
describe("Rendering UI", () => {

  it("Defaults properties correctly", () =>
    expect(shallow(<ColorList />).find('p').text())
      .toBe('No Colors Listed. (Add a Color)')
  )

})
```

Rendering the Color component without any properties not only covers line 8, it covers the default property value that is set in line 1 too (Figure 10-5).

Figure 10-5. Improved code coverage by testing empty colors

We are pretty close to having 100% of the `ColorList` component tested. The only things that we have not tested are the default functions for `onRate` and `onRemove`. If we did not provide these functions, these properties would be required. We can improve our test by rending the `ColorList` component without properties. We also want to simulate clicks on the first rating button and the last remove button:

```
describe("Rendering UI", () => {

    it("Defaults properties correctly", () =>
        expect(shallow(<ColorList />).find('p').text())
            .toBe('No Colors Listed. (Add a Color)')
    )

    it("Clicking default rate button does not cause Error", () => {
        mount(<ColorList colors={_testColors} />)
            .find('button.rate')
            .first()
            .simulate('click')
    })

    it("Clicking default remove button does not cause Error", () => {
        mount(<ColorList colors={_testColors} />)
            .find('button.remove')
            .first()
            .simulate('click')
    })
```

```
    })
```

The next time we run Jest with coverage reporting, we will see that we are now covering 100% of the code in the `ColorList` component (Figure 10-6).

Figure 10-6. 100% coverage for ColorList

But we still have a lot of work to do with the rest of the components in our project, as we can see in Figure 10-7.

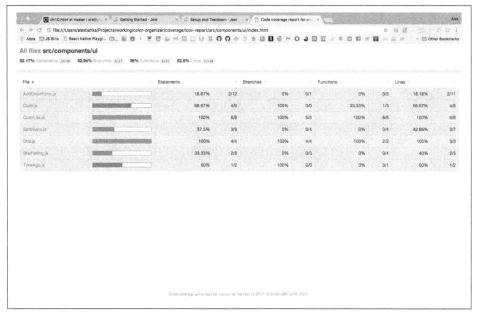

Figure 10-7. UI component test coverage after writing new tests for ColorList

You can use this report to help guide you through the process of improving your tests by improving the amount of code that is covered by testing.

You can also include coverage options in your *package.json* file:

```
"jest": {
    "setupFiles": ["./__tests__/global.js"],
    "modulePathIgnorePatterns": ["global.js"],
    "moduleNameMapper": {
      "\\.(scss)$": "<rootDir>/node_modules/jest-css-modules"
    },
    "verbose": true,
    "collectCoverage": true,
    "notify": true,
    "collectCoverageFrom": ["src/**"],
    "coverageThreshold": {
      "global": {
        "branches": 80,
        "functions": 80,
        "lines": 80,
        "statements": 80
      }
    }
}
```

The coverageThreshold field defines how much code should be covered before your testing passes. We have specified that 80% of all branches, functions, lines, and statements must be covered.

The collectCoverageFrom field is where you can specify which files should be covered. It takes an array of glob patterns. We have specified that all of the files in the *src* directory and any subdirectory should be covered.

Setting the collectCoverage option to true means that coverage data will be collected every time we run the jest command on this project. The notify field displays a notification box using your operating system. Finally, the verbose option displays a detailed report of each test every time you run Jest. The verbose report for the "<ColorList /> UI Component" suite looks like:

```
PASS  __tests__/components/ui/ColorList.test.js
  <ColorList /> UI Component
    Rendering UI
      ✓ Defaults Properties correctly (2ms)
      ✓ Clicking default rate button do not cause Error (6ms)
      ✓ Clicking default remove button do not cause Error (4ms)
    Rating a Color
      ✓ invokes onRate Handler
      ✓ rates the correct color (1ms)
    Removing a Color
      ✓ invokes onRemove Handler
      ✓ removes the correct color
```

It will take more testing to achieve 100% code coverage for the color organizer. The code found in the GitHub repository for this chapter does achieve 100% code coverage (Figure 10-8).

Figure 10-8. 100% code coverage

Code coverage is a great tool to measure the reach of your tests. It is one benchmark to help you understand when you have written enough unit tests for your code. It is not typical to have 100% code coverage in every project. Shooting for anything above 85% is a good target.[5]

---

5 See Martin Fowler's article "Test-Coverage" (*http://bit.ly/2kuXEsb*).

CHAPTER 11

React Router

When the web started, most websites consisted of a series of pages that users could navigate through by requesting and opening separate files. The location of the current file or resource was listed in the browser's location bar. The browser's forward and back buttons would work as expected. Bookmarking content deep within a website would allow users to save a reference to a specific file that could be reloaded at the user's request. On a page-based, or server-rendered, website, the browser's navigation and history features simply work as expected.

In a single-page app, all of these features become problematic. Remember, in a single-page app, everything is happening on the same page. JavaScript is loading information and changing the UI. Features like browser history, bookmarks, and forward and back buttons will not work without a routing solution. *Routing* is the process of defining endpoints for your client's requests.[1] These endpoints work in conjunction with the browser's location and history objects. They are used to identify requested content so that JavaScript can load and render the appropriate user interface.

Unlike Angular, Ember, or Backbone, React doesn't come with a standard router. Recognizing the importance of a routing solution, engineers Michael Jackson and Ryan Florence created one named simply React Router. The React Router has been adopted by the community as a popular routing solution for React apps.[2] It is used by companies including Uber, Zendesk, PayPal, and Vimeo.[3]

In this chapter, we will introduce the React Router and review how to leverage the HashRouter component to handle routing on the client.

---

1 Express.js documentation, "Basic Routing" (*http://bit.ly/2mJlIt5*).

2 The project has been starred over 20,000 times on GitHub (*http://bit.ly/2mJt4gk*).

3 See "Sites Using React Router" (*http://bit.ly/2mJbN6X*).

Incorporating the Router

To demonstrate the capabilities of the React Router, we will build a classic starter website complete with About, Events, Products, and Contact Us sections (Figure 11-1). Although this website will feel as though it has multiple pages, there is only one: it is an SPA.

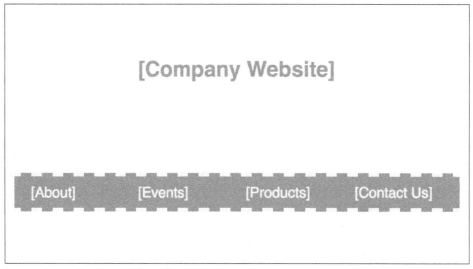

Figure 11-1. Company website home page

The sitemap for this website consists of a home page, a page for each section, and an error page to handle 404 Not Found errors (see Figure 11-2).

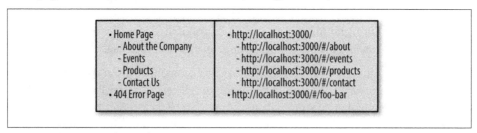

Figure 11-2. Page titles and routes

The router will allow us to set up routes for each section of the website. Each *route* is an endpoint that can be entered into the browser's location bar. When a route is requested, we can render the appropriate content.

HashRouter

`react-router-dom` provides a couple of options for managing the navigation history in single-page applications. The HashRouter was designed for the client. Traditionally, hashes in the location bar were used to define anchor links. When the # is used in the location bar, the browser does not make a server request. When using the HashRouter, the # is always required before all routes.

The HashRouter is a nice tool to use for new projects or for small client sites that do not require a backend. The BrowserRouter is a preferred solution for most production-ready applications. We will discuss the BrowserRouter in Chapter 12, when we cover universal applications.

Let's install `react-router-dom`, the package that we need to incorporate the router into our browser-based application:

```
npm install react-router-dom --save
```

We'll also need a few placeholder components for each section or page in the sitemap. We can export these components from a single file:

```
export const Home = () =>
    <section className="home">
        <h1>[Home Page]</h1>
    </section>

export const About = () =>
    <section className="events">
        <h1>[About the Company]</h1>
    </section>

export const Events = () =>
    <section className="events">
        <h1>[Events Calendar]</h1>
    </section>

export const Products = () =>
    <section className="products">
        <h1>[Products Catalog]</h1>
    </section>

export const Contact = () =>
    <section className="contact">
        <h1>[Contact Us]</h1>
    </section>
```

When the application starts, instead of rendering a single App component, we will render the HashRouter component:

```
import React from 'react'
import { render } from 'react-dom'

import {
  HashRouter,
  Route
} from 'react-router-dom'

import {
  Home,
  About,
  Events,
  Products,
  Contact
} from './pages'

window.React = React

render(
  <HashRouter>
    <div className="main">
        <Route exact path="/" component={Home} />
        <Route path="/about" component={About} />
        <Route path="/events" component={Events} />
        <Route path="/products" component={Products} />
        <Route path="/contact" component={Contact} />
    </div>
  </HashRouter>,
  document.getElementById('react-container')
)
```

The HashRouter component is rendered as the root component for our application. Each route can be defined within the HashRouter using the Route component.

These routes tell the router which component to render when the window's location changes. Each Route component has path and component properties. When the browser's location matches the path, the component will be displayed. When the location is /, the router will render the Home component. When the location is /products, the router will render the Products component.

The first route, the one that displays the Home component, has an exact property. This means that the Home component will only be displayed when the location exactly matches the root /.

At this point, we can run the app and physically type the routes into the browser's location bar to watch the content change. For example, type *http://localhost:3000/#/about* into the location bar and watch the About component render.

We do not expect our users to navigate the website by typing routes into the location bar. The `react-router-dom` provides a `Link` component that we can use to create browser links.

Let's modify the home page to contain a navigation menu with a link for each route:

```
import { Link } from 'react-router-dom'

export const Home = () =>
    <div className="home">
        <h1>[Company Website]</h1>
        <nav>
            <Link to="about">[About]</Link>
            <Link to="events">[Events]</Link>
            <Link to="products">[Products]</Link>
            <Link to="contact">[Contact Us]</Link>
        </nav>
    </div>
```

Now users can access every internal page from the home page by clicking on a link. The browser's back button will take them back to the home page.

Router Properties

The React Router passes properties to the components that it renders. For instance, we can obtain the current location via a property. Let's use the current location to help us create a 404 Not Found component:

```
export const Whoops404 = ({ location }) =>
    <div className="whoops-404">
        <h1>Resource not found at '{location.pathname}'</h1>
    </div>
```

The `Whoops404` component will be rendered by the router when users enter routes that have not been defined. Once rendered, the router will pass a location object to this component as a property. We can obtain and use this object to get the current pathname for the requested route. We will use this pathname to notify the user that we cannot find the resource that they have requested.

Now let's add the `Whoops404` component to the application using a `Route`:

```
import {
    HashRouter,
    Route,
    Switch
} from 'react-router-dom'

...

render(
  <HashRouter>
```

```
      <div className="main">
        <Switch>
          <Route exact path="/" component={Home} />
          <Route path="/about" component={About} />
          <Route path="/events" component={Events} />
          <Route path="/products" component={Products} />
          <Route path="/contact" component={Contact} />
          <Route component={Whoops404} />
        </Switch>
      </div>
    </HashRouter>,
    document.getElementById('react-container')
  )
```

Since we only want to display the Whoops404 component when no other Route matches, we need to use the Switch component. The Switch component only displays the first route that matches. This assures that only one of these routes will be rendered. If none of the locations match a Route, the last route—the one that does not contain a path property—will be displayed. If you were to enter the route http://localhost:3000/#/profits, you would see Figure 11-3.

Figure 11-3. 404 error page

This section introduced the basics of implementing and working with the React Router. All Route components need to be wrapped with a router, in this case the Hash Router, which selects the component to render based on the window's present location. Link components can be used to facilitate navigation. These basics can get you pretty far, but they just scratch the surface of the router's capabilities.

Nesting Routes

Route components are used with content that should be displayed only when specific URLs are matched. This feature allows us to organize our web apps into eloquent hierarchies that promote content reuse.

In this section, we will also look at how content can be organized into subsections that contain submenus.

Using a Page Template

Sometimes, as users navigate our apps, we want some of the UI to stay in place. In the past, solutions such as page templates and master pages have helped web developers reuse UI elements. React components can naturally be composed into templates using the children property.

Let's consider the simple starter website. Once inside, each section should display the same main menu. The content on the right side of the screen should change as the user navigates the website, but the content on the left side of the screen should remain intact (see Figure 11-4).

Let's create a reusable PageTemplate component that we can use as a template for these inside pages. This component will always display the main menu, but it will render nested content as users navigate the website.

First, we'll need the MainMenu component:

```
import HomeIcon from 'react-icons/lib/fa/home'
import { NavLink } from 'react-router-dom'
import './stylesheets/menus.scss'

const selectedStyle = {
    backgroundColor: "white",
    color: "slategray"
}

export const MainMenu = () =>
    <nav className="main-menu">
        <NavLink to="/">
            <HomeIcon/>
        </NavLink>
        <NavLink to="/about" activeStyle={selectedStyle}>
```

```
        [About]
    </NavLink>
    <NavLink to="/events" activeStyle={selectedStyle}>
        [Events]
    </NavLink>
    <NavLink to="/products" activeStyle={selectedStyle}>
        [Products]
    </NavLink>
    <NavLink to="/contact" activeStyle={selectedStyle}>
        [Contact Us]
    </NavLink>
</nav>
```

Figure 11-4. Inside Page: Events

The MainMenu component uses the NavLink component. The NavLink component can be used to create links that can be styled when they are active. The activeStyle property can be used to set the CSS to indicate which link is active or currently selected.

The MainMenu component will be used in the PageTemplate component:

```
import { MainMenu } from './ui/menus'

...

const PageTemplate = ({children}) =>
    <div className="page">
        <MainMenu />
        {children}
    </div>
```

The children of the PageTemplate component are where each section will be rendered. Here, we are adding the children just after the MainMenu. Now we can compose our sections using the PageTemplate:

```
export const Events = () =>
    <PageTemplate>
      <section className="events">
          <h1>[Event Calendar]</h1>
      </section>
    </PageTemplate>

export const Products = () =>
    <PageTemplate>
        <section className="products">
            <h1>[Product Catalog]</h1>
        </section>
    </PageTemplate>

export const Contact = () =>
    <PageTemplate>
        <section className="contact">
            <h1>[Contact Us]</h1>
        </section>
    </PageTemplate>

export const About = ({ match }) =>
    <PageTemplate>
        <section className="about">
            <h1>About</h1>
        </section>
    </PageTemplate>
```

If you run the application, you will see that each section now displays the same Main Menu. The content on the right side of the screen changes as you navigate through the interior pages of the website.

Subsections and Submenus

Next, we will nest four components under the About section using the Route component (see Figure 11-5).

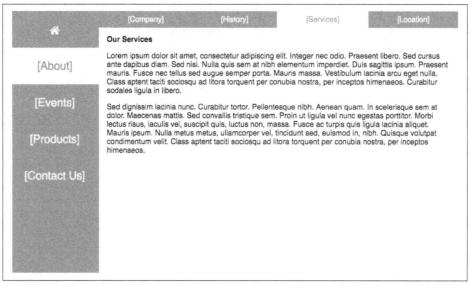

Figure 11-5. Subpages in the About section

We need to add pages for Company, History, Services, and Location. When the user selects the About section, they should be defaulted to the Company page under that section. The outline looks like this:

- Home Page
  - **About the Company**
    - **Company (default)**
    - **History**
    - **Services**
    - **Location**
  - Events
  - Products
  - Contact Us
- 404 Error Page

The new routes that we need to create will reflect this hierarchy:

- http://localhost:3000/
  - http://localhost:3000/#/**about**
    - http://localhost:3000/#/**about**

— http://localhost:3000/#/**about/history**

— http://localhost:3000/#/**about/services**

— http://localhost:3000/#/**about/location**

— http://localhost:3000/#/events

— http://localhost:3000/#/products

— http://localhost:3000/#/contact

- http://localhost:3000/#/foo-bar

Let's create a submenu for the About section. We will use NavLink components and set the activeStyle to the same activeStyle used in the MainMenu:

```
export const AboutMenu = ({match}) =>
    <div className="about-menu">
        <li>
            <NavLink to="/about"
                style={match.isExact && selectedStyle}>
                [Company]
            </NavLink>
        </li>
        <li>
            <NavLink to="/about/history"
                activeStyle={selectedStyle}>
                [History]
            </NavLink>
        </li>
        <li>
            <NavLink to="/about/services"
                activeStyle={selectedStyle}>
                [Services]
            </NavLink>
        </li>
        <li>
            <NavLink to="/about/location"
                activeStyle={selectedStyle}>
                [Location]
            </NavLink>
        </li>
    </div>
```

The AboutMenu component uses NavLink components to direct users to interior content under the About section. This component will be rendered using a Route which means that it receives routing properties. We will need to use the match property that is sent to this component from the Route.

All of the NavLink components use the activeStyle property except for the first one. The activeStyle will set the style property for the link when the location matches to the link's route. For instance, when the user navigates to `http://localhost:3000/about/services`, the Services NavLink will render a white background.

The first NavLink component does not use `activeStyle`. Instead, the style property is set to the `selectedStyle` only when the route matches exactly `/about`. The `match.isExact` property is `true` when the location is `/about` and `false` when the location is `/about/services`. Technically the `/about` route matches for both locations, but it is only an exact match when the location is `/about`.

Placeholder Components

We also need to remember to stub placeholder components for our new sections: Company, Services, History, and Location. Here is an example of the Services placeholder. It simply displays some Lorem Ipsum text:

```
export const Services = () =>
    <section className="services">
        <h2>Our Services</h2>
        <p>
            Lorem ipsum dolor sit amet, consectetur
            adipiscing elit. Integer nec odio.
            Praesent libero. Sed cursus ante dapibus
            diam. Sed nisi. Nulla quis sem at nibh
            elementum imperdiet. Duis sagittis ipsum.
            Praesent mauris. Fusce nec tellus sed
            augue semper porta. Mauris massa.
            Vestibulum lacinia arcu eget nulla.
            Class aptent taciti sociosqu ad litora
            torquent per conubia nostra, per inceptos
            himenaeos. Curabitur sodales ligula in
            libero.
        </p>
        <p>
            Sed dignissim lacinia nunc. Curabitur
            tortor. Pellentesque nibh. Aenean quam. In
            scelerisque sem at dolor. Maecenas mattis.
            Sed convallis tristique sem. Proin ut
            ligula vel nunc egestas porttitor. Morbi
            lectus risus, iaculis vel, suscipit quis,
            luctus non, massa. Fusce ac turpis quis
            ligula lacinia aliquet. Mauris ipsum.
            Nulla metus metus, ullamcorper vel,
            tincidunt sed, euismod in, nibh. Quisque
            volutpat condimentum velit. Class aptent
            taciti sociosqu ad litora torquent per
            conubia nostra, per inceptos himenaeos.
        </p>
    </section>
```

Now we are ready to add routes to the About component:

```
export const About = ({ match }) =>
    <PageTemplate>
        <section className="about">
            <Route component={AboutMenu} />
            <Route exact path="/about" component={Company}/>
            <Route path="/about/history" component={History}/>
            <Route path="/about/services" component={Services}/>
            <Route path="/about/location" component={Location}/>
        </section>
    </PageTemplate>
```

This About component will be reused across the entire section. The location will tell the app which subsection to render. For example, when the location is http://local host:3000/about/history, the History component will be rendered inside of the About component.

This time, we are not using a Switch component. Any Route that matches the location will render its associated component. The first Route will always display the AboutMenu. Additionally, any other Routes that match will render their components as well.

Using redirects

Sometimes you want to redirect users from one route to another. For instance, we can make sure that if users try to access content via http://localhost:3000/services, they get redirected to the correct route: http://localhost:3000/about/services.

Let's modify our application to include redirects to ensure that our users can access the correct content:

```
import {
  HashRouter,
  Route,
  Switch,
  Redirect
} from 'react-router-dom'

...

render(
  <HashRouter>
    <div className="main">
      <Switch>
        <Route exact path="/" component={Home} />
        <Route path="/about" component={About} />
        <Redirect from="/history" to="/about/history" />
        <Redirect from="/services" to="/about/services" />
        <Redirect from="/location" to="/about/location" />
        <Route path="/events" component={Events} />
```

```
            <Route path="/products" component={Products} />
            <Route path="/contact" component={Contact} />
            <Route component={Whoops404} />
        </Switch>
      </div>
    </HashRouter>,
    document.getElementById('react-container')
  )
```

The Redirect component allows us to redirect the user to a specific route.

 When routes are changed in a production application, users will still try to access old content via old routes. This typically happens because of bookmarks. The Redirect component provides us with a way to load the appropriate content for users, even if they are accessing your site via an old bookmark.

The React Router allows us to compose Route components anywhere within our application because the HashRouter is our root component. We can now organize our content in hierarchies that are easy to navigate.

Router Parameters

Another useful feature of the React Router is the ability to set up *routing parameters*. Routing parameters are variables that obtain their values from the URL. They are extremely useful in data-driven web applications for filtering content or managing display preferences.

Adding Color Details Page

Let's improve the color organizer by adding the ability to select and display one color at a time using the React Router. When a user selects a color by clicking on it, the app should render that color and display its title and hex value (see Figure 11-6).

Figure 11-6. Color Details screen

Every color has a unique ID. This ID can be used to find specific colors that are saved in state. For example, we can create a findById function that will find an object in an array by the id field:

```
import { compose } from 'redux'

export const getFirstArrayItem = array => array[0]

export const filterArrayById = (array, id) =>
    array.filter(item => item.id === id)

export const findById = compose(
    getFirstArrayItem,
    filterArrayById
)
```

This findById function follows the functional programming techniques discussed in Chapter 2. We can see that the findById method first filters the array by the ID and then returns the first item found in that filtered array. We can use the findById function to locate colors in state by their unique IDs.

Using the router, we can obtain the color ID via the URL. For example, this is the URL that we will use to display the color "Lawn" because the ID for the color lawn is being passed within the URL:

```
http://localhost:3000/#/58d9caee-6ea6-4d7b-9984-65b145031979
```

Router parameters allow us to capture this value. They can be defined in routes using a colon. For example, we could capture the unique id and save it in a parameter named id with the Route:

```
<Route exact path="/:id" component={UniqueIDHeader} />
```

The UniqueIDHeader component can obtain the id from the match.params object:

```
const UniqueIDHeader = ({ match }) => <h1>{match.params.id}</h1>
```

We can create parameters any time we want to collect data from the URL.

Multiple Parameters

Multiple parameters can be created and accessed on the same parameters object. The following sample route would create three parameters:

```
<Route path="/members/:gender/:state/:city"
       component="Member" />
```

These three parameters can then be initialized via the URL:

```
http://localhost:3000/members/female/california/truckee
```

All three values would be passed to the Member component via match.params:

```
const Member = ({ match }) =>
    <div className="member">
        <ul>
            <li>gender: {match.params.gender}</li>
            <li>state: {match.params.state}</li>
            <li>city: {match.params.city}</li>
        </ul>
    </div>
```

Lets create a ColorDetails component that will be rendered when the user selects a single color:

```
const ColorDetails = ({ title, color }) =>
    <div className="color-details"
        style={{backgroundColor: color}}>
        <h1>{title}</h1>
        <h1>{color}</h1>
    </div>
```

The ColorDetails component is a presentation component—it expects properties for the color's details. Since we are using Redux, we will need to add a new container that can find the selected color in state using a routing parameter:

```
export const Color = connect(
    (state, props) => findById(state.colors, props.match.params.id)
)(ColorDetails)
```

The Color container is created using the connect HOC. The first argument is a function that is used to set the properties of the ColorDetails based on a single color from state. Using the findById function that we defined earlier in this section, we will locate an individual color object in state with an id parameter that is obtained from the URL. The connect HOC will map the data from the located color object to the properties of the ColorDetails component.

The connect HOC also maps any properties sent to the Color container to the Color Details component. This means that all of the router properties will be passed to ColorDetails as well.

Let's add some navigation to the ColorDetails component using the router's history property:

```
const ColorDetails = ({ title, color, history }) =>
    <div className="color-details"
        style={{backgroundColor: color}}
        onClick={() => history.goBack()}>
        <h1>{title}</h1>
        <h1>{color}</h1>
    </div>
```

When users click the div.color-details element, the history.goBack() method will be invoked. The user will be navigated back to the previous location.

Now that we have a Color container, we need to add it to our app. First, we will need to wrap the App component with a HashRouter when it is initially rendered:

```
import { HashRouter } from 'react-router-dom'

...

render(
    <Provider store={store}>
        <HashRouter>
          <App />
        </HashRouter>
    </Provider>,
    document.getElementById('react-container')
)
```

Now we are ready to configure routes anywhere within our application. Let's add some routes to the App component:

```
import { Route, Switch } from 'react-router-dom'
import Menu from './ui/Menu'
import { Colors, Color, NewColor } from './containers'
import '../stylesheets/APP.scss'

const App = () =>
    <Switch>
```

```
                <Route exact path="/:id" component={Color} />
                <Route path="/"
                    component={() => (
                        <div className="app">
                            <Menu />
                            <NewColor />
                            <Colors />
                        </div>
                    )} />
            </Switch>

    export default App
```

The Switch component is used to render one of two routes: an individual color, or the main app components. The first Route renders the Color component when an id is passed in a URL. For instance, this route will match when the location is:

```
http://localhost:3000/#/58d9caee-6ea6-4d7b-9984-65b145031979
```

Any other location will match / and display the main application components. The second Route groups several components under a new anonymous stateless functional component. As a result, users will either see an individual color or a list of colors, depending upon the URL.

At present, we can test our application by adding the id parameter directly to the browser's location bar. However, users will need a way to navigate to the details view as well.

This time, the NavLink component will not be used to handle the navigation from the list of colors to a color's details. Instead, we will navigate by directly using the router's history object.

Let's add navigation to the Color component found in the *./ui* folder. This component is rendered by the ColorList. It does not receive routing properties from the Route. You could explicitly pass those properties all the way down the tree to the Color component, but it's easier to use the withRouter function. This ships with react-router-dom. withRouter can be used to add routing properties to any component that is rendered somewhere under a Route.

Using withRouter, we can obtain the router's history object as a property. We can use it to navigate from within the Color component:

```
    import { withRouter } from 'react-router'

    ...

    class Color extends Component {

        render() {
```

```
const {
    id,
    title,
    color,
    rating,
    timestamp,
    onRemove,
    onRate,
    history } = this.props

return (
    <section className="color" style={this.style}>
        <h1 ref="title"
            onClick={() => history.push(`/${id}`)}>
            {title}
        </h1>
        <button onClick={onRemove}>
            <FaTrash />
        </button>
        <div className="color"
            onClick={() => history.push(`/${id}`)}
            style={{ backgroundColor: color }}>
        </div>
        <TimeAgo timestamp={timestamp} />
        <div>
            <StarRating starsSelected={rating}
                onRate={onRate}/>
        </div>
    </section>
)
    }

}

export default withRouter(Color)
```

withRouter is an HOC. When we export the Color component, we send it to with Router which wraps it with a component that passes the router properties: match, history, and location.

Navigation is obtained by using the history object directly. When a user clicks the color title or the color itself, a new route is pushed into the history object. This new route is a string that contains the color's id. Pushing this route into history will cause the navigation to occur.

Single Source of Truth?

At present, the state of the color organizer is mostly handled by the Redux store. We also have some state being handled by the router. Specifically, if the route contains a color ID, the presentation state of the application is different than when it does not.

Having some state handled by the router may seem contradictory to Redux's requirement to store state in a single object: a single source of truth. However, you can think of the router as being the source of truth that interfaces with the browser. It is absolutely OK to allow the router to handle any state associated with the site map, including the filters required to look up data. Keep the rest of the state in Redux store.

Moving Color Sort State to Router

You do not have to limit the use of Router parameters. They can be more than filters for looking up specific data in state. They can also be used to obtain information necessary for rendering the UI.

The Redux store presently contains the information about how the colors should be sorted in state via the sort property. Would it make sense to move this variable from the Redux store to a route parameter? The variable itself is not data; it provides info about how the data should be presented. The sort variable is a string, which also makes it an ideal candidate for a route parameter. Finally, we want our users to be able to send the sort state to other users in a link. If they prefer to have the colors sorted by rating, they can send that info to other users in a link, or bookmark that content as is in the browser.

Let's move the sort state of the color wall to a route parameter. These are the routes that we will use to sort our colors:

/#/ default
    Sort by date

/#/sort/title
    Sort by title

/#/sort/rating
    Sort by rating

First, we need to remove the sort reducer from the *./store/index.js* file; we no longer need it. As a result:

```
combineReducers({colors, sort})
```

becomes:

```
combineReducers({colors})
```

Removing the reducer means that the state variable will no longer be managed by Redux.

Next, we can also remove the container for the Menu component from *./src/components/containers.js*. The container is used to link the state of the Redux store to the Menu presentation component. Sort is no longer stored in state, so we no longer need a container.

Additionally, in the *containers.js* file, we need to change the Colors container. It will no longer receive the sort value from state. Instead, it will receive sorting instructions as a route parameter that is passed to the Color component inside of the match property:

```
export const Colors = connect(
    ({colors}, {match}) =>
        ({
            colors: sortColors(colors, match.params.sort)
        }),
    dispatch =>
        ({
            onRemove(id) {
                dispatch(removeColor(id))
            },
            onRate(id, rating) {
                dispatch(rateColor(id, rating))
            }
        })
)(ColorList)
```

Now the colors are being sorted via a routing parameter before they are passed to the ColorList as a property.

Next, we need to replace the Menu component with one that contains links to our new routes. Much like the About menu that we created earlier in this chapter, the visual state of the menu will be controlled by setting the activeStyle property of the Nav Link:

```
import { NavLink } from 'react-router'

const selectedStyle = { color: 'red' }

const Menu = ({ match }) =>
    <nav className="menu">

        <NavLink to="/" style={match.isExact && selectedStyle}>
            date
        </NavLink>

        <NavLink to="/sort/title" activeStyle={selectedStyle}>
```

```
      title
    </NavLink>

    <NavLink to="/sort/rating" activeStyle={selectedStyle}>
      rating
    </NavLink>

  </nav>

export default Menu
```

Now users can sort the colors via the URL. When there is not a sort parameter available, the colors will be sorted by date. This menu will change the color of the link to indicate to the user how the data has been sorted.

We need to modify the App component. We need to handle sorting the colors via routes:

```
const App = () =>
  <Switch>
    <Route exact path="/:id" component={Color} />
    <Route path="/"component={() => (
      <div className="app">
        <Route component={Menu} />
        <NewColor />
        <Switch>
          <Route exact path="/" component={Colors} />
          <Route path="/sort/:sort" component={Colors} />
        </Switch>
      </div>
    )} />
  </Switch>
```

First, the Menu needs the match property, so we will render the Menu with a Route. The Menu will always render alongside the NewColor form and the list of colors because the Route does not have a path.

After the NewColor component, we want to display either the default list of colors, sorted by default, or the list of colors sorted by a parameter. These routes are wrapped in the Switch component to ensure that we only render one Colors container.

When users navigate to the home route, http://localhost:3000, the App component is rendered. By default, the Colors container is rendered within the App. The value of the sort parameter is undefined, so the colors are sorted by default.

If the user navigates to http://localhost:3000/sort/rating, the Colors container will also be rendered, but this time the sort parameter should have a value, and the colors should be sorted by that value.

Routing parameters are an ideal tool to obtain data that affects the presentation of your user interface. However, they should only be used when you want users to capture these details in a URL. For example, in the case of the color organizer, users can send other users links to specific colors or all the colors sorted by a specific field. Users can also bookmark those links to return specific data. If you want your users to save information about the presentation in a URL, then a routing parameter is your solution.

In this chapter, we reviewed the basic usage of the React Router. All of the examples in this chapter incorporated the HashRouter. In the next chapter, we will continue to use the router both on the client and the server with the BrowserRouter, and we'll use the StaticRouter to render the current routing context on the server.

CHAPTER 12

React and the Server

So far, we have built small applications with React that run entirely in the browser. They have collected data in the browser and saved the data using browser storage. This makes sense because React is a view layer. It is intended to render UI. However, most applications require at least the existence of some sort of a backend, and we will need to understand how to structure applications with a server in mind.

Even if you have a client application that is relying entirely on cloud services for the backend, you still need to get and send data to these services. Within the scope of Flux, there are specific places where these transactions should be made, and libraries that can help you deal with the latency associated with HTTP requests.

Additionally React can be rendered *isomorphically*, which means that it can be in platforms other than the browser. This means we can render our UI on the server before it ever gets to the browser. Taking advantage of server rendering, we can improve the performance, portability, and security of our applications.

We start this chapter with a look at the differences between isomorphism and universalism and how both concepts relate to React. Next, we will look at how to make an isomorphic application using universal JavaScript. Finally, we will improve the color organizer by adding a server and rendering the UI on the server first.

Isomorphism versus Universalism

The terms *isomorphic* and *universal* are often used to describe applications that work on both the client and the server. Although these terms are used interchangeably to describe the same application, there is a subtle difference between them that is worth investigating. *Isomorphic* applications are applications that can be rendered on multiple platforms. *Universal* code means that the exact same code can run in multiple environments.[1]

Node.js will allow us to reuse the same code that we've written in the browser in other applications such as servers, CLIs, and even native applications. Let's take a look at some universal JavaScript:

```
var printNames = response => {
  var people = JSON.parse(response).results,
      names = people.map(({name}) => `${name.last}, ${name.first}`)
  console.log(names.join('\n'))
}
```

The `printNames` function is universal. The exact same code can be invoked in the browser or on a server. This means that if we constructed a server with Node.js, we could potentially reuse a lot of code between the two environments. Universal JavaScript is JavaScript that can run on the server or in the browser without error (Figure 12-1).

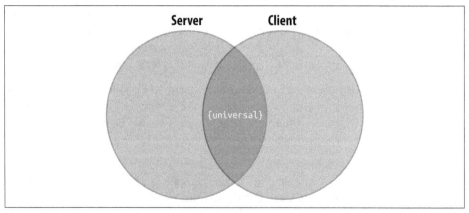

Figure 12-1. Client and server domains

The server and the client are completely different domains, so all of your JavaScript code will not automatically work between them. Let's take a look at creating an AJAX request with the browser:

```
const request = new XMLHttpRequest()
request.open('GET', 'https://api.randomuser.me/?nat=US&results=10')
request.onload = () => printNames(request.response)
request.send()
```

Here we are requesting 10 user records at random from the *randomuser.me* API. If we run this code in the browser and look at the console, we will see 10 random names:

---

1 Gert Hengeveld, "Isomorphism vs Universal JavaScript" (*http://bit.ly/2m0YDEY*), Medium.

```
ford, brianna
henderson, nellie
lynch, lily
gordon, todd
collins, genesis
roberts, suzanne
dixon, rene
ray, rafael
adams, jamie
bowman, mia
```

However, if we try to run the exact same code with Node.js, we get an error:

```
ReferenceError: XMLHttpRequest is not defined
    at Object.<anonymous> (/Users/...)
    at Module._compile (module.js:541:32)
    at Object.Module._extensions..js (module.js:550:10)
    at Module.load (module.js:458:32)
    at tryModuleLoad (module.js:417:12)
    at Function.Module._load (module.js:409:3)
    at Function.Module.runMain (module.js:575:10)
    at startup (node.js:160:18)
    at node.js:449:3
```

This error occurs because Node.js does not have an `XMLHttpRequest` object like the browser does. With Node.js, we can use the `http` module to make a request:

```
const https = require('https')
https.get(
    'https://api.randomuser.me/?nat=US&results=10',
    res => {

        let results = ''

        res.setEncoding('utf8')
        res.on('data', chunk => results += chunk)

        res.on('end', () => printNames(results))
    }
)
```

Loading data from an API with Node.js requires the use of core modules. It requires different code. In these samples, the `printNames` function is universal, so the same function works in both environments.

We could build a module that would print the names to the console in either a browser or a Node.js application:

```
var printNames = response => {
  var people = JSON.parse(response).results,
  names = people.map(({name}) => `${name.last}, ${name.first}`)
  console.log(names.join('\n'))
}
```

```
if (typeof window !== 'undefined') {

  const request = new XMLHttpRequest()
  request.open('GET', 'http://api.randomuser.me/?nat=US&results=10')
  request.onload = () => printNames(request.response)
  request.send()

} else {

  const https = require('https')
  https.get(
    'http://api.randomuser.me/?nat=US&results=10',
    res => {
      let results = ''
      res.setEncoding('utf8')
      res.on('data', chunk => results += chunk)
      res.on('end', () => printNames(results))
    }
  )

}
```

This JavaScript file is now isomorphic; it contains universal JavaScript. All of the code is not universal, but the file itself will work in both environments. It can run it with Node.js or include it in a <script> tag in the browser.

isomorphic-fetch

We have been using isomorphic-fetch over other implementations of the WHATWG fetch function because isomorphic-fetch works in multiple environments.

Let's take a look at the Star component. Is this component universal?

```
const Star = ({ selected=false, onClick=f=>f }) =>
    <div className={(selected) ? "star selected" : "star"}
        onClick={onClick}>
    </div>
```

Sure it is: remember, the JSX compiles to JavaScript. The Star component is simply a function:

```
const Star = ({ selected=false, onClick=f=>f }) =>
    React.createElement(
        "div",
        {
            className: selected ? "star selected" : "star",
            onClick: onClick
        }
    )
```

We can render this component directly in the browser, or render it in a different environment and capture the HTML output as a string. ReactDOM has a renderToString method that we can use to render UI to a HTML string:

```
// Renders html directly in the browser
ReactDOM.render(<Star />)

// Renders html as a string
var html = ReactDOM.renderToString(<Star />)
```

We can build isomorphic applications that render components on different platforms, and we can architect these applications in a way that reuses JavaScript code universally across multiple environments. Additionally, we can build isomorphic applications using other languages such as Go or Python. We are not restricted to Node.js.

Server Rendering React

Using the ReactDOM.renderToString method allows us to render UI on the server. Servers are powerful; they have access to all kinds of resources that browsers do not. Servers can be secure, and access secure data. You can use all of these added benefits to your advantage by rendering initial content on the server.

Let's build a basic web server using Node.js and Express. Express is a library that we can use to rapidly develop web servers:

```
npm install express --save
```

Let's take a look at a simple Express app. This code creates a web server that always serves the message "Hello World". First, information about each request is logged to the console. Then the server responds with some HTML. Both of these steps are contained in their own function and chained together with the .use() method. Express automatically injects request and response arguments into each of these functions as arguments.

```
import express from 'express'

const logger = (req, res, next) => {
    console.log(`${req.method} request for '${req.url}'`)
    next()
}

const sayHello = (req, res) =>
    res.status(200).send("<h1>Hello World</h1>")

const app = express()
    .use(logger)
    .use(sayHello)

app.listen(3000, () =>
```

```
    console.log(`Recipe app running at 'http://localhost:3000'`)
)
```

The `logger` and `sayHello` functions are middleware. In Express, middleware functions are chained together into a pipeline with the `.use()` method.[2] When a request occurs, each middleware function is invoked in order until a response is sent. This Express app logs details about each request to the console and then sends an HTML response: `<h1>Hello World</h1>`. Finally, we start the Express app by telling it to listen for incoming requests locally on port 3000.

In Chapter 10 we used the `babel-cli` to run our tests. Here we will use the `babel-cli` to run this Express app because it contains ES6 import statements that are not supported by the current version of Node.js.

 `babel-cli` is not a great solution for running apps in production, and we don't have to use to `babel-cli` to run every Node.js app that uses ES6. As of this writing, the current version of Node.js supports a lot of ES6 syntax. You could simply choose not to use import statements. Future versions of Node.js will support import statements.

Another option is to create a webpack build for your backend code. webpack can export a JavaScript bundle that can be ran with older versions of Node.js.

In order to run `babel-node`, there is a little bit of setup involved. First, we need to install the `babel-cli`, `babel-loader`, `babel-preset-es2015`, `babel-preset-react`, and `babel-preset-stage-0`:

```
npm install babel-cli babel-loader babel-preset-env
babel-preset-react babel-preset-stage-0 --save
```

Next, we need to make sure we add a *.babelrc* file to the root of our project. When we run `babel-node index-server.js`, Babel will look for this file and apply the presets that we have installed:

```
{
  "presets": [
    "env",
    "stage-0",
    "react"
  ]
}
```

---

2 Express Documentation, "Using Middleware" (*http://bit.ly/2m0Z2ax*).

Finally, let's add a `start` script to our *package.json* file. If you do not already have a *package.json* file, create one by running `npm init`:

```
"scripts": {
    "start": "./node_modules/.bin/babel-node index-server.js"
}
```

Now we can run our Express server with the command `npm start`:

```
npm start
```

```
Recipe app running at 'http://localhost:3000'
```

Once the server is running, you can open a web browser and navigate to *http://localhost:3000*. You will see the message "Hello World" in the page.

> `ctrl^c` will stop this Express server from running.

So far, our Express app responds to all requests with the same string: `"<h1>Hello World</h1>"`. Instead of rendering this message, let's render the Recipe app that we worked with back in Chapters 4 and 5. We can make this modification by rendering the `Menu` component with some recipe data using `renderToString` from ReactDOM:

```
import React from 'react'
import express from 'express'
import { renderToString } from 'react-dom/server'
import Menu from './components/Menu'
import data from './assets/recipes.json'

global.React = React

const html = renderToString(<Menu recipes={data}/>)

const logger = (req, res, next) => {
    console.log(`${req.method} request for '${req.url}'`)
    next()
}

const sendHTMLPage = (req, res) =>
    res.status(200).send(`
<!DOCTYPE html>
<html>
    <head>
        <title>React Recipes App</title>
    </head>
    <body>
        <div id="react-container">${html}</div>
```

```
    </body>
</html>
    `)

const app = express()
    .use(logger)
    .use(sendHTMLPage)

app.listen(3000, () =>
    console.log(`Recipe app running at 'http://localhost:3000'`)
)
```

First we import `react`, the `renderToString` method, the `Menu` component, and some recipes for our initial data. React is exposed globally, so the `renderToString` method can work properly.

Next, the HTML is obtained by invoking the `renderToString` function and sending it the `Menu` component.

Finally, we can create a new middleware function, `sendHTMLPage`, that responds to all requests with an HTML string. This string wraps the server-rendered HTML in boilerplate that is necessary for creating a page.

Now when you start this application and navigate to *http://localhost:3000* in a browser, you will see that the recipes have been rendered. We have not included any JavaScript in this response. The recipes are already on the page as HTML.

So far we have server-rendered the `Menu` component. Our application is not yet isomorphic, as the components are only rendered on the server. To make it isomorphic we will add some JavaScript to the response so that the same components can be rendered in the browser.

Let's create an *index-client.js* file that will run in the browser:

```
import React from 'react'
import { render } from 'react-dom'
import Menu from './components/Menu'

window.React = React

alert('bundle loaded, Rendering in browser')

render(
    <Menu recipes={__DATA__} />,
    document.getElementById("react-container")
)

alert('render complete')
```

This file will render the same `Menu` component, with the same recipe data. We know that the data is the same because it will already be included in our response as a string. When the browser loads this script, the __DATA__ will already exist in the global scope. The `alert` methods are used to see when the browser renders the UI.

We'll need to build this *client.js* file into a bundle that can be used by the browser. Here, basic webpack configuration will handle the build.

Don't forget to install `webpack`; we've already installed `babel` and the necessary presets:

```
npm install webpack --save-dev
```

Here, basic webpack configuration will handle the build:

```
var webpack = require("webpack")

module.exports = {
    entry: "./index-client.js",
    output: {
        path: "assets",
        filename: "bundle.js"
    },
    module: {
        rules: [
            {
                test: /\.js$/,
                exclude: /(node_modules)/,
                loader: 'babel-loader',
                query: {
                    presets: ['env', 'stage-0', 'react']
                }
            }
        ]
    }
}
```

We want to build the client bundle every time we start our app, so we'll need to add a prestart script to the *package.json* file:

```
"scripts": {
  "prestart": "./node_modules/.bin/webpack --progress",
  "start": "./node_modules/.bin/babel-node index-server.js"
},
```

The last step is to modify the server. We need to write the initial __DATA__ to the response as a string. We also need to include a `script` tag with a reference to our client bundle. Lastly, we need to make sure our server sends static files from the *./assets/* directory:

```
const sendHTMLPage = (req, res) =>
    res.status(200).send(`
<!DOCTYPE html>
<html>
    <head>
```

```
            <title>React Recipes App</title>
        </head>
        <body>
            <div id="react-container">${html}</div>
            <script>
                window.__DATA__ = ${JSON.stringify(data)}
            </script>
            <script src="bundle.js"></script>
        </body>
    </html>
        `)

const app = express()
    .use(logger)
    .use(express.static('./assets'))
    .use(sendHTMLPage)
```

script tags have been added directly to the response. The data is written to the first
script tag and the bundle is loaded in the second one. Additionally, middleware has
been added to our request pipeline. When the *bundle.js* file is requested, the
express.static middleware will respond with that file instead of the server-
rendered HTML because it is in the *./assets* folder.

Now we are isomorphically rendering the React components, first on the server and
then in the browser. When you run this app, you will see alert pop ups before and
after the components are rendered in the browser. You may notice that before you
clear the first alert, the content is already there. This is because it is initially rendered
on the server.

It may seem silly to render the same content twice, but there are advantages. This
application renders the same content in all browsers, even if JavaScript is turned off.
Because the content is loaded with the initial request, your website will run faster and
deliver necessary content to your mobile users more quickly.[3] It will not have to wait
for a mobile processor to render the UI—the UI is already in place. Additionally, this
app gains all of the advantages of an SPA. Isomorphic React applications give you the
best of both worlds.

Universal Color Organizer

In the last five chapters, we have been working on a color organization application.
Thus far, we've generated a lot of code base for this application, and it all runs in the
browser. We've coded React components, a Redux store, and tons of action creators
and helper functions. We've even incorporated the React Router. We already have a
lot of code that can be reused if we were to create a web server.

---

3 Andrew H. Farmer, "Should I use React Server-Side Rendering?" (*http://bit.ly/2m11mOI*)

Let's create an Express server for this application and try to reuse as much code as possible. First, we'll need a module that configures an Express application instance, so let's create *./server/app.js*:

```javascript
import express from 'express'
import path from 'path'
import fs from 'fs'

const fileAssets = express.static(
    path.join(__dirname, '../../dist/assets')
)

const logger = (req, res, next) => {
    console.log(`${req.method} request for '${req.url}'`)
    next()
}

const respond = (req, res) =>
    res.status(200).send(`
<!DOCTYPE html>
<html>
    <head>
        <meta charset="utf-8">
        <title>Universal Color Organizer</title>
    </head>
    <body>
        <div id="react-container">ready...</div>
    </body>
</html>
    `)

export default express()
    .use(logger)
    .use(fileAssets)
    .use(respond)
```

This module is the starting point for our universal application. The Express configuration uses middleware for logging and file assets, and eventually it responds to every request with an HTML page.

 Since we are serving HTML directly from this file, you'll need to remove the *./dist/index.html* file. If this file remains in place, it will be served before the response is reached.

Webpack allows us to import assets like CSS or image files, but Node.js will not know how to handle those imports. We'll need to use the ignore-styles library to make sure that we are ignoring any SCSS import statements. Let's install ignore-styles:

```
npm install ignore-styles --save
```

In the *./src/server/index.js* file, we will consume the Express app instance and start the server. This file represents the entry point for our Node.js server:

```
import React from 'react'
import ignoreStyles from 'ignore-styles'
import app from './app'

global.React = React

app.set('port', process.env.PORT || 3000)
    .listen(
        app.get('port'),
        () => console.log('Color Organizer running')
    )
```

This file adds React to the global instance and starts the server. Additionally, we've included the `ignore-styles` module, which ignores those imports so we can render components in Node.js without causing errors.

We now have a starting point: a basic Express app configuration. Any time we need to include new features on the server, they will need to make their way into this app configuration module.

For the remainder of this chapter, we will iterate on this Express application. We will use code universally to create an isomorphic/universal version of the color organizer.

Universal Redux

All of the JavaScript in the Redux library is universal. Your reducers are written in JavaScript and should not contain code that depends upon any environment. Redux was designed to be used as a state container for browser applications, but it can be used in all types of Node.js applications, including CLIs, servers, and native applications, too.

We already have the code in place for the Redux store. We'll use this store to save state changes to a JSON file on the server.

First, we need to modify the `storeFactory` so that it can work isomorphically. At present, the `storeFactory` includes logging middleware that will cause errors in Node.js because it utilizes the `console.groupCollapsed` and `console.groupEnd` methods. Neither of these methods are available in Node.js. If we create stores on the server, we'll need to use a different logger:

```
import { colors } from './reducers'
import {
    createStore, combineReducers, applyMiddleware
} from 'redux'
```

```
const clientLogger = store => next => action => {
    let result
    console.groupCollapsed("dispatching", action.type)
    console.log('prev state', store.getState())
    console.log('action', action)
    result = next(action)
    console.log('next state', store.getState())
    console.groupEnd()
    return result
}

const serverLogger = store => next => action => {
    console.log('\n  dispatching server action\n')
    console.log(action)
    console.log('\n')
    return next(action)
}

const middleware = server =>
    (server) ? serverLogger : clientLogger

const storeFactory = (server = false, initialState = {}) =>
    applyMiddleware(middleware)(createStore)(
        combineReducers({colors}),
        initialState
    )

export default storeFactory
```

Now the storeFactory is isomorphic. We created Redux middleware for logging actions on the server. When the storeFactory is invoked, we'll tell it which type of store we want and the appropriate logger will be added to the new store instance.

Let's now use this isomorphic storeFactory to create a serverStore instance. At the top of the Express configuration, we'll need to import the storeFactory and the initial state data. We can use the storeFactory to create a store with initial state from a JSON file:

```
import storeFactory from '../store'
import initialState from '../../data/initialState.json'

const serverStore = storeFactory(true, initialState)
```

Now we have an instance of the store that will run on the server.

Every time an action is dispatched to this instance, we want to make sure the *initialState.json* file is updated. Using the subscribe method, we can listen for state changes and save a new JSON file every time the state changes:

```
serverStore.subscribe(() =>
    fs.writeFile(
```

```
        path.join(__dirname, '../../data/initialState.json'),
        JSON.stringify(serverStore.getState()),
        error => (error) ?
            console.log("Error saving state!", error) :
            null
    )
)
```

As actions are dispatched, the new state is saved to the *initialState.json* file using the
fs module.

The serverStore is now the main source of truth. Any requests will need to communicate with it in order to get the current and most up-to-date list of colors. We'll add
some middleware that will add the server store to the request pipeline so that it can
be used by other middleware during a request:

```
const addStoreToRequestPipeline = (req, res, next) => {
    req.store = serverStore
    next()
}

export default express()
    .use(logger)
    .use(fileAssets)
    .use(addStoreToRequestPipeline)
    .use(htmlResponse)
```

Now any middleware method that comes after addStoreToRequestPipeline will
have access to the store on the request object. We have used Redux universally. The
exact same code for the store, including our reducers, will run in multiple environments.

There are complications associated with building web servers for
large applications that are not addressed by this example. Saving
data to a JSON file is a quick solution for data persistence, but production applications use actual databases. Using Redux is a possible
solution that may meet requirements for some applications. However, there are complications associated with forking node processes that need to be addressed in larger applications. You can
investigate solutions like Firebase and other cloud providers for
assistance in working with databases that can scale smoothly.

Universal Routing

In the last chapter, we added the react-router-dom to the color organizer. The router
decides which component to render based on the browser's current location. The
router can be rendered on the server as well—we just need to provide the location or
route.

So far, we've used the `HashRouter`. The router automatically adds a # before each route. To use the router isomorphically, we need to replace the `HashRouter` with the `BrowserRouter`, which removes the preceding # from our routes.

When we render our application, we need to replace the `HashRouter` with the `BrowserRouter`:

```
import { BrowserRouter } from 'react-router-dom'

...

render(
    <Provider store={store}>
        <BrowserRouter>
          <App />
        </BrowserRouter>
    </Provider>,
    document.getElementById('react-container')
)
```

Now the color organizer is no longer prefacing each route with a hash. At this point, the organizer still works. Start it up and select one color. The `Color` container is rendered, and it changes the background of the entire screen using the `ColorDetails` component.

The location bar should now look something like:

```
http://localhost:3000/8658c1d0-9eda-4a90-95e1-8001e8eb6036
```

There is no longer a # in front of the route. Now let's refresh the page in the browser:

```
Cannot GET /8658c1d0-9eda-4a90-95e1-8001e8eb6036
```

Refreshing the page causes the browser to send a GET request to the server using the current route. The # was used to prevent us from sending that GET request. We use the `BrowserRouter` because we want the GET request to be sent to the server. In order to render the router on the server, we need a location—we need the route. This route will be used on the server to tell the router to render the `Color` container. The `BrowserRouter` is used when you want to render routes isomorphically.

Now that we know what content the user is requesting, let's use it to render the UI on the server. In order to render the router on the server, we'll have to make some significant changes to our Express configuration. To start, we'll need to import a few modules:

```
import { Provider } from 'react-redux'
import { compose } from 'redux'
import { renderToString } from 'react-dom/server'
import { StaticRouter } from 'react-router-dom'
```

We need the `Provider`, a `compose` function, the `renderToString` function, and the `StaticRouter`. On the server, the StaticRouter is used when we want to render our component tree to a string.

In order to generate an HTML response, there are three steps:

1. Create a store that runs on the client using the data from the `serverStore`.
2. Render the component tree as HTML using the `StaticRouter`.
3. Create the HTML page that will be sent to the client.

We create one function for each of these steps and compose them into a single function, the `htmlResponse`:

```
const htmlResponse = compose(
    buildHTMLPage,                        // Step 3
    renderComponentsToHTML,               // Step 2
    makeClientStoreFrom(serverStore)      // Step 1
)
```

In this composition, the `makeClientStoreFrom(serverStore)` is a higher-order function. Initially, this function is invoked with the `serverStore` once. It returns a function that will be invoked on every request. The returned function will always have access to the `serverStore`.

When `htmlResponse` is invoked, it expects a single argument: the `url` that has been requested by the user. For step one, we will create a higher-order function that packages the `url` with a new client `store` created using the current state of the `server Store`. Both `store` and `url` are passed to the next function, step 2, in a single object:

```
const makeClientStoreFrom = store => url =>
    ({
        store: storeFactory(false, store.getState()),
        url
    })
```

The output from the `makeClientStoreFrom` function becomes the input for the `ren derComponentToHTML` function. This function expects that the `url` and `store` have been packaged into a single argument:

```
const renderComponentsToHTML = ({url, store}) =>
    ({
        state: store.getState(),
        html: renderToString(
            <Provider store={store}>
                <StaticRouter location={url} context={{}}>
                    <App />
                </StaticRouter>
            </Provider>
        )
    })
```

The `renderComponentsToHTML` returns an object with two properties: `state` and `html`. The `state` is obtained from the new client store and the `html` is generated by the `renderToString` method. Since the app still uses Redux in the browser, the `Provider` is rendered as the root component, and the new client store is passed to it as a property.

The `StaticRouter` component is used to render the UI based upon the location that is being requested. The `StaticRouter` requires a `location` and `context`. The requested `url` is passed to the `location` property and an empty object is passed to `context`. When these components are rendered to an HTML string, the location will be taken into account, and the `StaticRouter` will render the correct routes.

This function returns the two necessary components to build the page: the current state of the organizer, and the UI rendered to an HTML string.

The `state` and the `html` can be used in the last composed function, `buildHTMLPage`:

```
const buildHTMLPage = ({html, state}) => `
<!DOCTYPE html>
<html>
    <head>
        <meta charset="utf-8">
        <title>Universal Color Organizer</title>
    </head>
    <body>
        <div id="react-container">${html}</div>
        <script>
            window.__INITIAL_STATE__ = ${JSON.stringify(state)}
        </script>
        <script src="/bundle.js"></script>
    </body>
</html>
`
```

Our color wall is now isomorphic. It will render the UI on the server and send it to the client as text. It will also embed the initial state of the store directly into the response.

The browser initially displays the UI obtained in the HTML response. When the bundle loads, it re-renders the UI and the client takes over from there. From this point on, all user interactivity including navigation will happen on the client. Our single page application will function as it always has, unless the browser is refreshed, at which point the server rendering process starts all over again.

Here is all of the current code from the Express app module, the entire file:

```
import express from 'express'
import path from 'path'
import fs from 'fs'
import { Provider } from 'react-redux'
```

```javascript
import { compose } from 'redux'
import { StaticRouter } from 'react-router-dom'
import { renderToString } from 'react-dom/server'
import App from '../components/App'
import storeFactory from '../store'
import initialState from '../../data/initialState.json'

const fileAssets = express.static(
    path.join(__dirname, '../../dist/assets')
)

const serverStore = storeFactory(true, initialState)

serverStore.subscribe(() =>
    fs.writeFile(
        path.join(__dirname, '../../data/initialState.json'),
        JSON.stringify(serverStore.getState()),
        error => (error) ?
            console.log("Error saving state!", error) :
            null
    )
)

const logger = (req, res, next) => {
    console.log(`${req.method} request for '${req.url}'`)
    next()
}

const addStoreToRequestPipeline = (req, res, next) => {
    req.store = serverStore
    next()
}

const makeClientStoreFrom = store => url =>
    ({
        store: storeFactory(false, store.getState()),
        url
    })

const renderComponentsToHTML = ({url, store}) =>
    ({
        state: store.getState(),
        css: defaultStyles,
        html: renderToString(
            <Provider store={store}>
                <StaticRouter location={url} context={{}}>
                    <App />
                </StaticRouter>
            </Provider>
        )
    })
```

```
const buildHTMLPage = ({html, state}) => `
<!DOCTYPE html>
<html>
    <head>
        <meta charset="utf-8">
        <title>Universal Color Organizer</title>
    </head>
    <body>
        <div id="react-container">${html}</div>
        <script>
            window.__INITIAL_STATE__ = ${JSON.stringify(state)}
        </script>
        <script src="/bundle.js"></script>
    </body>
</html>
`

const htmlResponse = compose(
    buildHTMLPage,
    renderComponentsToHTML,
    makeClientStoreFrom(serverStore)
)

const respond = (req, res) =>
    res.status(200).send(htmlResponse(req.url))

export default express()
    .use(logger)
    .use(fileAssets)
    .use(addStoreToRequestPipeline)
    .use(respond)
```

Our app now allows users to bookmark URLs and send URLs to other users that will be rendered isomorphically. The router decides which content to render based upon the URL. It does so on the server, which means that our users can access our content rapidly.

Isomorphic applications have the best of both worlds: they can take advantage of the speediness, control, and security that server rendering provides, while benefiting from the low bandwidth and speed that is gained from single page applications. An isomorphic React application is essentially a server-rendered SPA, which lays the foundation for you to build efficient applications that will be cool but also fast and efficient.

Incorporating server-rendered styles

At present, we are rendering the HTML on the server, but the CSS does not get rendered until the bundle is loaded in the browser. The result is a strange flicker. Initially we will see all of the unstyled content in the browser before the CSS is loaded. When

JavaScript is turned off in the browser, users will not see any CSS styles at all because they are embedded in the JavaScript bundle.

The solution is to add the styles directly to the response. To do this, we must first extract the CSS from the webpack bundle into its own separate file. You will need to install the `extract-text-webpack-plugin`:

```
npm install extract-text-webpack-plugin
```

You will also need to require this plugin in your webpack configuration:

```
var webpack = require("webpack")
var ExtractTextPlugin = require("extract-text-webpack-plugin")
var OptimizeCss = require('optimize-css-assets-webpack-plugin')
```

Also, in the webpack configuration, we need to replace the CSS and SCSS loaders with loaders that use the `ExtractTextPlugin`:

```
{
    test: /\.css$/,
    loader: ExtractTextPlugin.extract({
        fallback: "style-loader",
        use: [
            "style-loader",
            "css-loader",
            {
                loader: "postcss-loader",
                options: {
                    plugins: () => [require("autoprefixer")]
                }
            }
        ]
    })
},
{
    test: /\.scss/,
    loader: ExtractTextPlugin.extract({
        fallback: "style-loader",
        use: [
            "css-loader",
            {
                loader: "postcss-loader",
                options: {
                    plugins: () => [require("autoprefixer")]
                }
            },
            "sass-loader"
        ]
    })
}
```

And we need to include that plugin in our configuration inside of the plugins array. Here, when the plugin is included, we specify the filename of the CSS file to extract:

```
plugins: [
    new ExtractTextPlugin("bundle.css"),
    new OptimizeCss({
        assetNameRegExp: /\.optimize\.css$/g,
        cssProcessor: require('cssnano'),
        cssProcessorOptions: {
            discardComments: {removeAll: true}
        },
        canPrint: true
    })
]
```

Now when webpack runs, it will not include the CSS in the JavaScript bundle; it will instead extract all of the CSS into a separate file, *./assets/bundle.css*.

We also need to modify the Express configuration. When the organizer starts, the CSS is saved as a global string. We can use the filesystem or fs module to read the contents of a text file into the variable staticCSS:

```
const staticCSS = fs.readFileSync(
    path.join(__dirname, '../../dist/assets/bundle.css')
)
```

Now we have to modify the buildHTMLPage function to write the CSS directly to the response inside of a <style> tag:

```
const buildHTMLPage = ({html, state}) => `
<!DOCTYPE html>
<html>
    <head>
        <meta charset="utf-8">
        <title>Universal Color Organizer</title>
        <style>${staticCSS}</style>
    </head>
    <body>
        <div id="react-container">${html}</div>
        <script>
            window.__INITIAL_STATE__ = ${JSON.stringify(state)}
        </script>
        <script src="/bundle.js"></script>
    </body>
</html>
`
```

CSS is now directly embedded into our response. There is no longer a strange, style-less flicker. When JavaScript is turned off, the styles remain in place.

We now have an isomorphic color organizer that shares a lot of universal JavaScript. Initially, the color organizer is rendered on the server, but it is also rendered on the browser after the page is finished loading. When the browser takes over, the color organizer behaves as a single-page application.

Communicating with the Server

At present, the color organizer is rendering UI on the server and re-rendering UI in the browser. Once the browser takes over, the organizer functions as a single-page application. Users dispatch actions locally, the local state changes, and locally the UI is updated. Everything is working well in the browser, but the dispatched actions are not making it back to the server.

In this next section, we will not only make sure that this data gets saved on the server, we will make sure that the action objects themselves are created on the server and dispatched to both stores.

Completing Actions on the Server

In the color organizer, we will integrate a REST API for handling our data. Actions will be initiated on the client, completed on the server, and then dispatched to both stores. The serverStore will save the new state to JSON, and the client store will trigger a UI update. Both stores will dispatch the same actions universally (#fig1202).

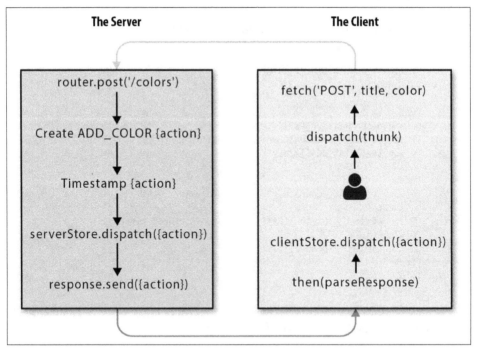

Figure 12-2. Creating a universal action

Let's take a look at an example of the complete process for dispatching an ADD_COLOR action in the proposed solution:

---

1. Dispatch action creator `addColor()` with new title and color.
2. Send data to server in new POST request.
3. Create and dispatch the new `ADD_COLOR` add color action on the server.
4. Send the `ADD_COLOR` action in the response body.
5. Parse the response body and dispatch the `ADD_COLOR` action on the client.

The first thing that we need to do is build the REST API. Let's create a new file called *./src/server/color-api.js*.

Every action created is handled the same way: it is dispatched on the server and then it is sent to the client. Let's create a function that dispatches the action to the `server` `Store` and sends the action to the client using the response object:

```
const dispatchAndRespond = (req, res, action) => {
    req.store.dispatch(action)
    res.status(200).json(action)
}
```

Once we have an action, we can use this function to dispatch the action and send a response to the client.

We will need to create some HTTP endpoints using the Express `Router` that can handle various HTTP requests. We will create routes to handle `GET`, `POST`, `PUT`, and `DELETE` requests on the route */api/colors*. The Express `Router` can be used to create these routes. Each route will contain the logic to create a different action object and send it to the `dispatchAndRespond` function along with the request and response objects:

```
import { Router } from 'express'
import { v4 } from 'uuid'

const dispatchAndRespond = (req, res, action) => {
    req.store.dispatch(action)
    res.status(200).json(action)
}

const router = Router()

router.get("/colors", (req, res) =>
    res.status(200).json(req.store.getState().colors)
)

router.post("/colors", (req, res) =>
    dispatchAndRespond(req, res, {
        type: "ADD_COLOR",
        id: v4(),
        title: req.body.title,
        color: req.body.color,
```

```
        timestamp: new Date().toString()
    })
)

router.put("/color/:id", (req, res) =>
    dispatchAndRespond(req, res, {
        type: "RATE_COLOR",
        id: req.params.id,
        rating: parseInt(req.body.rating)
    })
)

router.delete("/color/:id", (req, res) =>
    dispatchAndRespond(req, res, {
        type: "REMOVE_COLOR",
        id: req.params.id
    })
)

export default router
```

Each function added to the router object handles a different request for *http://localhost:3000/api/{route}*:

GET '/colors'
Responds with the current color array from the server's state. This route is added just so we can see the listed colors; it is not used by the frontend.

POST '/colors'
Creates a new color action object and sends it to dispatchAndRespond.

PUT '/color/:id'
Changes the rating of a color. The color's ID is obtained from route paramaters and used in the new action object.

DELETE '/color/:id'
Removes a color based upon the ID sent in the routing parameters.

Now that we have defined the routes, we need to add them to the Express app configuration. First, we install the Express body-parser:

```
npm install body-parser --save
```

The body-parser is used to parse incoming request bodies and obtain any variables sent to the routes. It is necessary to obtain the new color and rating information from the client. We'll need to add this middleware to our Express app configuration. Let's import the body-parser and our new routes into the *./server/app.js* file:

```
import bodyParser from 'body-parser'
import api from './color-api'
```

Let's add the bodyParser middleware and the API to our Express app. It is important to add the bodyParser before the API so that the data can be parsed by the time the request has been handled by the API:

```
export default express()
    .use(logger)
    .use(fileAssets)
    .use(bodyParser.json())
    .use(addStoreToRequestPipeline)
    .use('/api', api)
    .use(matchRoutes)
```

The bodyParser.json() is now parsing incoming request bodies that have been formatted as JSON. Our color-api is added to the pipeline and configured to respond to any routes that are prefixed with */api*. For example, this URL can be used to obtain the current array of colors as JSON: *http://localhost:3000/api/colors*.

Now that our Express app has endpoints that can respond to HTTP requests, we are ready to modify the frontend action creators to communicate with these endpoints.

Actions with Redux Thunks

One problem with client/server communication is latency, or the delay that we experience while waiting for a response after sending a request. Our action creators need to wait for a response before they can dispatch the action, because in our solution the action itself is being sent to the client from the server. There is middleware for Redux that can help us with asynchronous actions: it is called redux-thunk.

In this next section, we will rewrite out action creators using redux-thunk. These action creators, called thunks, will allow us to wait for a server response before dispatching an action locally. Thunks are higher-order functions. Instead of action objects, they return other functions. Let's install redux-thunk:

```
npm install redux-thunk --save
```

redux-thunk is middleware; it needs to be incorporated into our storeFactory. First, at the top of *./src/store/index.js*, import redux-thunk:

```
import thunk from 'redux-thunk'
```

The storeFactory has a function called middleware. It returns the middleware that should be incorporated to the new store in a single array. We can add any Redux middleware to this array. Each item will be spread into the arguments of the applyMiddleware function:

```
const middleware = server => [
    (server) ? serverLogger : clientLogger,
    thunk
]
```

```
const storeFactory = (server = false, initialState = {}) =>
    applyMiddleware(...middleware(server))(createStore)(
        combineReducers({colors}),
        initialState
    )

export default storeFactory
```

Let's take a look at the current action creator for adding colors:

```
export const addColor = (title, color) =>
    ({
        type: "ADD_COLOR",
        id: v4(),
        title,
        color,
        timestamp: new Date().toString()
    })

...

store.dispatch(addColor("jet", "#000000"))
```

This action creator returns an object, the addColor action. That object is immediately dispatched to the store. Now let's look at the thunk version of addColor:

```
export const addColor = (title, color) =>
    (dispatch, getState) => {

        setTimeout(() =>
            dispatch({
                type: "ADD_COLOR",
                index: getState().colors.length + 1,
                timestamp: new Date().toString()
                title,
                color
            }),
            2000
        )
    }

...

store.dispatch(addColor("jet", "#000000"))
```

Even though both action creators are dispatched the exact same way, the thunk returns a function instead of an action. The returned function is a callback that receives the store's dispatch and getState methods as arguments. We can dispatch an action when we are ready. In this example, a setTimeout is used to create a two-second delay before we dispatch a new color action.

In addition to dispatch, thunks also have access to the store's getState method. In this example, we used it to create an index field based upon the current number of colors in state. This function can be useful when it is time to create actions that depend upon data from the store.

 Not all of your action creators have to be thunks. The redux-thunk middleware knows the difference between thunks and action objects. Action objects are immediately dispatched.

Thunks have another benefit. They can invoke dispatch or getState asynchronously as many times as they like, and they are not limited to dispatching one type of action. In this next sample, the thunk immediately dispatches a RANDOM_RATING_STARTED action and repeatedly dispatches a RATE_COLOR action that rates a specific color at random:

```
export const rateColor = id =>
    (dispatch, getState) => {

        dispatch({ type: "RANDOM_RATING_STARTED" })
        setInterval(() =>
            dispatch({
                type: "RATE_COLOR",
                id,
                rating: Math.floor(Math.random()*5)
            }),
            1000
        )
    }

...

store.dispatch(
    rateColor("f9005b4e-975e-433d-a646-79df172e1dbb")
)
```

These thunks are simply samples. Let's build the real thunks that the color organizer will use by replacing our current action creators.

First, we'll create a function called fetchThenDispatch. This function uses isomorphic-fetch to send a request to a web service and automatically dispatch the response:

```
import fetch from 'isomorphic-fetch'

const parseResponse = response => response.json()

const logError = error => console.error(error)
```

```
const fetchThenDispatch = (dispatch, url, method, body) =>
    fetch(
        url,
        {
            method,
            body,
            headers: { 'Content-Type': 'application/json' }
        }
    ).then(parseResponse)
     .then(dispatch)
     .catch(logError)
```

The `fetchThenDispatch` function requires the `dispatch` function, a URL, the HTTP request method, and the HTTP request body as arguments. This information is then used in the `fetch` function. Once a response is received, it will be parsed and then dispatched. Any errors will be logged to the console.

We'll use the `fetchThenDispatch` function to help us construct thunks. Each thunk will send a request to our API, along with any necessary data. Since our API responds with action objects, the response can be immediately parsed and dispatched:

```
export const addColor = (title, color) => dispatch =>
    fetchThenDispatch(
        dispatch,
        '/api/colors',
        'POST',
        JSON.stringify({title, color})
    )

export const removeColor = id => dispatch =>
    fetchThenDispatch(
        dispatch,
        `/api/color/${id}`,
        'DELETE'
    )

export const rateColor = (id, rating) => dispatch =>
    fetchThenDispatch(
        dispatch,
        `/api/color/${id}`,
        'PUT',
        JSON.stringify({rating})
    )
```

The `addColor` thunk sends a POST request to *http://localhost:3000/api/colors* along with the title and hex value of the new color. An `ADD_COLOR` action object is returned, parsed, and dispatched.

The removeColor thunk sends a DELETE request to the API with the ID of the color to delete provided in the URL. A REMOVE_COLOR action object is returned, parsed, and dispatched.

The rateColor thunk sends a PUT request to the API. The ID of the color to rate is included in the URL as a route parameter, and the new rating is supplied in the body of the request. A RATE_COLOR action object is returned from the server, parsed as JSON, and dispatched to the local store.

Now when you run the application, you can see actions being dispatched to both stores in the console log. The browser console is a part of the developer tools and the server console is the terminal where the server was started (Figure 12-3).

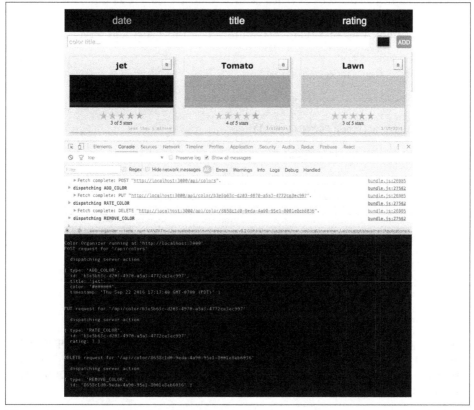

Figure 12-3. Browser console and server console

Using Thunks with Websockets

The color organizer uses REST to communicate with the server. Thunks can also be used with *websockets* to send and receive. Websockets are two-way connections between the client and the server. Websockets can send data to a server, but they also allow the server to send data to the client.

One way to work with websockets and thunks is to dispatch a connect action creator. For example, let's say we wanted to connect to a message server:

```
store.dispatch(connectToMessageSocket())
```

Thunks can invoke dispatch as much as they want. We can create thunks that listen for incoming messages and dispatch NEW_MESSAGE actions when they are received. This next sample uses socket.io-client to connect to a socket.io server and listen for incoming messages:

```
import io from 'socket.io-client'

const connectToChatSocket = () => dispatch => {

    dispatch({type: "CONNECTING"})

    let socket = io('/message-socket')

    socket.on('connect', () =>
        dispatch({type: "CONNECTED", id: socket.id})
    )

    socket.on('message', (message, user) =>
        dispatch({type: "NEW_MESSAGE", message, user})
    )

}

export default connectToMessageSocket
```

As soon as the connectToChatSocket is invoked, a CONNECTING action is dispatched. We then attempt to connect to the message socket. Once connected, the socket will respond with a connect event. When this happens, we can dispatch a CONNECTED action with information about the current socket.

When the server sends new messages, message events are raised on the socket. We can dispatch NEW_MESSAGE actions locally every time they are sent to this client from the server.

Thunks can work with any type of asynchronous process, including websockets, socket-io, Firebase, setTimeouts, transitions, and animations.

Just about every React application that you build will require the existence of some type of web server. Sometimes you will only need a web server to host your application. Other situations require communications with web services. And then there are high-traffic applications that need to work on many platforms that will require different solutions entirely.

Advanced Data Fetching

If you are working on high-traffic applications that share data on multiple platforms, you may want to look into frameworks like Relay and GraphQL or Falcor. These frameworks provide more efficient and intelligent solutions for providing applications with only the data that they require.

GraphQL (*http://graphql.org*) is a declarative data querying solution developed at Facebook that can be used to query data from multiple sources. GraphQL can be used by all types of languages and platforms. Relay (*https://facebook.github.io/relay/*) is a library, also developed at Facebook, that handles data fetching for client applications by linking GraphQL queries with React or React Native components. There is a bit of learning curve associated with GraphQL and Relay, but it is well worth it if you really like declarative programming.

Falcor (*https://netflix.github.io/falcor/*) is a framework developed at Netflix that also addresses issues associated with fetching and efficiently using data. Like GraphQL, Falcor allows you to query data from multiple services in a single location. However, Falcor uses JavaScript to query data, which likely means less of a learning curve for JavaScript developers.

The key to React development is knowing when to use the right tools. You already have many of the tools needed to build robust applications in your toolbelt. Only use what is needed. If your application does not depend upon a lot of data, don't use Redux. React state is a great solution that is perfect fit for the right size app. Your application may not require server rendering. Don't worry about incorporating it until you have a highly interactive app that has a lot of mobile traffic.

When setting forth to develop your own React applications, we hope that this book will serve as a reference and a great foundation. Though React and its related libraries will almost certainly go through changes, these are stable tools that you can feel confident about using right away. Building apps with React, Redux, and functional, declarative JavaScript is a lot of fun, and we can't wait to see what you'll build.

Index

and data transformations, 41-47
defined, 187
in functional programming, 36-38
imperative programming, 34-36
inheritance
classes and prototypical inheritance, 26
ES6, 26
inverse data flow, 121-122
isomorphic-fetch, 159, 300, 323
isomorphism
advantages of isomorphic applications, 315
defined, 297
universalism vs., 297-301
Istanbul, 262

J

JavaScript
D3 and, 160-166
ES6 (see ES6)
Fetch and, 159
functional programming with, 31-52
(see also functional programming)
JSX and, 83
lexical variable scoping, 10
library integration with React, 158-166
modules, 27
semicolons in, 15
Jest
code coverage, 262-272
environment setup, 245-247
manual mocks, 254-257
mocks, 252-254
setup/teardown features, 243
join(), 41
jQuery, 158
JSBin, 4
JSX, 81-107
Babel and, 84
Babel presets, 92
className, 83
evaluation, 83
JavaScript expressions, 83
mapping arrays to, 83
nested components, 82
React elements as, 81-83
recipes and, 85-92
tips for working with, 82
webpack and, 93-107
(see also Webpack)

L

lambda calculus (λ-calculus), 26
latency, 159
let (ES6 keyword), 10-12
lexical variable scoping, 10
lifecycles (see component lifecycles)
linting, 229
(see also ESLint)
Lisp, 31
loaders, webpack, 94
localStorage, 202
loops, recursion vs., 50

M

manual mocks, 254-257
map(), 43
mapping arrays, 83
middleware
applying to store, 207-209
as higher-order functions, 208
Redux, 206-209
redux-thunk, 321-327
minifying code, 104
mixins, 166
mocking, 249-257
HOC testing, 249-252
Jest mocks, 252-254
manual mocks, 254-257
modularity, webpack and, 93
module bundler, 93
(see also webpack)
modules, ES6, 27
mounting lifecycle, 142-146

N

nesting
page templates, 279-281
placeholder components, 284
routes, 279-286
subsections and submenus, 281-286
network performance, webpack and, 93
Node.js
CommonJS and, 28
installing, 6

O

Object.keys(), 44
objects

About the Authors

Alex Banks is a software engineer, instructor, and cofounder of Moon Highway, a curriculum development company in Northern California. As a software consultant, he has developed applications for the Chicago Marathon, MSN, and the Department of Energy. Alex also assisted in the development of the continuous delivery curriculum that is delivered to every Yahoo new hire. In addition, he's authored several classes for *Lynda.com*.

Eve Porcello is a software architect and cofounder of Moon Highway. Prior to Moon Highway, Eve worked on software projects for 1-800-Dentist and Microsoft. She is an active corporate trainer, speaker, and author on *Lynda.com*.

Colophon

The animal on the cover of *Learning React* is a wild boar and its babies (*Sus scrofa*). The wild boar, also known as wild swine or Eurasian wild pig, is native to Eurasia, North Africa, and the Greater Sunda Islands. Because of human intervention, they are one of the widest-ranging mammals in the world.

Wild boars have short thin legs and bulky bodies with short, massive trunks. Their necks are short and thick, leading to a large head that accounts for up to a third of the body's length. Adult sizes and weights vary depending on environmental factors such as access to food and water. Despite their size, they can run up to 25 mph and jump to a height of 55–59 inches. In the winter, their coat consists of coarse bristles that overlay short brown downy fur. These bristles are longer along the boar's back and shortest around the face and limbs.

Wild boars have a highly developed sense of smell; they have been used for drug detection in Germany. It also has an acute sense of hearing, which contrasts with its weak eyesight and lack of color vision. It is unable to recognize a human standing 30 feet away.

Boars are social animals that live in female-dominated groups. Breeding lasts from around November to January. Males go through several bodily changes in preparation of mating, including the development of a subcutaneous armor that helps confront rivals; they travel long distances, eating very little on the way, to locate a sow. Average litters contain 4–6 piglets.

Many of the animals on O'Reilly covers are endangered; all of them are important to the world. To learn more about how you can help, go to *animals.oreilly.com*.

The cover image is from *Meyers Kleines Lexicon*. The cover fonts are URW Typewriter and Guardian Sans. The text font is Adobe Minion Pro; the heading font is Adobe Myriad Condensed; and the code font is Dalton Maag's Ubuntu Mono.

Learn from experts.
Find the answers you need.

Sign up for a **10-day free trial** to get **unlimited access** to all of the content on Safari, including Learning Paths, interactive tutorials, and curated playlists that draw from thousands of ebooks and training videos on a wide range of topics, including data, design, DevOps, management, business—and much more.

Start your free trial at:

oreilly.com/safari

(No credit card required.)